Learning Difficulties
A Guide for Teachers

LEARNING DIFFICULTIES

A GUIDE FOR TEACHERS

WALDORF INSIGHTS AND PRACTICAL APPROACHES

EDITED BY

Mary Ellen Willby

RUDOLF STEINER COLLEGE PRESS

The contents of this book are based on the concepts of Spiritual Science
as conceived by Rudolf Steiner (1861-1925).

Cover: The Flower-Rod Exercise from *The Extra Lesson*

First Edition 1998
Second Edition 1999
Second Edition, revised 2005
© Rudolf Steiner College

ISBN 0-945803-40-0

All rights reserved. No part of this book may be copied in any form
whatsoever without the written consent of the publisher.

The content of this book represents the views of the authors
and should not be taken as the official opinion or policy
of Rudolf Steiner College or Rudolf Steiner College Press.

Book orders may be made through Rudolf Steiner College Bookstore.
Tel 916-961-8729, Fax 916-961-3032, E-mail bookstore@steinercollege.edu.
See catalog at www.steinercollege.edu.

Rudolf Steiner College Press
9200 Fair Oaks Blvd.
Fair Oaks, CA 95628

*Dedicated
to
the Sophia Being
in her Threefold Aspect*

ACKNOWLEDGEMENTS

TO

Ingun Schneider, for her devotion in helping children with the Extra Lesson, as a class teacher and individually. Ingun's colleagueship and insight during the preparation of this handbook has been a major factor in helping the editor.

Gayle Davis, faculty member and financial officer at Rudolf Steiner College, for her support of the publication of this handbook.

Audrey McAllen, for her patient diligence as silent editor.

Hallie Bonde, for the typing and layout of this handbook, and her much appreciated humor.

Mark Herndon, for his many hours of typing.

The librarians at the Rudolf Steiner Library, in Ghent, New York, who fulfilled all my wish lists.

Daisy Aldan, for permission to publish one of her favorite poems 'Vertical, I Walk a Horizontal Line'.

Betty Lou Kratoville, for permission to quote from the publications of Academic Therapy Press.

Keith Critchlow, for permission to quote from *Resurgence*.

All contributors, in gratitude for their permission to republish their work.

Contents

Foreword	*- Audrey E. McAllen*	- vii
Editor's Note: Profile of Audrey E. McAllen	*- Mary Ellen Willby*	- ix

Section I: Deeper Insights by Audrey E. McAllen

The Structural Physical Body as Archetype of Man's Spiritual Being	- 1
Twofold Man as Archetype	- 5
Identity and Personality	- 10
On the Imprinting of Man's Structural Physical Body's Spiritual Archetype into the Etheric Body of the Earth	- 15
The Mirroring Process in Relation to Two- and Three-Dimensional Space	- 28
The Postural System	- 35
School Entry	- 41

Section II: Factors in the Causes of Learning Difficulties

The Nine-Year Change	*- James A. Dyson MD*	- 49
The Picture on Both Sides of the Atlantic — An Interview with Rosemary Gebert	*- Audrey E. McAllen*	- 52
Causes of Learning Troubles	*- Else Göttgens*	- 55
Observing in the Classroom	*- Audrey E. McAllen*	- 58
An Immature Movement Pattern Which Interferes with Reading and the Vertical Midline Barrier	*- Dee J. Coulter*	- 60

Dominance	- *Audrey E. McAllen*	- 64
Comments and extracts - Neuropsychological Fundamentals in Learning Disabilities by J. B. de Quiros, O. L. Schrager	- *Audrey E. McAllen*	- 75
Osteopathy for Children	- *Elizabeth C. Hayden*	- 80
Goethe's Color Theory Applied	- *Mary Nash-Wortham*	- 94

SECTION III: EXERCISES AND LESSONS WITH STUDENTS

Have You Seen Your Own Star	- *Kyle Morton*	- 99
Variation on the 'Ball Throwing' Exercise	- *Gaby Wensink*	- 104
The Extra Lesson in Triform — An Interview with Janet McGavin	- *Audrey E. McAllen*	- 107
The Extra Lesson for Children in an EBD School in England	- *John Marking*	- 111
Into the Future Here I Go	- *Kyle Morton*	- 115
Remedial Tutorial Lessons	- *Mary Jo Oresti*	- 118
Strengthening the Reading Process	- *Mary Jo Oresti*	- 121
Exercises Researched by the Dutch Group of Teachers of Children with Specific Learning Difficulties	- *Joep Eikenboom*	- 124
Three Dimensions of Space Around Me	- *Marieke Lofvers*	- 126
Aaron's Story — A Third Grade Student	- *Mary Ellen Willby*	- 129
Andrew and His Sense of Touch	- *Mary Jo Oresti*	- 131
Laura's Story — A High School Student	- *Mary Ellen Willby*	- 135
David's Story — A High School Student	- *Lalage Craig*	- 138
Nancy's Story — A University Student	- *Lalage Craig*	- 143
Exercise List from *The Extra Lesson*		- 146

Section IV: Questions and Answers

Visual Sense Impressions	- 147
Tension in Writing	- 148
Writing with the Foot	- 148
Person - House - Tree	- 149
Copper Ball Exercise	- 149
Lyre with Copper Ball Exercise	- 150
Lying and Stealing	- 150
Artistic Element in Remedial Lessons	- 151
Blue and Red	- 151
Strengthening Memory	- 152
Memory Problem	- 152
Writing on the Blackboard	- 152
Pictures on the Blackboard	- 153
Restlessness in Class Two	- 153
Three Dimensions of Space	- 154
The Scribbled Whirl	- 154
Older Children with Learning Difficulties	- 155
Lens Mirroring	- 155

Section V: Exercises for Classes

'Vertical, I Walk a Horizontal Line'	*-Daisy Aldan*	- 157
Standards of Movement Skills Classes One to Four	*- Ester Buekers*	- 159
Remedial Exercises	*- Else Göttgens*	- 163
Exercises for Groups and Individual Children	*- Gymnasts*	- 166
Pioneering the Extra Lesson in a Waldorf School	*- Howard Schrager*	- 169
How Many Feet Are You?	*- Ester Buekers*	- 172
Body Geography through the Grades	*- Ingun M.Schneider*	- 175

From the Classroom	*- Mary Ellen Willby*	- 181
Children's Games	*- Susan Goldstein*	- 185
Stacking Sticks	*- Howard Schrager*	- 187
Bean Bag Exercises in the Morning Circle	*- Patrick Marooney*	- 189
Care of Desks and Exercises	*- Daena Ross*	- 189
Classroom Exercises for Helping Eye Movement in Relation to Writing and Reading	*- Audrey E. McAllen*	- 193
Exercises with a Sixth Grade	*- Patrick Wakeford-Evans*	- 195
Bean Bags in First Grade	*- Jackie Treinen*	- 196
Verses to go with Jean Hunt's Bean Bag Exercises	*- Various Teachers*	- 198

Section VI: Guidance for Teachers in the Classroom

Guidance for New Teachers	*- Else Göttgens*	- 207
Child Study and Assessment	*- Audrey E. McAllen*	- 210
Suggestions from Else Göttgens	*- Ingun M. Schneider*	- 214
Suggestions for Pedagogical Economy	*- Audrey. E. McAllen*	- 219
Helping Through the Feet	*- Jannebeth Roëll*	- 224
Teachers Look to Your Handwriting	*- Irene N. Ellis/ Audrey E. McAllen*	- 225
Hints for Waldorf Teachers in the Early Grades	*- Irene N. Ellis*	- 230
Guidelines for the Teaching of Writing, Spelling and Reading in the Early Grades	*- Teachers' notes and lectures by - Audrey E. McAllen*	- 234
Language from the Whole to the Part	*- Else Göttgens*	- 239

Section VII: Kindergarten

Forces of the I AM	- René M. Querido	- 243
Birth to Seven Years	- Audrey E. McAllen	- 245
Movement in the Earliest Years	- Joan Caldarera	- 247
Suggestions for Interviewing Parents	- W. K. Kerney/ S. Temple	- 250
For Kindergarten Teachers	- Margret Meyerkort	- 254
On First Grade Readiness	- Margret Meyerkort	- 257

Section VIII: On Left Handedness

An Interview with Else Göttgens	- Audrey E. McAllen	- 263
Rudolf Steiner's Indications for Confirming Dominance	- Audrey E. McAllen	- 266
Confirming Dominance — with a Child	- Melinda Turner	- 268
Confirming Dominance — with an Adult	- Mary Ellen Willby	- 271

Glossary — 275

Editor's Afterword — 279

Resource Information — 281

Bibliography and Works Cited — 283

Foreword

During this latter half of the 20th century, an increasing number of children with no lack of intelligence show an inability to manage the skills of Writing, Reading and Arithmetic, much to the distress of their parents and the bewilderment of their teachers. In the day to day living with their children, parents become aware that something basic is wrong, even to the extent of founding associations to research the problem. The teachers, on their side, see many behavioral problems and lack of concentration in their pupils to account for this condition. Since, in Waldorf education, our concern is with the soul of the individual and its incorporation into the body, this condition of learning difficulty is considered a particular problem of that individual. The surprising phenomenon that contradicts this psychological aspect is that the child is well aware that he is different in his learning capacity from his peers; therefore, it is not behavior problems that are preventing the child from learning, but rather learning difficulties that cause psychological reactions. The reactions are secondary to his disability and not the producer of the disability.

These facts were also not recognized in State Schools until those doctors and neurologists, working from the discoveries by Sir Charles Sherrington (1861-1952) of the physiology of the nervous system, became engaged in research into this growing epidemic of children who had what is now termed Specific Learning Difficulties (SLD). Shortly before he died, Sir Charles gave an introductory talk to a series of radio broadcasts on the findings of neurological research. This listener recognized that he spoke about sense perception as Rudolf Steiner had in his book *Intuitive Thinking As A Spiritual Path — A Philosophy of Freedom*. The nervous system, which engaged Sherrington's studies, is an archetype common to all human beings, and Steiner, in his 1909 lectures *Anthroposophy*, gives the spiritual origins of this archetype: its creation, development and how it is integrated into the spiritual body of the Earth.

Mrs. Mary Ellen Willby, herself a parent with a Waldorf teacher training, realized that Waldorf teachers need to know and to find the connection between their spiritual scientific knowledge of man and the findings of modern neuropsychology. Out of her experience of working in Waldorf education with children who had these problems, she had the enthusiasm to initiate the *Bulletin* of the Remedial Research Group. For five years, with the support of Rudolf Steiner College, she edited the *Bulletin* for Waldorf teachers; she also published a newsletter for Extra Lesson teachers. Now, in her retirement, Mrs. Willby has selected articles from issues of the *Bulletin*, together with other new and relevant material, to produce this handbook. Those of us working in this field are indeed indebted to her for her devotion and love for Waldorf education.

Audrey E. McAllen
Stroud, England
Winter 1998

Editor's Note:
Profile of Audrey McAllen

Many have heard of Audrey McAllen only through her work called *The Extra Lesson*. Therefore, it was thought that some background of the destiny that led Audrey to develop her seminal work for children with specific learning difficulties would be welcome.

She was born in Southhampton — the south coast of England — during the holy nights of 1920. Her father was a young officer in a passenger shipping company serving the African continent. Audrey was nourished with stories of the sea by her father and often visited the ship when it was in port. She wanted to become a writer, but her mother encouraged her to take a teaching post. It was in a small boarding school that the fundamental question of education was posed; one child everyone loved, the other irritated and annoyed everyone. Why, and how could one learn to love the unlovable? Destiny in the shape of the war intervened. Audrey returned home and was asked to form a tutorial class for children who had not been evacuated from this coastal danger area. An advertisement in *The Teachers World* on a short course for problem children at The Sunfield Children's Home introduced her to Anthroposophy. She then met Eileen Hutchins who told her about the Steiner Schools for normal children and Audrey recognized immediately that this was the way for her. She took the teacher training course sponsored by Eileen Hutchins, Elly Wilke and teachers of the Elmfield Steiner (Waldorf) School in Stourbridge (near Birmingham). Elly Wilke was one of the first eurythmy teachers of the original Waldorf school in Stuttgart, Germany. When the war came, Elmfield school was evacuated and moved to Sunfield Children's Homes in Clent near Stourbridge, which had a normal school, a school for the handicapped and training programs. The training had as its basis lectures which included the senses and the currents which flow through the human being. These lectures, called *Anthroposophy,* were given by Rudolf Steiner in 1909 in Berlin, Germany. Audrey was then 21 years old.

At the end of the school year she stayed on to see the St. John's festival and so missed the blitz of Southhampton. At the time of the blitz, her mother was in a neighbor's shelter, fortunately, for later three bombs were found in the McAllen's shelter. Audrey's father, too, survived the war. He had been reassigned to captain another vessel days before his original ship was destroyed.

Meanwhile, the group of children Audrey had left in the care of another teacher had grown, and when Walburga Hauschka, a eurythmist, came to work with her, a sign bearing the name of Rudolf Steiner was displayed outside the school. The children's work so impressed the inspector of schools that Audrey was exempted from military service and Miss Hauschka, who was Austrian, was exempted from internment. Eileen Hutchins and other teachers came regularly to give guidance and talks to parents, and Francis Edmunds visited.

Years later, Audrey asked Elly Wilke why she chose and translated these particular 1909 lectures for the teacher training course; her answer was that it had been 33 years since Steiner had given them and she wondered what the new generation would be able to make of them. Later when Audrey observed children, she saw their movements in relation to these lectures. The school continued to grow; new premises were needed but no funds were forthcoming. So, although new pupils were coming to the school, other factors brought about the decision to close in 1947. The ages of the children — kindergarten through fifth grade — made it possible for them to be easily placed in other schools. One of the established Steiner schools offered two scholarships which made it possible for two of the pupils to have a Steiner education from kindergarten through class twelve.

After the school closed Audrey went to Holland and studied speech formation with the late Mrs. Tamo Tymstra of the Hague Teacher Training Course. There she also met Herr Gümbel Zeiling, the original 'Strader' in the first productions of the Mystery Plays by Rudolf Steiner; she had speech lessons with him. On her return to England she became a class teacher for ten years at Michael Hall, the Steiner (Waldorf) school in Forest Row. During the time she was a class teacher she continued her speech training (see acknowledgements in Audrey's book *The Listening Ear*). After this, she moved to Gloucester to take care of her mother.

A boy who was having learning difficulties was sent by his class teacher to Dr. Norbert Glas, the school doctor at Wynstones School. Dr. Glas found nothing wrong with him medically. Since Wynstones was near Gloucester, he asked Audrey to work with the child; she again turned to the notes from her teacher training year. The research that eventually emerged was made possible by the confidence and generosity of the college of teachers at Wynstones. She was sent other pupils, and her research to meet the deep and pressing needs of the children continued for about twelve years.

Around 1973, Audrey gave a talk at a teachers conference; there she met Eva Frommer who had been a pupil at Michael Hall and had become a physician and a member of the Anthroposophical Society. She directed a clinic at St. Thomas Hospital in London. After Audrey's talk, Dr. Frommer congratulated her on having the neurology correct. This was a surprise to Audrey for she had arrived at this 'correct' neurology by studying Dr. Steiner's lectures. Dr. Frommer and her associate Dr. M. MacAuslan, head of the dyslexia department at St. Thomas Hospital, as well as several Steiner school teachers, encouraged Audrey to make her work available to teachers, thus, *The Extra Lesson*, the 'blue book', was first published in 1974. This first edition had only one chapter as an introduction to the exercises, called 'How Do I Get into My Body'. This innovative work of Audrey McAllen springs from morally permeated inventiveness, resulting from the perception of concrete life situations, which developed new solutions based on actual perception and on individually active imagination.

It was 1974 when my youngest child entered Wynstones School. His teacher recommended I take him to Audrey McAllen for assessment, after both the doctor and psychologist had diagnosed him as severely dyslexic, holding forth little hope for him to read . . . ever. At this time, Audrey no longer saw children for individual lessons but was available for consultation. From 1978 to 1983, Audrey was also responsible for the course on speech for the teachers in the Kindergarten Training Course at Wynstones School.

My first impression of Audrey was her gentle, light-filled eyes, her smile of welcome and the warmth that came from this charming lady. It was through her encouragement that I began helping my child with the exercises from *The Extra Lesson* which turned around the gloomy forecast of the doctors. Being present at the magical moment when my son began to read — he was 12 and one half years old — inspired my efforts later to help the children at the Sacramento Waldorf School in Fair Oaks, California.

Later, I began teaching the exercises from *The Extra Lesson* to the teacher trainees at Rudolf Steiner College. Audrey was invited to the college by director René Querido former colleague at Michael Hall. She returned to teach classes for several years at Rudolf Steiner College, worked with teachers in several Waldorf schools on the West Coast and presented a workshop to Extra Lesson teachers at the West Coast Teachers Conference in 1986. The founding of the Remedial Research Group in these years eventually led to the Remedial Education Program at Rudolf Steiner College. This program, currently (2005) in its seventh cycle, is directed by Ingun Schneider who was a founding member of the Remedial Research Group.

Audrey also taught a three-week course at the Rudolf Steiner Institute in Maine. She was invited to speak on movement at a conference sponsored by the Camphill Association for Healing Education at Camp Glenbrook, New Hampshire. She gave a workshop at the East Coast Teacher's Conference, Spring Valley, New York and worked with schools on the East Coast. In England, she taught at Emerson College and the Tobias School of Art in Sussex. Invitations from New Zealand, Canada, Finland, France and Holland brought Audrey to all of these countries. After the publication of *The Extra Lesson* she was invited by Else Göttgens and the late Annerie Marx to address class teachers at their annual tutorial seminar in Zutphen, Holland, and continued this for several years. There she met Joep Eikenboom, a class teacher at the Rotterdam Waldorf School, who when he had finished his class made himself responsible for the Extra Lesson work at the Dutch Teacher Training at the Hogeschol, Helicon, Zeist. [Although, in 2004, Joep is still a class teacher, he continues this work with groups in the Netherlands, the United States, and Germany where this initiative is under the direction of Uta Stolz.]

In Australia Lalage Craig, another Waldorf teacher, discovered Extra Lesson and traveled to England to study with Audrey. This resulted in an invitation from the Glenaeon Steiner School in Sydney to visit Australia where, together with Lalage she gave a full foundational course on Extra Lesson educational support to class teachers and those working in therapy.

In the United States Mary Jo Oresti, teacher of children with these difficulties in the Detroit Waldorf School, was invited to the first conference held in England on this subject at Emerson College where she heard Audrey lecture. From her new enthusiasm for the Extra Lesson work, Mary Jo founded and now co-directs with Joan Ingle the Waldorf Remedial Education Program on the East coast (US). (For information on training centers see resource page.)

'Retired' Audrey maintains an extensive correspondence; the many teachers who come to her also keep her busy. She also lectures in the two-year Extra Lesson training workshops led by Monica Ellis in Gloucester.

This profile would be incomplete without mentioning Audrey McAllen's relation to the work and person of Rudolf Steiner whom she recognized as her teacher and guide. Anthroposophy formed for her the basis of her own spiritual orientation, personal destiny, scientific thinking, work and research.

* * * * *

In the lectures given by Rudolf Steiner in 1909 (see above), he spoke of the senses for the first time, describing them from the viewpoint of the phases of Earth's evolution as development of the vessel (body) to contain the Ego (see Steiner's *An Outline of Esoteric Science*). Later, Steiner related the senses to soul development, the biological and psychological growth expressed in thinking, feeling and willing. A lecture cycle by Steiner illuminating this latter viewpoint is *Man as a Being of Sense and Perception*. The exercises in *The Extra Lesson* are derived from Steiner's description of the archetypal form of the physical body seen as spirit. The physical body is of primary focus as are developmental hindrances to it which are the root causes of learning difficulties. Thus, teachers are dealing with the body as spirit in order for the soul to use it as its instrument, which differentiates this approach from most other therapies. In this view, psychological issues are secondary. Current findings in neuropsychological research match Audrey McAllen's pedagogical insights of over a score of years ago.

In the years since its first publication in 1974, and its subsequent translation into several languages, *The Extra Lesson* (now 5th English expanded and revised edition and second revised German edition *Die Extra Stunde*) has become a well-worn book in the hands of teachers world wide when applied to the children in their care. The aspect which most distinguishes a Waldorf/Steiner school is its spiritual stream. Audrey McAllen is an inspiring guardian of that stream. This can be seen clearly in her book *The Extra Lesson*, as well as in other publications which further and elucidate the concepts that lie behind it. These publications are: *Sleep: an Unobserved Element in Education; The Listening Ear; Teaching Children Handwriting;* and *Reading Children's Drawings: The Person, House and Tree Motifs.*

In the 1980's, she contributed to the *Bulletin*, the bi-annual publication of the Remedial Research Group, and although the publication of the *Bulletin* has ended, demand for them continued. The need was seen to bring the contents of the various issues of the *Bulletin* under one cover. As editor of the *Bulletin*, this task fell to me; this handbook is the response to this need. The articles chosen from the *Bulletin* issues have been revised and updated by the authors, and new articles have been added. I am grateful to have been able to contribute to the work of those striving toward education for the future of mankind.

Mary Ellen Willby
Fair Oaks, California, 2005

"Our age is the first period of time in which the Gods put man's own, free spiritual activity to the test. True, the Gods do not refuse their help, but they vouchsafe it only when by the strength of aspiration developed in the soul through a number of incarnations, men make themselves worthy to receive the forces streaming to them from above. What we ourselves have to create is essentially new — in the sense that we must work with forces differing altogether from those in operation in bygone times. We have to create out of the free activity of our own human souls. The hallmark of our age is consciousness —it is the epoch of the Consciousness Soul. If the future is to receive from us such works of culture and of art as we have received from the past, we must create out of full and clear consciousness, free from any influence arising from the subconscious life. . . . Only if we know upon what laws and fundamental and spiritual impulses our work must be grounded, only if what we do is in line and harmony with the evolutionary forces operating in mankind as a whole — only then will achievement be within our reach."

— Rudolf Steiner
Berlin, December 12, 1911

I

Deeper Insights

The Structural Physical Body As Archetype of Man's Spiritual Being

Audrey E. McAllen

In schools the world over, teachers are facing the problem that they can no longer expect the capacity in children to learn to write, read and do arithmetic as a natural faculty. The number of children per class who are lacking these basic abilities on which learning depends is increasing to such proportions that, in the American state system class teachers are being encouraged to accept specialist teachers into the classroom as part of their classroom 'equipment'.

It is beginning to be recognized that learning problems are connected with a lack of spatial orientation; the child does not perceive how he moves in space, neither does he recognize his own bodily relationship to it. This can be characterized by his inability to understand the meaning of the preposition, the part of speech which guides us in space. "Go to the door — put the ball in the basket — stand on the stairs." This is an outer element. Inwardly, he cannot connect the movements between himself and his body. "Touch your head with your right hand." Such a direction requires thought-time before there is a response. Neither can he, on his own recorder, spontaneously copy the movements of the teacher's fingers.

What is this inability to learn which is spreading through children like a new disease? What is it telling us? It is an 'Orwellian' end-of-the-century challenge.

In Waldorf education we have to ask the question, "What does this phenomenon mean?" Powers are at work to destroy, to distort man's sense of his ego which is based on *the archetype of the physical body*. These same powers would prevent the healthy development of the consciousness soul — the member of the soul without which the human being cannot grasp, through his will forces, his own and the world's spiritual being.[1]

In a very important lecture on the senses, Rudolf Steiner defines the physical body as the sum total of the senses in their working together.[2] The structural sensing form of the physical body in its connection with the constellations of the zodiac[3] is *archetypal* and is formed from the cosmic forces working in surrounding space. While planets work into the interior organic process via the etheric body,[4] the zodiac works through physical forces.[5] The structure of the physical body is common to everyone, whether one is Chinese, English, American, or Indian. The bones of the skeleton are the same in number and proportion and function, the muscular system has the same type of muscles to move this skeleton, and all human beings have the same brain structure and nervous system to perceive their movements and the effects of their movements. All this, the writer would designate as the *structural physical body* which is concerned with spatial perceptions, while the organs with their planetary connections can be defined as the *physiological constitutional* element.[6] The ego has the capacity to use this *archetype* with all its manifold variations in size, weight, agility and constitution.

Let us consider that the *structural physical body* is designed to stand, move and perceive in three-dimensional space. The fact that the baby lifts itself into the upright position and is thereby able to move to the left or the right, forward and backward, to look and move up and down is the signature of the ego. This physical-spatial organism was designed as an ego-bearer. This fact is clearly stated in the book *An Outline of Esoteric Science* by Rudolf Steiner. It was at the end of the Saturn period of evolution that the Saturn 'Earth' body and its structures developed the capacity to manifest as an ego-bearing organism.

This *structural physical* organization is the vessel for the individual ego and gives it the ability to function in three-dimensional space. This ego relationship to space is carried over into the time element in that the physical body is that vehicle from which the ego awakens into the consciousness soul.[7] The consciousness soul which is developed between the ages of 35 and 42 years is defined by Steiner as that part of the soul in which the ego is able to recognize and grasp itself as a spiritual being and to understand that the same spirit is working in the outer world around him. One might say that this is the reason for having a sense organization able to perceive the world around it.[8]

There is the need for class teachers to understand the steps of development in the first seven years of a child's life just as thoroughly as a kindergarten teacher does.* We also have to recognize that a remedy for incomplete or interrupted development of the *physical-spatial coordination system* of the physical body will have to take into account the spiritual Being of the planet Earth and the archetypal movements of its spiritual bodies and their laws.[9]

We must not regard the laws pertaining to the physical world, either bodily or in space, as being purely mechanical; we have to remember, in many other connections, that Steiner has also told us that the laws of Nature are — in higher Devachan — moral laws, the will forces of the spiritual Beings with whom the eternal core of our being — the Ego — lives between death and rebirth. The archetypal structure of the sensing, moving physical body is likewise formed out of these same moral laws. It is from the embodiment of these moral forces, which we carry in our body of formative forces (see p. 276), that we are revitalized during sleep when we are in the environment of the spiritual body of our Earth planet.[10]

Meeting this attack on the *spiritual archetype* of the physical body requires that we take into account the supersensible forces in space and how man's body is integrated into the physical, etheric and astral bodies of the Earth. The exercises of *The Extra Lesson* are an attempt in this direction.

---

* In the first seven-year period the 'education' of the physical body takes place; the pre-school child lives entirely in sensory experiences and in their effects on the will, and by the change of teeth the teachers expect that the faculties to learn to write, to read and to calculate will spring naturally from the physical organism. (See article p. 28.)

1 Rudolf Steiner, *Deeper Insights into Education*; Audrey E. McAllen, *Sleep*.
2 R. Steiner, *The Zone of the Senses*, December 30, 1918.
3 R. Steiner, *The Shaping of the Human Form Out of Cosmic and Earthly Forces*, November 26, 1920.
4 R. Steiner, *Planetary Spheres and Their Influence on Man's Life on Earth and in Spiritual Worlds*, lecture August 22, 1922.
5 R. Steiner, *Cosmic Forces in Man*; Ernst Marti, *The Four Ethers*, pp. 5-8.
6 R. Steiner, *The World of the Senses, the World of the Spirit*, lecture 4.
7 R. Steiner, *Metamorphoses of the Soul*; *Paths of Experience*, Vol. 2, lect. 7; Gilbert Childs, *An Imp on Either Shoulder*, chapter 6, 'The Age of the Consciousness Soul'; Owen Barfield, *Romanticism Comes of Age*, see essay 'On The Consciousness Soul'.
8 R. Steiner, *An Outline of Esoteric Science*, chapter 1.
9 R. Steiner, *A Psychology of Body, Soul and Spirit*, lectures given October 23-27, 1909.
10 R. Steiner, *The Three Stages of Sleep*, lecture given March 24, 1922; *Man's Experiences in Sleep*, lecture given November 13, 1921 in Dornach; *The Etherization of the Blood*, lecture given October 1, 1911 in Basel; Audrey E. McAllen, *Sleep*.

Twofold Man as Archetype

Audrey E. McAllen

It is quite clear that the causes of learning problems in the normal child are connected with the developmental stages of the first seven years. With this in mind, the writer would like to consider learning problems in relation to the *heredity body*. The heredity body is the model body that the child receives from his parents.

It is known from Rudolf Steiner and from our own observations that, from the time of birth, it requires three times about two and a third years for the 'cognitive development' to mature and become a faculty for learning.

In most of Europe and Scandinavia, the ego is centered in the etheric body and in the development of the intellectual soul. This occasions a particular sensitivity to the requirements of the etheric body. The innate wisdom of these people brought it about that children did not start school and 'learning' until they were seven, the age at which the independent etheric body is born. It can then be expected that the *soul-spirit* has transformed the heredity model body into one suited to its own requirements.

In the West (the English-speaking world) where the ego development is centered in the *structural physical body* and therewith the development of the *consciousness soul*,[1] this wisdom connected with the formative forces of the body (see Rudolf Steiner, *Theosophy*, chapter 1) has been eclipsed by an expectation of early intellectual attainment. Learning which is based on 'cognitive development' is stressed, and the faculties arising from the physical body are used prematurely. School starts at five years, just when the third stage in the first seven years of development is starting, and the first beginning of a 'head-thinking' consciousness shows itself; instead of allowing this to consolidate in the bodily processes, it is seized upon for learning. The West has become so fanatical for learning attainment that children are being 'prepared for school' in play groups.

Newell C. Kephart's[2] hypothesis is that the children who begin well in the early grades (that is, children who are still in the imitative kindergarten stage which has not been allowed to mature in the body) and then fail in the later grades are those with poor sensory-motor integration. So, let us look at the sensory-motor system as it is given in the heredity body.

When we consider the human being from this point of view, Rudolf Steiner says it is necessary to look at him from a twofold aspect — head and trunk.[3] The head as the Earth; the body, limbs and organs as the Cosmos. Consider then this 'instrument' which the ego will eventually use for its cognitive development: the structural body of bones, muscles, and nerves which are the 'instrument' of perception of itself and of the space around it. Is there a twofolding to be seen? The content of the lectures *The World of the Senses and the World of the Spirit* indicates that there is. The nervous system has two functions: sensing (sense perception through the sense organs) and perceiving by 'inner-sensing' our response to this outer sense perception. Neurology describes how, with the help of chemical processes, electrical impulses pass across the synapses, or gaps between nerve endings. Spiritual science describes how the spiritual world interpenetrates the human being at the points of the synapses and makes it possible for the act of will to flash into consciousness.[4] This gives us a clue to a cause for the difficulties in those children who do not perceive their own movements.

The nervous system is the physical organ of perception. Steiner describes the nervous system as a spiritual sheath which, due to the 'Fall of Man', has been filled with matter. Seen spiritually, this nervous system is the work of the Spirits of Wisdom (Kyriotetes) and is a construction of their 'Intuitions'. Similarly, our muscles, now filled with substance, were originally intended to be sounding, like the swaying movements of music. The muscles are formed of the 'Inspirations' of the Spirits of Movement (Dynamis). Likewise our visible bones are the solidified 'Imaginations' of the Spirits of Form (Exusiai). (See Glossary p. 275.) The supersensible physical body of the human being has been filled with matter and become visible to the senses.[5]

The spiritual substance of this supersensible archetype was the gift of the Spirits of Will (Thrones). They poured out their own warmth at the beginning of our evolution to form the first spiritual body of the Earth planet — the 'body' of Old Saturn. This body was formed by the Hierarchies to receive in the course of time the ego of the human being and to become a mirror in which one could recognize oneself as a spiritual being.

This spiritual structural body, the work of the Primal Creative Beings of the universe, is the archetype which is imprinted into the stream of physical heredity. Between death and rebirth, we live in this spiritual archetype. On entering incarnation, we bring this archetypal picture with us. The soul and spirit of the child has to integrate this picture with the parental heredity body, which also carries the spiritual evolutionary archetype, solidified into form.* The educational task is to help the child accomplish this integration to the best of the teachers' and child's ability.[6]

We are perceiving and moving in the physical condensation of the Intuitions, Inspirations, and Imaginations which is the wrought work of the Hierarchies.[7] Earlier forms of consciousness knew this and recognized it in ceremony and ceremonial clothing. A study of armor and costumes through the ages is most revealing. Even the present day delight in materials with gold and silver thread, or with sequins can be seen as a remnant of the awareness of spiritual light and of the activity connected with the spiritual aspect of processes within the synapses.[8] Do human beings not sparkle as they move? Is this why 'sparklers' are a delight to children?

Just as the nerve-senses are twofold, so are the muscles: extensors and flexors — those muscles which stretch out to grasp the object, the others which lift. The soul, as it enters into the body, unites with these activities in movement and gesture. It enters gravity[9] and releases itself. The 'stretching man' is connected with sensory activity; the 'lifting man' is connected with motor movements. The 'stretching man' is the organ of day-wake consciousness of the present work-a-day ego. 'Lifting man', the deeply embedded subconsciousness of the individuality of the previous incarnations, is at work in the will. The blood is the bearer of this individuality and carries in its stable temperature the warmth of the Old Saturn period. Steiner gives the sequence of blood almost becoming muscle,[10] muscle becoming nerve, and nerve becoming bone.[11] The skeleton carries the muscle/nerve 'stretching-lifting man' and is the organ of the ego in three-dimensional space. The rounded bones of the skull

---

* The body which comes from the womb is the end result of Saturn, Sun, and Moon evolution (see *An Outline of Esoteric Science*), the spiritual archetype solidified into form. The potential *heredity* will be the substance and aberrations of this archetype, ie., healthy organs (liver, etc.) or distorted organs.

protect the brain in which are incorporated the formative forces; the radial bones of the limbs enter into gravity, making man an inhabitant of the Earth.

In children with specific learning difficulties, the lack of both development and integration of movement and sensory activity during the first seven years of life requires us to penetrate the problem with the understanding of *spiritual science*. We can then distinguish, for example, the difference between offering the children contrived or natural experiences, the difference between playing with plastic bricks or with real logs and sticks and between fitting geometrical shapes into corresponding templates or running and drawing these shapes; between simulated movements and movements based on spiritual scientific laws.

Contemplation of spiritual facts leads to finer observation and recognition of health-giving activity for the child, so that he can find his way to use this 'cosmos' of trunk-limb which has been given him by the Hierarchies. This activity can then be written into the 'earth-head' and thence become cognitive faculty for use in learning in daily life. The summary on the facing page is to aid contemplation of these facts.[12]

1 Rudolf Steiner, *The Challenge of the Times*, lecture 6, December 8, 1918.
2 Newell C. Kephart (1911 - 1973), *Learning Disability: an Educational Adventure*.
3 Rudolf Steiner, *Anthroposophical Life - Gifts*, p. 275.
4 R. Steiner, *The Foundations of Human Experience* (formerly *The Study of Man*) lecture 2; *Psychology of Body, Soul, and Spirit, A*, lectures October 23, 25, 26, 27, 1909.
5 R. Steiner, *The World of the Senses and The World of the Spirit*, lecture 5; *From Jesus to Christ*, chapter 6; and *The Etherization of the Blood*.
6 R. Steiner, *Practical Advice for Teachers*, p 9; Glossary p. 275.
7 See notes 4 and 5.
8 See note 4.
9 R. Steiner, *Initiation, Eternity, and the Passing of the Moment*, lecture 2.
10 The sixth grade is a milestone: the boys come quite heavily into their bony structure; the girls balance this phenomenon with more experience of the muscular/blood system so they find it easier to cope; one can see previously disguised difficulties emerge with boys and girls at this age.

11 R. Steiner, *An Outline of Esoteric Science* and *The World of the Senses and the World of the Spirit.*
12 R. Steiner, *Kindgom of Childhood*, lecture 5.

TWOFOLD MAN AS ARCHETYPE

'Stretching Man'		'Lifting Man'
sensory	**NERVES**	motor
daylight	light	shining in the darkness
	INTUITION	rainbow
extensor	**MUSCLES**	flexor
speaking	sound	singing
consonants	**INSPIRATION**	vowels
major		minor
radial	**BONES**	curved
past	warmth	future
	IMAGINATION	

'day-wake' consciousness　　　　　　　'sleep' consciousness

work-a-day ego　　　　　　　　　　karma-bearing ego
temporal personality　　　　　　　　of the individuality

subconscious by night　　　　　　　subconscious by day

SPIRITUAL-PHYSICAL FORM OF MAN — A WARMTH BEING FILLED WITH LIGHT AND TONE

IDENTITY AND PERSONALITY

Audrey E. McAllen

Specific learning problems require the teachers to look at the contrast between the *structural* movement system of the body (the bones, muscles, and nerves) and the *constitutional* composition of the body (the breathing, circulation, digestion and internal organs).

Developmentally the two systems stand in contrast to one another. The structural components complete their development in the first months of life; the fetus can sneeze in the womb. Sneezing is only possible if the nervous system can function as a whole. In contrast to this, the circulation, digestion and organs, although formed during this time, are not mature at birth and require the first seven years of life to complete their development. They have to be 'hatched out' by the love and warmth the child receives from his environment.[1]

The time when the individuality asserts himself as an earthly being is the great moment when he overcomes gravity and can stand upright. He is now free to move in all the directions of space, forward and back, up and down, left and right. It is this upright posture and movement in space which reflects to him his own identity; this is the act of the ego, the spirit being, which goes from one incarnation to the next and which is the judge of the soul (astral body) in the life after death.[2] This *eternal I* now lives in a state of pure consciousness with the whole of his surroundings and includes his body as an object of observation. Agatha Christie, in her autobiography, gives a very graphic instance of this. While watching her grandson, Mathew, walking downstairs at the age of two and one-half years, she noted that this was a new achievement of which he was very proud, although scared. He was muttering to himself, "This is Mathew going downstairs, Mathew going downstairs, this is Mathew going downstairs." She then comments, "I wonder if we all start life thinking of ourselves, as soon as we can think of ourselves at all, as a separate person, as it were, from the one observing. Did

I say over to myself, 'This is Agatha in her party sash going downstairs to the dining room.' It is as though the body in which we have found our spirit lodged is at first strange to us, an entity, we know its name, we are on terms with it, but are not yet fully identified with it. We are Agatha going downstairs. We *see* ourselves rather than *feel* ourselves. Then one day the next stage happens. Suddenly it is no longer, 'This is Mathew going downstairs.' Suddenly it has become 'I' am going downstairs.' The achievement of 'I' is the first step in the progress of a personal life."[3]

The consciousness that observes itself from outside is the *eternal I* that has been accompanying the Hierarchies as they have prepared man's future body and that of the Earth through the evolution of the Old Saturn, Old Sun, and Old Moon periods. *The nervous system which supports our consciousness has been evolved from the zodiac of the fixed stars; the zodiac is the archetype of this aspect of the physical body.* The structural movement system which supports our upright position is the basis of the consciousness soul into which the *eternal I* awakens between 35 and 42 years of age. It is mankind's task to transform — by the inner work of his ego — this structural physical body into Spirit Man in the far distant future. All this development potential is condensed into the first year of life.

In contrast, it takes three years before the child designates himself "I", the achievement of which, as Agatha Christie says, "is the first step in the process of a personal life." Every mother is aware of this stage; the toddler will not go to the newcomer so readily; he discovers the word "no" and can fill it with all the forces of his will!

This personal aspect of the ego — the soul being — belongs to the *constitutional organization* of the physical body where the processes are at work which develop the life organs. The planetary forces at work here are the seat of the soul of the *temporal I*, the personal one which is different in each incarnation and is conditioned by the karma of previous lives through the heredity body and the environment into which one is born. One's talents for the present incarnation arise from this *temporal I*. Observe the differences between the personal-temporal I of the individualities in the series Rudolf Steiner gives in *Karmic Relationships* (eight volumes) and in his mystery dramas.[4] This *soul I* is the consciousness with which we normally function; it is the seat of the intellect in our present time.

The seat of the *eternal I*, the spirit, is centered in the deepest senses: the 'visceral' (somatic) sense — sense of life; proprioception — sense of self-movement; and vestibular system — sense of balance; these are also the senses connected with the evolving Spirit Self, Life Spirit and Spirit Man.[5] These senses are the basis for the skills we develop; their 'organizer' is the *eternal I* — the spirit that grasps itself as a spiritual entity in the consciousness soul. The *soul I* is the part which has been sucked into the astral body and thereby has become embroiled in personal thinking, feeling and will, instead of using these soul capacities of thinking, feeling and will as organs of objective faculties.[6] One could say that all through life there is the struggle between the *eternal I* and the *personal soul I*. The *soul I* can choose between following the intentions of its spiritual being (*eternal I*) or allowing itself to be sucked in too deeply into the desires of the body beyond the body's natural needs.

The result of this tension is resolved during the period which the *soul I* and *eternal I* spend in Kamaloca in the life after death. The soul attributes of ideals, moral strivings and virtues are imprinted into the ethereal seed of the constitution of the new body which the *eternal I* will require for the next incarnation. All the will forces dissipated by the *soul I* in earthly gratification remain behind to burden the spiritual bodies of the Earth. The *eternal I* enters into the spiritual world to work with the Hierarchies in preparing the destiny and body for the coming earthly life.[7]

In his lectures called *Deeper Insights Into Education*,[8] Steiner gives to the teachers the educational and medical implications of these two systems, the *structural* and the *constitutional*. He defines an outer and inner physical body, an outer and inner etheric body and their interconnection with the astral (soul) body. The outer and inner physical body and outer etheric body is the concern of the teacher, while the astral (soul) body working within the organs, blood, breathing, and circulation is the province of the doctor. He then directs the teachers' attention to certain physical-chemical processes in the human being and their relationship to those in the world around. Such processes have now been noted and researched by scientists, and the Earth is being recognized as a self-renewing living organism.[9] Through this we have to realize that man is intimately related to the spiritual bodies of the Earth. Thus, we have a double identity — man as a picture of the Cosmos and man as a picture of the Earth. Keith Critchlow, as interviewed by Vicky Cruickshank, responded as follows;

> "Here we have it, don't we? The top and the bottom: what is a city spiritually and what is a city in relation to its food? — the beginning and the end are the same, and of equal importance. Work on one and you are immediately improving the other." Keith Critchlow: "Exactly, because the huge mystery about investing in materialism is that it is always unsatisfactory, because 'matter' is always in a state of change. Take, for example, the body, which we all identify with. If you think about it, with almost every cell changing every seven years and no piece of skin or flesh being more than eighteen months old, it all points to the remarkable fact that you as a person are totally impermanent and therefore basically a 'pattern' or an identity. The thing that is travelling through this curiously changing body of ours, is an identity, and once you invest in 'change' rather than in that pattern, everything breaks down: the identity of both the city and its citizens is gone...."[10]

Just as the Christ Being supports the *eternal I* in the first three years of life,[11] so does He now carry our Earth forward into its next evolutionary stages. And just as our environment imprints itself into our etheric body through the outer physical structural body, so does this *archetypal* structure of man have to be imprinted into the ethereal body of the evolving Earth.[12]

From this one can recognize that in Waldorf educational work the teacher has the responsibility to see that the child incarnates not only into the *archetypal* physical body, which has been given to him by the Hierarchies, but also into the *objective* physical and spiritual bodies of the Earth, the sphere in which the Christ is now working. The crucial time for the process of incarnation is during the first seven years. *If this process is not completed, then the necessary recapitulation becomes a matter of specific education.*

---

1   Rudolf Steiner, *The Education of the Child*, Part 1.

2 R. Steiner, *The Moral Configuration of Man in Sleep,* November 12-13, 1921. Die Gestaltung des Moralish-Geistigen des Menschen im Schlafe, the translation in English is available in typewritten form in the national Rudolf Steiner Libraries in various countries.
3 Agatha Christie (1890-1976), *An Autobiography,* p. 55.
4 R. Steiner, *Karmic Relationships* — eight volumes; R. Steiner, *The Four Mystery Plays.*
5 See diagram in Section I article 'Postural System'.
6 Zeylmans van Emmichoven, "The Seven Rhythms" in *The Foundation Stone of the Anthroposophical Society,* ; Rudolf Steiner, *The World of the Senses and the World of the Spirit.*
7 Audrey McAllen, *Sleep.*
8 R. Steiner, *Deeper Insights Into Education,* lecture 2.
9 James Lovelock, *A New Look at Life on Earth: The Gaia Hypothesis.*
10 Keith Critchlow, 'Wholesome Cities', from an interview by Vicky Cruickshank published in *Resurgence,* May/June 1995. No. 170. Professor Keith Critchlow is a Director at the Prince of Wale's Institute of Architecture, London, England.
11 R. Steiner, *The Spiritual Guidance of the Individual and Humanity* —essential reading for understanding the concepts in this handbook.
12 R. Steiner, *The Gospel of St. John in Relation to the Other Gospels,* lecture 10.

On the Imprinting of Man's Structural Physical Body's Spiritual Archetype into the Ethereal Body of the Earth

Audrey E. McAllen

Rudolf Steiner has described the physical body as the 'sum total of the senses'.[1] In doing this, he is drawing our attention to something very specific: an aspect of the physical body to which, because of the usual Anthroposophical picture of man, Waldorf teachers have not paid sufficient attention.

When we think of our physical body, we often associate it with something that has gone wrong and is causing us discomfort or worse! This is the 'process' aspect of the physical body.

What Steiner is referring to above is the *archetypal structural* element, which goes back to Old Saturn at the beginning of our planetary evolution. It was at this time that the senses were laid down, everything which during the following planetary stages would metamorphose into the bones, muscles and nerves on our present Earth — the structural aspect of our body. This 'structure' at the end of the Old Saturn time was so organized that inwardly it manifested as 'smell', and outwardly it could be apprehended — recognized — as a structure formed in such a way that it represented 'ego-ity' in the cosmos. That is, it was formed in such a way that it could be a 'cup' for the future ego that the gods intended to create. This evolution started in warmth. Today the primal archetypal warmth is contained in the blood. It is our blood[2] that is the connecting link between the two aspects of the physical body: 1) its constitutional process of matter-transforming activity on which our ego needs to 'press' in order to obtain an awareness of ego consciousness and 2) the structural 'cup' which is to contain this ego so that it can know itself in space (spatial orientation) and inwardly visualize its structure (body geography/body schema). Spatial orientation and inner visualization are the basis for a healthy experience of the nine-year change where one recognizes oneself as an 'I-ego', and that the world is something separate. In the parlance of modern research — this factor of spatial orientation and inward visualization of the body's structure, together with the integration of the postural system (i.e. vestibular sense and proprioception) — "is the basis of a fundamental psychological process, i.e. the ability to differentiate between external space and the body schema which is actually the core of consciousness and the pivot of interaction between 'ego' and 'nonego', subject and object." F. S. Rothschild, 1963.[3]

This physio-psychological point in development the writer would suggest is the culmination of the first stage of childhood. Then the second stage, the soul aspect, takes over and the developing rhythmic system is ready for educational use.

The child enters the first grade when the birth of the ethereal body has taken place. This means that the coordination in the physical body has been completed and consolidated so that the child can repeat out of his own forces what has been nurtured in the kindergarten stage. In the words of neuropsychology, the child has attained:

> — Purposeful equilibrium, body image and the integration of the postural system (*the sense of balance and the sense of self-movement*)* which are basic for the use of instruments or objects (*for example pencils, rulers, etc.*);
> — Independence of both halves of the body (*to know your right hand from left hand, how to turn right and left - necessary for eurythmy*);
> — Learning of non-conditioned language (*learning to speak fluently*);
> — The possibility of developing creativity;
> — The capacity for higher-level learning.[4]

These faculties are the ones which the child needs if he is to learn to draw, to write, to retell stories, in short all that is given in the curriculum for first grade which is, in the writer's view, based on the recapitulation of the first seven years of life. This evolutionary principle of repetition occurs before the next stage of development takes place; hence, it is important that children are mature in the co-ordination of their physical organization. They should be at least six and

---

* Italics are comments added by writer.

a half years of age when they commence schooling. These extra months are essential, even if medically the constitutional processes of the physical body are complete and the child may *appear* ready for school.

The class teachers in a Waldorf School are accustomed to working with the concepts of the constitutional body of the child. They learn to recognize the temperament, how to balance the incorporation of the ego into the etheric body and to be aware of the change of soul when the nine-year change comes (this is the time when the digestive processes which have been controlled by the head pass over to the stomach, and the regulation of breathing to heartbeat in its adult rhythm is established).

The above developmental sequences relate to constitutional physiology, a revelation of the working of the ego into the etheric body and astral body according to the individual's life plan (karma).

What can we learn about the *structural* development which is the foundation in the body for the production of the skills needed to *draw*, to *write* and to *read*? Here we have much to learn from the large body of research contributed by occupational and physical therapists and doctors who have specialized in neuropsychology, having in some cases spent a lifetime devoted to helping children with specific learning difficulties.

In lectures[5] by Rudolf Steiner, he says we can look at the human organization from a twofold aspect — head and trunk. It was from this indication that the writer recognized the connections between this new science developed during her lifetime and the picture of the first seven years with which Waldorf teachers are all familiar. We can also see the human being as a twofold entity from the structural and the constitutional aspect — the 'cup' and its content.

The structural body is archetypal, that which we have in common with all men, and which is complete at birth — the nerves, muscles and bones. This is in contrast to the archetype of the organs, whose growth and functions are not completed until the end of the seventh year, with the rhythm of circulation and breath completed during the tenth year.[6]

This structural body is the oldest part of us; it was laid down in the Old Saturn evolution and has been carried through the work of Higher Beings throughout the evolution of the planetary system and has metamorphosed into what we know now as our structural system of muscle, bones and nerves.

Medically, it is difficult to see the structural archetype, for doctors and curative educators are faced with such extreme distortions. For the normal child and adult, we are given a 'wrought work' which goes through a specific development which is the same whether we are large-headed, small-headed, or have a cosmic or earthly constitution. This archetypal path of development needs more of our attention now-a-days, because it culminates in the two physiological requirements for ego awareness, namely *spatial orientation* and *body geography* (body schema).

How is this spatial orientation and inner picture of one's body attained? Steiner has pinpointed the moment of standing upright as being the signature of the ego; he then goes on to develop our awareness of the interconnection between walking and speech, leading as they do to social integration, using imitation and imagination. When the child raises himself into the vertical, he is free to move left and right, up and down, forward and back; in these planes of dimension, the signature of threefold man is implicit. He defines these planes as the thinking plane, the feeling plane, and the willing plane.[7] As soon as there is a duality, eg. left-right, the ego focus comes into play where the two meet. Here, again, the body of Old Saturn is seen as the 'cup' for the ego. Also, we know from Steiner's lectures given in 1923[8] that through movement the physical body is inserted into the etheric body. It is via the sense of self-movement that the body geography is imprinted into the etheric body. This imprinting process is the crucial situation for the nine-year change (between age nine and ten).[9]

This *outer imprinting* should ideally match the *archetypal imprinting* which the individuality is inserting into the etheric body from *within* via the objective element in his astral body which he has brought with him from his life between death and rebirth.[10] Problems can arise if there is weakness or discrepancies from either of these *imprinting* activities.

Children with learning difficulties have problems in just this area of spatial orientation and the imprinting of the body geography. One-to-one help is needed to make good this developmental gap, for it does not take place of its own accord after the change of teeth.[11] When recapitulated, the wonderful laws of movement within our body educate the soul. For example, the modern lifestyle plunges the soul too strongly and one-sidedly into the movement system. In an exercise like the Moving Straight Line and Lemniscate (*The Extra Lesson*, 62-63) one can see how the movement laws inherent in the structure of the body take over and school the soul. All activities of handwork, craft and instrument playing do this, as well. In effect, all the exercises in *The Extra Lesson* address spatial orientation and body geography, through the movement laws defined by Rudolf Steiner : 'the astral body moves in the opposite direction of the unified physical and etheric bodies' and 'the astral body moves in a spiral through the physical and etheric bodies during the day.'[12] The writer's research shows that this spiral has a clockwise movement.

The facts of spatial orientation and body geography are well known in educational therapy, and there are many types of movement exercises devised to remedy their lack of development. Teachers working out of Anthroposophy have something unique to add with the exercises in *The Extra Lesson*; these exercises have been developed from Steiner's indications in lectures given in 1909[13] and take into account the movements of the supersensible spiritual bodies of the Earth in relation to those of man. This objective element — which enables the soul to find its archetypal relationship to its own body in relationship to that of the Earth — has been a consoling factor to the frustrations in the incarnating process which the individuality has experienced.

There is the need to be aware that the Earth planet also carries in it the picture of *Man* — early Christian consciousness was aware of this, as seen in the maps portraying the Earth as the Body of Christ.[14] It is in the spiritual bodies of the Earth that the Christ — *The Ego of our Planet* — is now working.[15]

The importance of imprinting the structural image of man into his etheric body is highlighted in Chapter Seven, *East in the Light of the West*:

> "Mankind is entering a condition in which the ether body is to a certain extent drawing itself out of the physical body again; but it must not be thought that it now receives spontaneously everything which in earlier times it possessed as an ancient heritage. If nothing else happened but its withdrawal, the ether body of man would just leave the physical body and would retain in itself none of the forces

which it formerly possessed. In the future it will be born from out of the human physical body. If the human physical body did not add something to it, this ether body would be empty, barren. The future of human evolution will be that men will, as it were, allow their ether body to leave their physical bodily nature, and they will eventually have the possibility of being able to send it out empty. What does that mean? The ether body is the force-bearer, the energizer of all that takes place in the physical body.[16] It must not only provide forces for the physical body when it is entirely concealed within it, but at all times; it must provide forces for the physical body even when it is again partly outside it. If the ether body is left empty it cannot react upon the physical body, for it would then have no strength with which to react. The ether body must, after it has passed through the physical body, have obtained its forces from within the physical body. The forces with which the ether body can react again upon the physical body, must have been drawn from within the latter. The task of present-day humanity is to absorb into itself that which can only be acquired through activity in a physical body. That which is gained within the physical body accompanies evolution, and when man in future incarnations lives in organisms wherein the ether body is to a certain extent released from the physical body, he will experience in his consciousness a kind of memory through the partially liberated ether body."[16]

Where do we see the archetype for this imprinting? It is in the Gospel accounts of the Resurrection where the Christ shows his disciples the imprint of the wounds of the nails in His hands and feet and that of the spear in His side. Here we see the resurrected spiritual archetypal structure of the physical body imprinted into an ethereal body. This is a new phenomenon in earthly history.[17]

Nowadays everything connected with our physical structural body is exploited. The sensory organization is stimulated in every possible way. In consequence, the movements of our astral body cannot maintain their balancing activity, so it is possible to get all kinds of tensions in our muscular system, and these, in turn, block the neurological pathways that carry the stimulus to the brain for the soul to use.

Again, the writer wants to link this with planetary development. We are told that, at the end of the Old Saturn evolution, the planet manifested the future structure of the physical body inwardly as the sense of 'smell'. (This sense enables man to experience within his entire organism what comes to him from outside. It is an objective process, one that connects us to the world around us and to which we respond: objective and subjective processes are one.)[18] Steiner links this sense with the *consciousness soul*.[19] This is the soul member which becomes our possession by the age of forty-two. The consciousness soul gives us the faculty of recognizing that the Spirit has organized the body we live in, and that this same Spirit has created the world.[20] Furthermore, the basis for the consciousness soul is the physical body, whose education we are responsible for during the first seven years.[21]

The writer links this with the Old Saturn evolution. Within the warmth body of this preliminary stage of the Earth's planetary development, the Spirits of Personality (Archai) were engaged in forming what was to become the sense organs of the future human physical body. This activity enabled the Archai during that time period to develop the consciousness which present day human beings experience — an ego consciousness. Completing their work on Old Saturn, the Spirits of Personality were able to continue their development through Old Sun and Old Moon planetary evolutions in metamorphosing the warmth body of Old Saturn into what is now under their particular care in our present Earth stage, the bony structure of our body — the skeleton. When one sleeps, one's astral body and ego leave one's physical body and etheric body, and it is necessary for members of the Hierarchies to maintain these bodies. It is the spiritual structure of the physical body that the Spirits of Personality (Archai) protect, so that one's soul and spirit can pick the physical body up again when one awakens; hence, it is important that the sensory aspect of the physical body is recognized, because, since the beginning of his regency in 1879, the Archangel Michael is ascending to the rank of a Spirit of Personality (Archai). He is thus entering into direct connection with the warmth/will forces that formed the archetype of the sensory structural body of the human being on Old Saturn.

Rudolf Steiner tells us that, during the Old Moon evolution, certain beings within the ranks of the Hierarchies rebelled against the plan of the creator Godhead and attempted to seize them for their own purposes. This rebellion was defeated by those members of the Hierarchies who remained faithful to the evolutionary purpose of the Godhead. Michael was their leader.

Now in our time, another attempt is being made by these rebellious beings to separate the human being (ninefold man) from the Godhead, again trying to seize these will forces which formed the warmth body of Old Saturn.[22] Today, these will forces have been metamorphosed into our sensory structural physical body.

The attack on the sensory aspect of the physical body is something to be taken very seriously, as our senses have a twofold activity. By day, they are used for the perception of the world around us; by night, their function is to revive the formative forces of the body so that we awake refreshed each morning.[23] This process and the structural element of the physical body come under the domain of Michael as he enters into his new Hierarchical rank, and the development of the consciousness soul becomes paramount.

This new regency of Michael — his first since the Death and Resurrection of Christ — signifies that the cosmic Sun Forces (the Sun Intelligence) should penetrate directly into the physical and etheric body of the human being. Before the incarnation of Christ Jesus, the cosmic Sun Forces worked into the ego and astral body which then brought about changes in the physical and ethereal bodies of the human being.[24] Until this present period (when the consciousness soul develops), the astral body and ego were only gradually inserting themselves into the physical/etheric organizations.

The quote below is from Steiner's lectures on the Gospel of St. John which shows this wonderful connection between the Christ Being and Michael; or, one could almost say, what the Christ has done for Michael in preparation for this time when he will become a Spirit of Personality (Archai):

> "Through the entrance of Christ into the body of Jesus of Nazareth the individuality of Christ gained dominion over the bony structure itself with its physical and chemical processes. As a result there once lived on Earth a body able to use its forces in such a way that it caused the spiri-

tual form of the bony structure to become embedded into the evolution of the Earth. The sum of everything that man has undergone would be irretrievably lost, unless he were able to incorporate the noble form of his bony structure into the evolution of the Earth, as an evolutionary law of which he could by degrees gain mastery. No vestige of Earth-future evolution would be carried over into the future if the bony frame were not preserved. The form of the bony structure conquers death in a physical sense."[25]

In our modern life we can see how this attack on Michael results in an inability to properly use the body of the senses. One aspect is the very fact that the integration of the postural system, that is the vestibular system (balance sense) and the proprioceptive system (sense of self-movement), is interfered with during the development of the *first three years* (see article 'Postural System'). This integration takes place by the time the child says "I"; it is during these three years that the Christ Being supports every child.[26]

In the lectures which Steiner gave in Stuttgart in 1923, he said that we must understand Michael's struggle with the dragon in a particular sphere.[27] We need to recognize the interconnection of the senses with their spiritual functions (the connection of these functions with the Earth and its spiritual organization, and the inner soul relationship between the Earth and the senses).[28] *It is these relationships which teachers must take into account at the present time. In understanding this, we realize that we are then working for the healing of humanity in the future.*

To integrate the human being and the world as part of their developmental process is really the whole reason for our Earth incarnation.[29] This is why we are here on the Earth, because it is only from the Earth that we can gain the forces for the future. Again from the lectures on the Gospel of St. John, Steiner says:

> "At the moment of Golgotha the Logos began to unite with the Earth, the Earth aura changed. Anyone who understands the profound meaning of this mystery will feel not only that one's physical body is united with the physical Earth, but that one's psycho-spiritual being is united with Christ Himself, how Christ as the Spirit of the Earth flows through one's body."[30]

The above thoughts given at the course for children with specific learning difficulties in Land-en-Bosch, Holland, 1989, to teachers and doctors, have been revised by the lecturer.

UPDATE WITH REFERENCE TO ABOVE

A particular epoch has a particular task. Ours is to see that the double trinities penetrate properly.[30]

The diagram on the facing page shows this double trinity — the interrelationships of the spiritual members of the human being (ninefold man) with those of the Earth (as Gaiasophia).

In correlating the triads with each other (see the following instructions), and by adding the corresponding facts from the preceding articles and references, one can become aware of the totality of the Sophia Being in her threefold manifestation as Theosophia, Anthroposophia, and Gaiasophia sustained since the Resurrection by the Creative Word.

Trace the diagram using a sheet of tracing paper. Fold it in half horizontally. Correlate the triads with each other:

— Consciousness arising between the sentient soul and sentient body (astral organization) is grasped by the ego.

— The Intellectual Soul is awakened in the etheric body.

— The Consciousness Soul is awakened from the physical body.

— Likewise, Spirit Man is embedded in the mineral kingdom via the Consciousness Soul.

— The Life Spirit is the transformation of the Intellectual Soul connected to the plant kingdom and etheric body.

— The Spirit Self is the transformation by the ego of the sentient soul and sentient body (astral body) of the animal kingdom.

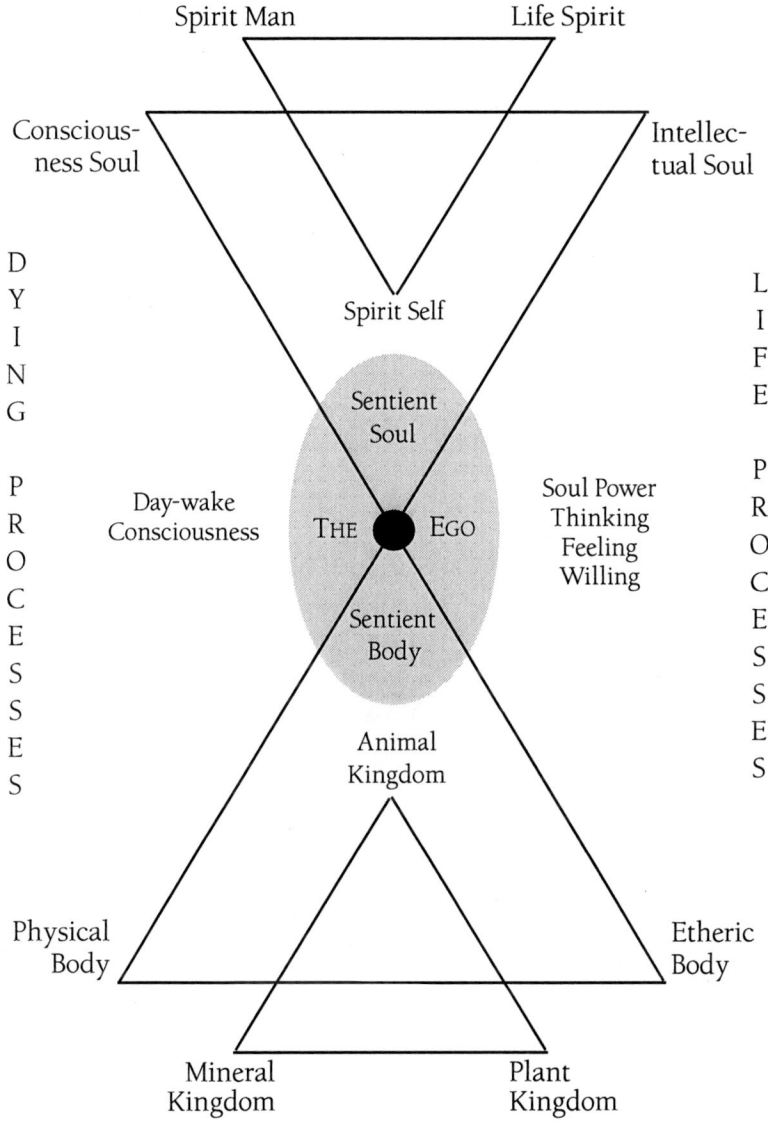

Imagine this total complex in movement within the human organization as a circulation of tone and speech: the Creative Word sounding from the Earth planet since the Resurrection.

1. Rudolf Steiner, *A Psychology of Body, Soul, and Spirit*, Lectures given October 23-27, 1909; and The Zone of the Senses.
2. R. Steiner, *The World of the Senses and the World of the Spirit*.
3. Julio B. de Quiros and Orlando L. Schrager, *Neuropsychological Fundamentals in Learning Disabilities*. Cited in *Learning Difficulties* pp. 75-79.
4. de Quiros and Schrager, op. cit., Chapter Two, Section 12, p. 27.
5. R. Steiner, *The Mission of the Archangel Michael*.
6. R. Steiner, *The Renewal of Education through the Science of the Spirit*, Lecture 8.
7. R. Steiner, *Mystery of the Universe: The Human Being, Image of Creation*.
8. R. Steiner, *Deeper Insights into Education*.
9. See James A. Dyson, Section III, 'Nine-Year Change'.
10. R. Steiner, *The Inner Nature of Man and Our Life between Death and Rebirth*.
11. Audrey E. McAllen, Two-Year Research Report of Children with Learning Difficulties in Waldorf/Steiner Schools, available from the Remedial Education Program Director at Rudolf Steiner College.
12. R. Steiner, *Planetary Spheres and Their Influence on Man's Life on Earth and in Spiritual Worlds*, pp. 58 - 59; *Mystery of the Universe: The Human Being, Image of Creation* (see information on the spiral and lemniscate); Margarete Kirchner-Bockholt, MD, *Fundamental Principles of Curative Eurythmy*, p. 83; Audrey E. McAllen, *Sleep*, p. 17.
13. Rudolf Steiner, *A Psychology of Body, Soul, and Spirit*, Lectures given October 23-27, 1909; and *The Zone of the Senses*.
14. Richard De Bello, Mappa Mundi, 13th Century, Hereford Cathedral, Hereford, Herefordshire, England.
15. See A. E. McAllen, Section I, 'Identity and Personality' (quote from Keith Critchlow); D. J. van Bemmelen, 'The First Goetheanum As a Mystery Temple', *Anthroposophical Quarterly*, 1964, Vol. 9 #1; Robert Lawlor, *Sacred Geometry*, in Chapter 9 'Anthropos', gives the geometrical construction of all archetypes within the human body.
16. R. Steiner, *East in the Light of the West*, pp. 133-134; *The Apocalypse of St. John*, lecture 12.
17. R. Steiner, *From Jesus to Christ*, Lectures 7 - 8.
18. R. Steiner, *Man as a Being of Sense and Perception*, 1958 ed., pp. 16-17.
19. See number 1.
20. R. Steiner, *The Michael Letters*.

21 R. Steiner, *Metamorphoses of the Soul*, Vol. 2, Lecture 5; Rahima Baldwin, *You are your Child's First Teacher*; John Thomson, *Natural Childhood*.
22 R. Steiner, *An Outline of Esoteric Science*, Chapter 'World Evolution' — Moon phase — Earth recapitulation.
23 R. Steiner, *The Etherization of the Blood*, p. 12.
24 R. Steiner, *Karmic Relationships*, Esoteric Studies, Vol. 8, Lectures 2 and 3; *The Invisible Man Within Us*.
25 R. Steiner, *The Gospel of St. John in Relation to the Other Gospels*, pp. 182, 183.
26 R. Steiner, *Spiritual Guidance of the Individual and Humanity*, Lect. 1; René Querido, *The Wonder of Childhood*.
27 R. Steiner, *Deeper Insights into Education; Man as a Being of Sense and Perception*.
28 R. Steiner, *World of the Senses and the World of the Spirit*.
29 R. Steiner, *The Foundations of Human Experience*, Lecture 1; Adrian Andersen, *Living a Spiritual Year*.
30 R. Steiner, *The Gospel of St. John in Relation to the Other Gospels*; For further study, see R. Steiner, 'The Twelve Senses and the Seven Life Processes in Man', August 12, 1916, Dornach (Switzerland); and 'The Significance of the Senses After Death', August 13, 1916, Dornach, published in *The Golden Blade* 1975, RSP, London.

The Mirroring Process in Relation to Two- and Three-Dimensional Space

Audrey E. McAllen

When looking at oneself in the mirror, surprisingly one sees one's left hand mirrored to ones left hand, right hand to right hand — this is a symmetrical mirror picture which appears in a flat mirror and in a convex mirror. Landscapes and maps are similarly described. One calls what is left and right on the map according to the left and right side of one's own body. This means that in *these situations* there is no depth, no three-dimensional element which requires the diagonal line of perspective (the will line). Only when we *face another person* and describe what is to our left as his right side, do we *inwardly* transfer *our* right side to *his* right side crosswise (diagonally). In this situation, we do not have the symmetrical mirror picture, but we cross over. This is a picture we can see in a concave mirror, like the inside of a large, shiny spoon: the right hand is mirrored on the left of the spoon, left hand on the right. Hold a concave mirror — the bowl of a round spoon — vertically to yourself, i.e. at 180^0, and the concave image will appear upside down, as well as 'reversing' left to right (see *The Extra Lesson* 15, 16).[1] Thus, behind perspective (three-dimensional space) is concealed a concave situation, as when we look into the concave bowl of the sky. But note that when this concave mirror — the inside of a large spoon — is held at a right angle to paper that is flat on a table (for instance at the top of this flat page and at an angle of 90^0 to this text), at a certain central point no reversals or upside-down reflecting occurs. We see our writing appear exactly as it is written. This never happens with either flat mirrors, like hand or wardrobe mirrors, or with convex mirrors, as for instance the back of a large spoon, either at 180^0 or 90^0. Concave and convex mirroring are connected with the *ability to change from a three-dimensional space to a two-dimensional one*.

This ability to change between three and two dimensions is needed for the skills of writing and reading. Drawing diagonal lines (including clock- and anti- clockwise curves) represents the third dimension (perspective) in a two-dimensional situation, i.e. on paper. Letters are made up of vertical and horizontal as well as diagonal lines and curves. We have to be aware of the fact that in writing and reading we are dealing with the sense of self-movement as much as with the sense of sight. The eyes in their sockets can move left-right, up-down and in a circle; this we can reproduce in two dimensions. To bring the eyes into the perspective situation of near and far, we have to use our limb system to carry them forward and back (the diagonal line in two-dimensional space). The eye itself is a convex globe. If we observe our movements in a mirror, the inner adjustments which we make, as for example in dance choreography, turn the mirror into an 'eye'. We watch ourselves and adjust, as from the mirrored image; we 'look' from the mirror back at ourselves. Rudolf Steiner describes that, to 'spiritual sight', the back of the head is open to the spiritual world. If we, as an ego, look into our head from this spiritual aspect, then by closing our eyes and imagining that the eyelids act as the silvering of the mirror, we can look from 'within' into our eye as in a concave aspect.

Therefore, we have to differentiate between astral mirroring and etheric mirroring. Steiner has also described astral mirroring as three-five-four being reflected as four-five-three. We have the following possibilities. A L M can be reflected in two and three dimensions as follows: Stand facing a convex mirror (180°), then a concave mirror (180°) holding a card with the written letters A L M. The reflection appears as in *Figure 1a*.

Fig. 1a

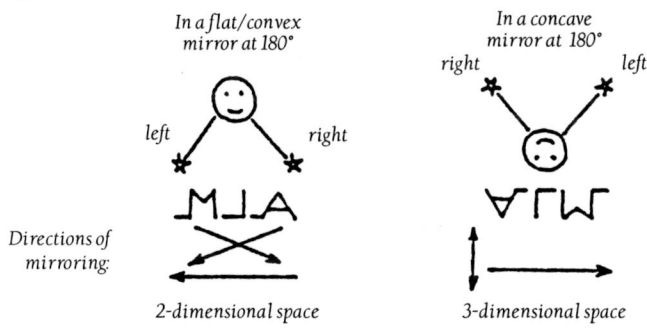

Place the written card A L M flat on the table before you (horizontal surface). Hold first a convex and then a concave mirror at 90⁰ beyond the writing at the top of the page. Reflection is as in *Figure 1b*.

Fig. 1b

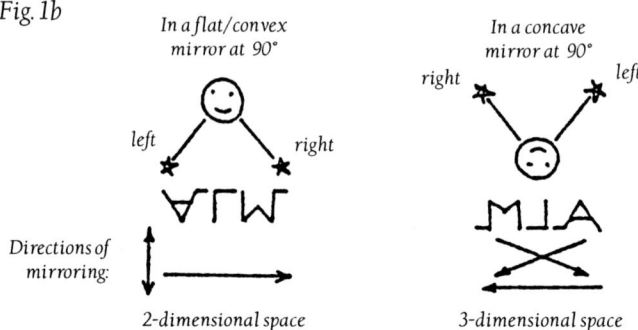

REFLECTIONS OF A L M AS A PALINDROME:
A L M in two-dimensional space as seen in *figure 2* as follows:

Fig. 2

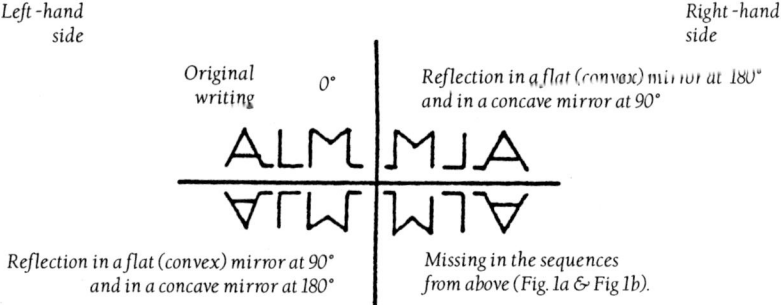

Rudolf Steiner differentiates between the right and left sides of the etheric body. From my observations of children's movements and drawings, it appears that the function of the left and right sides of the etheric body is to act as mirrors;[2] independently, yet simultaneously, the two sides of the etheric body mirror each movement we make. If one side does this without the other, the reflection sequence is distorted. We can give the sequence of reflections in man's spiritual bodies as follows, in *figure 3*:

Section I: Deeper Insights   31

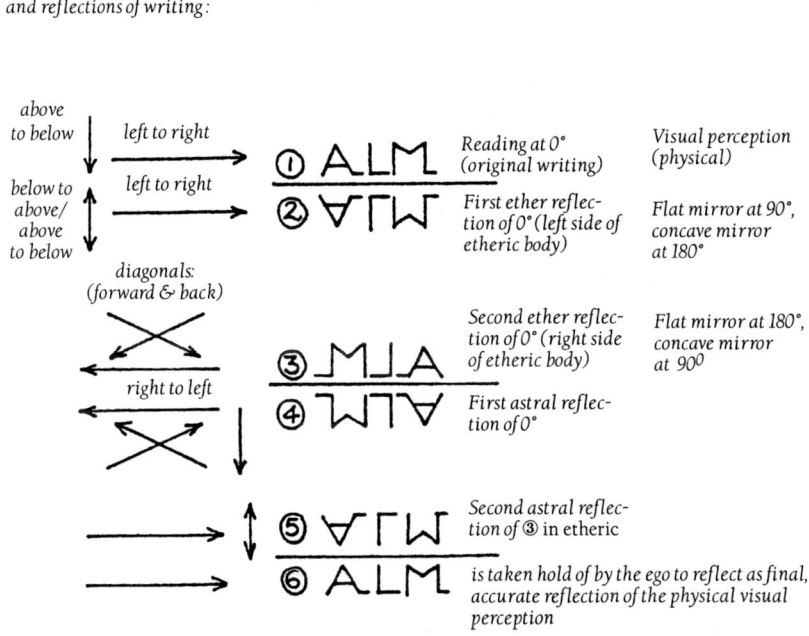

Fig. 3: Sequence of reflections. (Steps 3 and 4 are the crucial problems in reading difficulties).

In the course of discussions, I am often asked why there are adults and children who have cross or mixed dominance, yet who can still read, while for a larger number of others this dominance factor seems to be a stumbling block.

An answer comes to light if we consider the difference between the result from the usual form of dominance check[3] with that of the Handedness Pattern assessment.[4]

In the usual dominance test, teachers use a kaleidoscope or a paper with a hole in the center, and they observe the child as he raises this to his eye. A watch or a shell can be used for checking ear dominance. For hand dominance, the teacher observes which hand is used for writing or picking up an object, and for foot dominance, which foot is used to hop on. These findings are recorded and then compared with the child's use of foot, hand, and/or eye in the Handedness Pattern.

Assessment with the Handedness Pattern requires the child to sit on the floor in front of a basic symmetry form. Each form is drawn on a large (22" x 30" - 55cm x 75cm) card which is placed upright against the wall. Facing the vertical symmetry form,[5] the child is directed to move as described in *The Extra Lesson*, (p. 44). As the child moves, he has to cross the vertical midline[6] and is aware subconsciously of left and right. It is on subconscious levels that we automatically carry out movements while we are consciously thinking or speaking, i.e. in writing, we are thinking about the content, but not how the hand does the writing, or in reading while knitting we are thinking about the content, but not about how the hands do the knitting.[7] If foot, hand and eye dominance is not fully established on subconscious levels, the bizarre choice of foot, hand, and/or eye and the choice of different starting places on the form show that there are disturbances in the dominance patterns. These disturbances of dominance cause mirroring problems between the physical/etheric bodies and the responsive movements of the astral body.

A similar challenge to subconscious levels is made on the horizontal form[8] when space is divided into above and below, and the horizontal midline has to be crossed. Here, the child becomes aware subconsciously of above and below.

If the choice of foot, hand and/or eye on the Handedness Pattern corresponds to that of the usual dominance test (even when there is cross dominance), and the movements are from left to right and from above to below, the dominance pattern, even when 'crossed', is being consistently carried in a stable pattern throughout all the mirroring processes in the supersensible bodies — that is, *the supersensible activities are held in balance* (see *figure 3*). With this stable pattern, there are no conflicting mirror images arising from the subconscious, the child can write and read as the required motor activity is being carried on in the lower subconscious levels, and the instrument of the brain is free for the ego to use for learning and thinking.*

---

* 'Splinter Skills' — if a child cannot write with ease while thinking about the content of what he's writing, ie. he uses more tension than necessary for the process of moving the pencil on the paper to write, this activity (skill) is not subconsciously performed. 'Splinter skills' are those skills where the child has to bring conscious focus to an activity which he should be able to perform subconsciously.[9]

We know the supersensible currents[10] are reacting to the visual image without any control on the subconscious level when the child responds to the Handedness Pattern with bizarre choices of foot, hand and/or eye; the child traces the patterns from right to left and from below to above or without any consistent pattern; hence, the ego is faced with conflicting images which it cannot condense into one image corresponding to the percepts which eye and movement convey.

To make this clear, take the palindrome diagram (*figure 2*) and draw it onto a tracing paper. Now fold it on the vertical line and you will see that the left and right sides fit over each other — center is the vertical midline (Note: This is why the Mesker exercises[11] where the child draws a form with both hands simultaneously onto a double-sided black board — placed vertically in the symmetry plane before him — is so effective).

Now open up the diagram and fold it from above to below — horizontal midline aspect — again the letters cover each other.

Now fold the paper in both directions left-right, above-below, and again, there is a total match. This is the normal perceptional pattern for the ego: Both sides of the etheric body reflecting harmoniously, together, in relation to the astral body, see diagram of movement directions (*figure 3*).

When one of these sequences is interrupted due to disturbances in the dominance patterns, the reflection sequence is distorted and confusion results. We can then see the discrepancies from the normal in the Handedness Patterns as described in *The Extra Lesson*.[12] We can see in the Flower-Rod drawings illustrated in *The Extra Lesson*[13] how the flat mirroring, convex mirroring and concave mirroring are opposing reflections of each other in the movement system. We can therefore understand the confusion in the child's perception.

---

1   Audrey E. McAllen, *The Extra Lesson*, chapter 2.
2   Rudolf Steiner, *Metamorphoses of the Soul*, Vol. 1, Lecture 5.
3   See A. E. McAllen, Section II 'Dominance'; Dee J. Coulter, p.60.
4   A. E. McAllen, *The Extra Lesson*, pp. 42-51.
5   Ibid., pp. 43-44.
6   See number 3.
7   R. Steiner, *A Modern Art of Education*, Lecture 3.
8   A. E. McAllen, *The Extra Lesson*, p. 43.

9   See number 7.
10 R. Steiner, *A Psychology of Body, Soul, and Spirit*, Lectures October 23-27, 1909.
11 P. Mesker, *De Menselyke Hand*, 1980, Dekker & v. d. Vegt, Nijmegen, Holland.
12 A. E. McAllen, *The Extra Lesson*, pp. 42-51.
13 Ibid., pp. 51-55.

The Postural System

Audrey E. McAllen

"The postural system, what's that? Standing and sitting properly? Surely, this is for the gym and eurythmy teacher, nothing to do with me ; I'm a class teacher." But it is for the class teacher. Quietly over the last three decades, neuropsychologists, as well as occupational and physical therapists[1] have studied the causes for the crop of difficulties which stand in the way of learning. The following is one of their findings:

> Purposeful equilibrium, body image, the integration of the postural system are basic for:
> 1. The use of instruments or objects,
> 2. Independence of both sides of the body,
> 3. Learning to speak fluently,
> 4. The possibility of developing creativity,
> 5. The capacity for higher-level learning.[2]

All basic classroom requirements! So what about Tom who can't manage to draw a straight line with a ruler? Mary who still needs two hands to catch a ball? Bob who muddles his sentences, and that little group who never knows what to do until you tell each one of them? Then, there is Tim who copies everything from someone else and periodically falls off his chair when the class is listening quietly to the lesson. And what about Susan who always leans against the desk when the class stands for recitation?

Signs and Symptoms

These are all very ordinary things when spread out over the class, but if a child has two or three of these characteristics, then we must look at his Main Lesson books. Is the writing, spacing and cleanliness of the book passable? Is the memory good? Not too bad for him, one may think; but is it a child who, you think, could do better if he exerted himself? If that thought is at the back of your mind, then the child is in need of specific help. A characterization which the writer heard is that the children who sit so badly with limbs thrust forward while the body flops back onto the chair are ones who are pushing away the benefits which the pedagogy brings and who have a weak ego incarnation. *This is not a sufficient or necessarily correct reading of the child's condition.*

What is the situation of the children with specific learning difficulties? Again, teachers can learn from the research of neuropsychology:

"When higher levels of the brain are forced to enter into action in order to maintain posture, learning possibilities decrease."[3] In other words, the formative forces at work on the body during the first seven years have not been freed from their organic task in order to become usable for thinking and imagination.

The Postural System

Of what does the postural system consist? It is the two senses of self-movement and balance — in technical language the sense of self-movement is termed 'proprioception' and the term 'vestibular system' is used for the sense of balance. These are the basis of the postural system. These two senses, together with the sense of life, work in the deepest unconscious of our being. The working together of the senses of balance and self-movement perception are needed in order to stand upright. Once the human being attains verticality, walking becomes possible; from this, movement and speech arises. This is a process of ego activity metamorphosing to a higher level a specific sense function, i.e., the sense of speech is a metamorphosis of the sense of self-movement while the concept sense is a metamorphosis of the life sense.[4] The senses of the postural system should be integrated by about the age of three. This is the time at which the ego of the child manifests its first stage of coming into consciousness with the possibility of saying "I," so we see how deeply these senses are related to ego development. (See diagram page 39.)

Physiological Research

Since Steiner first spoke about the senses in 1909,[5] their physiological basis has been thoroughly researched. Work based on the discoveries of Sir Charles Sherrington[6] show that the proprioceptive organization is a series of responses within the muscles and tendons where nerve endings are arranged in the forms of spirals and flower sprays. These integrated impulses, in turn, interconnect with impulses from the two parts of the vestibular organs, i.e., the semi-circular canals (which are concerned with balance, acceleration and deceleration in space) and the gravity receptors (which are responsible for holding the head upright in relation to the trunk). These integrated impulses work back onto the muscle tone of the body.

If this very complicated system is not properly integrated, then what the child learns does not go into the subconscious, i.e., *into the ethereal body* — to mature and be available for recall. Learning is then only taken into the areas of the brain which respond to short-term memory. This means the child has to consciously relearn the same things day after day; thus, the contents of his lessons do not mature into faculty.[7] (See footnote 'Splinter Skills', page 32.)

If these facts are applied to eurythmy, we can perhaps understand some of the difficulties certain children have in this lesson. If the postural system is not functioning properly, there will be difficulty in transferring the movement control from the lower body to the new center of the shoulders for leading the movement. Forms will be the center of consciousness, and as soon as gesture is required, the form, such as a triangle or star, will be be lost; the child will experience that his body will not obey the gesture of his soul. He feels awkward and stupid and consequently behaves badly during eurythmy.

When I watched this happen, I was told that this boy was very good at mathematics, so he knew what a triangle was; he only couldn't get it into his feet! These are children who are in tension between their will and the response of their body, *creating a frustration which produces behavior problems.*

LACK OF DEVELOPMENT

In child study, teachers usually focus on the behavioral problems and their psychological cause. Today, there are causes that stem from a lack of proper development of the first seven years. One example of an interference in the development of standing is the use of baby walkers. The result of this lack of proper development of the first seven years is found in the children in today's classes.

Movement Assessment

How can the teacher meet this situation out of Anthroposophical research? The class teacher can ask that the child be given a movement assessment as indicated in *The Extra Lesson*[8]; this assessment will show whether or not the first seven years' development has been properly completed. The appropriate exercises can be used for a term, then the pupil can be re-assessed. By this time, the teachers will have learned a great deal about the child; this knowledge will help them to see how they should proceed.

Another finding of neuropsychology is that the unfinished stages of the development of the first seven years do not correct themselves during the child's later education. The stages have to be recapitulated in a one-to-one situation.[9] Sadly, this is also true in Waldorf education, as experience and research has shown.[10]

Apart from the obvious necessity for the teaching in Waldorf schools to be effective, what responsibility do teachers have as Anthroposophists in remedying this condition?

Basis of Sense Experience

The senses of self-movement and balance (together with the sense of life) are supported in the human organism by very high spiritual members of the total organization of the human archetype — ninefold man.[11] According to Rudolf Steiner, human beings, out of their ego organization, cannot sustain the activity of these senses. It is done for them through these senses being membered into the organization of spiritual beings; the human ego will awaken into these spiritual beings in the far distant future. It is the Spirit Self (Manas) which ensouls our sense of balance, and the Life Spirit (Buddhi) that ensouls our sense of self-movement; the Spirit Man (Atman) ensouling our sense of life.[12] (See Diagram on the facing page.)

We know from Rudolf Steiner that these members are part of the supersensible bodies of the Christ Being who supports every child from birth until the child is able to say "I" out of his own forces.[13]

When we observe how these senses responsible for the postural system are assaulted by our modern lifestyle and technology, we see the Adversary again attacking that which has been rescued for us through the Mystery of Golgotha.[14] Here lies the challenge to meet the needs of the preschool/playschool child and later to recognize his need for help in the classroom.

Section I: Deeper Insights

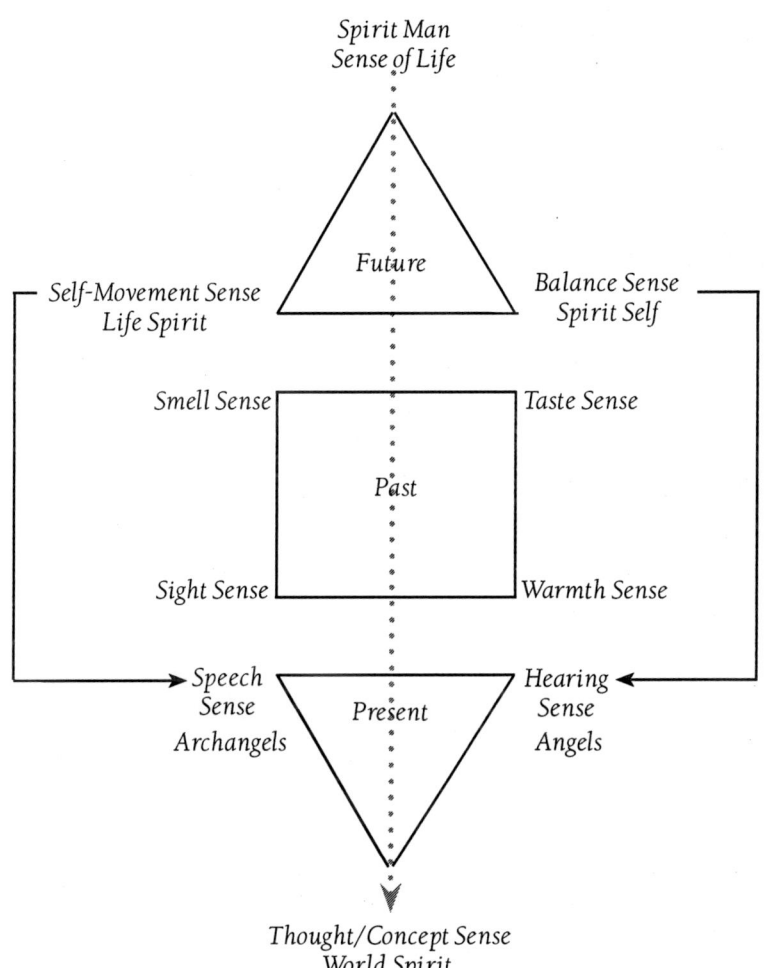

Senses	Sustained by	Development Stage
Smell, Taste, Sight, Warmth	The Present Human Ego	PAST
Speech, Hearing, Thought	The Angels, Arch-Angels and World Spirit	PRESENT
Life, Self-Movement, Balance	Spirit Man, Life Spirit and Spirit Self	FUTURE

Reference: Lectures by Rudolf Steiner entitled *Anthroposophy* (ten senses and higher astral senses) October 23-27, 1909, Berlin, published in *Wisdom of Man, of the Soul and of the Spirit* (Anthroposophic Press 1971), republished as *A Psychology of Body, Soul and Spirit* (Anthroposophic Press 1999).

1. A. Jean Ayres, *Sensory Integration and the Child* (for Teachers and Parents); *Sensory Integration and Learning Problems* (written for Medical Practioners and Physical/Occupational Therapists).
2. Julio B. de Quiros and Orlando L. Schrager, *Neuropsychological Fundamentals in Learning Disabilities*, Chapter Two, Section 12, p 27.
3. Ibid., Chapter Four, Section 22.
4. Rudolf Steiner, *A Psychology of Body, Soul and Spirit*, lectures given October 23-27, 1909
5. Ibid.
6. C. S. Sherrington, *Man On His Nature*.
7. Rudolf Steiner, *A Modern Art of Education*, Lecture 3.
8. Audrey E. McAllen, *The Extra Lesson*, 6th edition, Chapter Four, p. 27.
9. Ibid.
10. *Two-Year Research Report of Children with Learning Difficulties in Waldorf/Steiner Schools*, available from Remedial Education Program Director at Rudolf Steiner College; Reuven Kohen-Roz, *Learning Disabilities and Postural Control*.
11. See Glossary.
12. Rudolf Steiner, *A Psychology of Body, Soul and Spirit*, lectures given October 23-27, 1909.
13. Rudolf Steiner, *The Spiritual Guidance of the Individual and Humanity*.
14. Rudolf Steiner, *From Jesus to Christ* [These lectures are essential reading for understanding the concepts in this handbook and are expanded by the quotations on pp. 22, 23; see also p. 27 notes 26 and 31.]

School Entry

Audrey E. McAllen

When should a child enter class one? Spiritual science says that when the formative forces have completed their work in the building up of the organs of the physical body, they are free to be used for memory and the first pictorial thinking. This building process completes itself about the time the child reaches the age of seven. School entry at this age presented no problems on the European continent, but in the United Kingdom — and its associates New Zealand, Australia — and in North America, Waldorf schools have had to struggle against the accepted educational norm of starting formal learning as early as five years of age. Considerable tact and talk over the last fifty years have been required to persuade parents that it is better to wait until their child is at least six years old before starting school!

This parental and societal pressure has meant that the Waldorf/Steiner school movement has had to compromise on this important issue. Gradually, the recognition of the significance and signs of the decisive step between the kindergarten stage of childhood and the school child has been eroded.

The morning verse in Waldorf school classes says that we come to school that we may 'love to work and learn.' What has happened to this will to work and learn?

Over the last decades, a decisive point being the '60s, the formative forces of the young child have gradually been sapped by our modern lifestyle. The child's senses have been overstimulated, and the will has not been sufficiently activated through play, the result being that the body does not produce its inherent faculties in the spontaneous way it did thirty, forty years ago. The crucial time for the child's body to *complete its development* and so produce the required skills, is the five to seven years phase when the final spurt of growth for the period from birth to age seven takes place. The proportions of the body attain their threefold structure of head, rhythmic system and limbs. Coupled with this is the vital phase of imprinting this structural form into the etheric body[1] of the child through the sensory organization being activated via the senses of balance and self-movement and by manual skills. If this outer imprinting is weak or even lacking, the formative forces working from within outwards, that is from the ego into the astral body and etheric body, have no foothold in the physical body. The structural physical body is therefore not reflected back into the etheric body and inserted into the processes of the formative forces.[2] It is this imprinting of the picture of threefold man from both sides — the outer and the inner — which gives the basis for the self-identity necessary for passing harmoniously through the nine-year change and the repetitive stages which follow.[3]

It is not necessary to go into further details. Rather, it would be better for schools to look at the birthday dates in their classes and see where they cluster. Are there more birthdays from around September-April (so that the children were six and a half by the time school began)? Are there children whose birthdays fall in the summer months, so that they were six years and five months old to only six years old when they started Class One in the autumn?[4] Having done this, look at the attainments of these latter children in their classes during the class teaching period and beyond.

There are three criteria for school entry which have to be considered; the medical, the social and the individual circumstances. They all play into the decision process. Medically, the body and its organs may be immature — this is often the case. But, the kindergarten teacher may be well aware that socially the child is not ready, and school entry will affect the child's further progress. This is the first area of 'conflict'. Then comes the pressure from the parents to start school; the question of the karma of the group adds further complications. This is a well known sequence of factors which arises year after year.

CONSOLIDATION

Where can we find some kind of fulcrum for this situation? The writer thinks there has not been sufficient attention given to the *need for the consolidation of developmental processes*. The necessity for this consolidation the writer learned over the years by watching the progress of children through the school and from the observations of children's drawings. In these drawings, one can witness, inscribed graphically, the whole process of the growth and development of the first seven years.⁵ What is so striking is the principle that when a new stage is reached, a 'regression' to earlier motifs takes place in the drawings; from there, all the phases are repeated until the recent attainment is consolidated, and another new step is made. In effect, we are seeing the same process that Rudolf Steiner describes in the chapter on 'World Evolution' in *An Outline of Esoteric Science* when every stage of development is *recapitulated* before the new one can take place; therefore, when it appears from a medical constitutional point of view that all is in order, that the child is 'bright' and would be able to cope, although by age he would be less than six and a half years old on school entry, we have to give greater regard to what the kindergarten teacher says about his social and individual development, as well as to the need for the body to consolidate its development phase. Far, far too many times the writer has seen how, when these younger children enter Class One from kindergarten, this change-over halts the activity of the formative forces in their bodily work, and the final imprinting of the threefold picture of man into the ethereal body is not fulfilled. This has its repercussion in poor self-identity at the nine-year change and soul weakness at the eleven-year old stage. What is serious is that this inner picture of the form of the body is seldom 'made up' during school life.⁶

It is of the greatest importance for the future of our pupils that the five to seven year stage of development is consolidated. At this stage, the capacity of creative play begins to wane because the formative forces have changed their activity and are now engaged in the overall growth of the body, bringing its threefold harmonious structure to completion. The children now want to *exercise their limbs in work and in gaining bodily skills*. They need activities which absorb and direct their energy into their bodies. They should not have this stage of their development arrested by entry into school and by being faced with learning, however ideal and artistic it may be. This puts a heavy responsibility on our Waldorf kindergartens to provide the older age group with the right facilities, as without them the children become rambunctious, a sign that has often been mistakenly attributed to 'school readiness'.

This may be disputed, but one has to be aware that many educators are also making their observations. Fortunately, early play learning groups are the 'in thing', and there is an influential body of educational research that delineates the three stages of development of the pre-school child; this research recognizes that academic work before children are seven years of age is detrimental to their later progress.[7]

> "Brain growth at age seven is one of the biggest spurts. Remember that the child's matrix is shifting from environment to knowledge of the world. This is the time when child development specialists who base their theories on Piaget's work, such as Pearce, Hymes, and Elkind, believe it is appropriate to introduce formal academic instruction, *and not before.*"[8]

A wider area of research on scholastic attainment has found that children with summer birthdays (May-September) who start school in the autumn, lag behind their classmates for all of their school time. This has an effect on their picture of themselves and on their potential as adults.[9]

So, again there is empirical research confirming spiritual scientific facts; teachers in Waldorf schools could eventually be in danger of being told they are not carrying out their own principles.

THE FOUR SEASONS AND THE ARCHANGELS

In the last lecture (October 13, 1923) of the cycle *The Four Seasons and the Archangels*, we gain an insight as to why this consolidation from age five to seven is so intimately bound up with the activity of the formative forces. At the end of this lecture, Rudolf Steiner says that the souls about to incarnate during the next year enter the gate of the moon between Christmas and Easter. Every spring the Easter moon gives nature its 'push' for growth. Man's life forces are interwoven with those of the Earth, never more so than in the first seven years of life. Therefore teachers could take as their criterion that every child should have experienced the 'life-push' of seven Easter moons before entering Class One. This would help to recognize the 'variables' which teachers meet in a group of children, as some will have had their birthdays before Easter in the year of their birth and some afterwards. In the year 1991, for example, Easter was in March, therefore all April-born children should be ready for Class One in September, 1997. In contrast, out of those who were born in 1992 when Easter was April 17th, only some of the April born children will have had this push of life forces towards maturity for September, 1998. Needless to say, one should not become dogmatic, as other factors are always at work, but the above fact can be one which gives us insight into the choice of birth by the incarnating individuality and can be the pivot around which other considerations may be viewed. (See the interesting work of David A. Phillips, Ph. D., author of *Secrets of the Inner Self.*)

---

1. Rudolf Steiner, *The East in the Light of the West*. Also see Audrey E. McAllen, Section I, 'On the Imprinting of Man's Structural Physical Body's Spiritual Archetype into the Etheric Body of the Earth'.
2. Ernst Marti, *The Four Ethers* regarding the differences and connections between the etheric body, the four ethers and the formative forces.
3. See James A. Dyson, Section IV, 'Nine-Year Change'.
4. J. Gilmore, J. Uphoff, R. Huber, *Summer Children — Ready or Not for School; The Rape of Childhood — No Time to Be a Kid*.
5. Michaela Strauss, *Understanding Children's Drawings*, pp. 83-91, 'Notes on the Study of Man', by Wolfgang Schad.
6. A. E. McAllen, *Two-Year Research Project on Children with Learning Problems in Waldorf Schools* available from Remedial Education Program director at Rudolf Steiner College.
7. J. Gilmore, et al, *Summer Children — Ready or Not for School*.
8. Diablo Valley Directors, *Growing Up, A Plea for Development Readiness*.
9. See number 7.

"The whole impulse, the whole spirit of our spiritual science must enter the culture of our age. Now spiritual science seeks to relate man to the great laws of the cosmos. The deepest impulses of spiritual science will be understood in their truest sense only when men will have grasped the actual range of this search for the relation between man and the laws, the mighty supersensible laws of the universe."

— *Rudolf Steiner*
July 11, 1916, Dornach, Switzerland (GA 169)

II

CAUSES OF LEARNING DIFFICULTIES

NINE-YEAR CHANGE

notes from a lecture by
James A. Dyson, MD

Dr. Dyson opened his talk with pictures from his own schooldays. He looked back to the school he attended — a very small school, yet one in which the high ideals and outstanding achievements of the students over a wide field of activities could be seen as the fruit of an education cultivated by prescription and hierarchy, a confident expression of the wisdom of the past. There is, of course, no way back even if it were to be desired, but he asked us to look carefully at what we have lost. It would be a social task, not an educational one, to recover the values which were formerly transmitted by authority and prescription.

    The early grades could be seen simply as the preparation for and subsequent dealing with the nine-year change.[1] Some of the most common illnesses which presented themselves to him in his practice he recognized as failures in the management of this process; these illnesses include anorexia, drug abuse, psychosis and post-viral syndrome ('chronic fatigue'). The upper school cannot deal with these problems, and indeed, they are educational problems only in the sense that they take the children out of school. As the illnesses become more prevalent, however, we will find ourselves with fewer and fewer students in our schools. Further, the illnesses, which are manifestations of young persons being brought prematurely to the 'threshold' of the spiritual world, are only extreme versions of the condition most young people are in today. If the 'Rubicon' of the nine-year change is not crossed properly, then the earthly forces meet the astral in an inadequate state and the astral itself is not thereafter fully able to do its proper work. The astral contains in itself all of the forces of the 'Fall', and therefore, in its naked working, one has to meet and deal with one's own guilt.[2]

There are *NO* simple medical solutions to these conditions — *the healing process requires a total re-membering of the sick youngster.* Worse, this dangerous path may have to be taken by all young people in the future. What then might be a preventive milieu to help children with these predispositions? The damage done to the four lower senses — balance sense, self-movement sense, life sense and touch sense[3] — has a serious effect on the deeper forces of the soul. Recognition of having been there oneself, however, connects more or less consciously with the person who is ill. Education of the lower senses, which was in the past the task of Spiritual Beings, has now to become an act of self-consciousness. Perhaps, we may therefore see that the prevailing human condition should not be seen in negative terms. It is the ultimate challenge to us to cross the 'threshold' consciously.

We are witnessing the total collapse of the old world. We are challenged to take the next step. The question facing us is, "How can the principle of initiation[4] become the principle of civilization?" Dr. Dyson quoted the verse by Rudolf Steiner:

DARKNESS, LIGHT, LOVE

To bind oneself to matter
Means to grind the soul to dust

To find oneself in the spirit
Means to unite human beings

To behold oneself in man
Means to build worlds.[5]

Dr. Dyson said that this was as far as our predecessors in the Waldorf school movement could reach — a vital stage but one which doesn't *change* anything; in it we are reconnected with the spiritual world but do not 'build worlds'. "To behold the Self in Man" — that is the real challenge by which we will be called to meet the Ego in the other being in its true guise with its spiritual sheaths fallen away.

Dr. Dyson concluded his talk with a quotation from Rudolf Steiner, "In the new mysteries the whole earth becomes a temple. The hidden tragedy and triumph of the pupil become external fact. Men's friends become for him, whether he knows it or not, the terrible and wonderful actors in the ceremony of his initiation."

The above notes were revised by Doctor James A. Dyson, founder of Park Attwood Clinic, Trimpley Bewdley, Worcestershire, England, who is also lecturing and giving courses for doctors and has a private practice in the U.K.

---

1 Rudolf Steiner, *The Renewal of Education Through the Science of the Spirit*, Lecture 8.
2 R. Steiner, *The Festivals and Their Meaning*, Lecture 1.
3. R. Steiner, *A Psychology of Body, Soul, and Spirit*, Lecture II, p. 24, "The sense of touch proper must be sought higher up in the sense of equilibrium...."
4 R. Steiner, *Karmic Relationships*, Vol. V.
5 René Querido, *The Esoteric Background of Waldorf Education: The Cosmic Christ Impulse*, pp. 13-14.

The Picture on Both Sides of the Atlantic: An Interview with Rosemary Gebert

Audrey E. McAllen

Audrey McAllen:
Now that you have spent nearly two years back in the United Kingdom with the responsibility for learning problems at Michael Hall (the largest Waldorf school in the English-speaking world), can you give us a picture of the needs and the action which should be taken on both sides of the Atlantic in order that we Waldorf teachers can help children who have learning difficulties?

Rosemary Gebert:
To begin with, everyone needs to recognize that Waldorf education can indeed help children with learning difficulties; yet, it is important to avoid overestimating what our educational methods can do. Many Waldorf schools have taken the first step in recognizing that a major problem exists, that there are many kinds of learning difficulties, and that many children with learning difficulties are coming to Waldorf schools because parents recognize that the intellectual orientation of mainstream education is harmful.

So, the first step is to see the problem facing us and, equally vital, to recognize its dimensions. This next step requires our schools to give a high priority when planning staffing, use of space and use of funds for teaching children with learning difficulties. This matter is urgent.

Audrey McAllen:
What role do you see for the Waldorf/Steiner teacher training centers?

Rosemary Gebert:
Parallel with the two steps for the schools is the need for teacher training centers to recognize the problem. An extensive course on

learning difficulties should be given in every teacher training center, preferably by someone currently working in the field. Also important is for the teachers to be able to recognize which children have problems as well as when to seek further advice and expertise.

Audrey McAllen:
Do you see a problem with the growing numbers of children with difficulties applying to Waldorf schools?

Rosemary Gebert:
Yes, we have to protect the schools from being swamped by children with problems, as Waldorf education is primarily there to fructify the cultural/spiritual life of the times we live in. We, therefore, have to look at the admission of these children in relation to each class, especially when the class has a first-time class teacher. It is better that the preliminaries (interviews) are done by an experienced group such as representatives from the lower and upper school, a eurythmist, an Extra Lesson teacher, and the admission secretary with the school doctor as consultant. They will research the child's background (such as school and psychological reports), interview the parents; and the Extra Lesson teacher will assess the child's potential before the future class teacher or class guardian is called in.

Even if the group recommends that the child be admitted, the class teacher or class guardian has the final word as to accepting the child or not doing so. I would also recommend that children in the Kindergartens not be automatically accepted for first grade.

Finally, there seems to me to be two sides to this specialized work. One deals with the symptoms directly; that is, teach the children, unravel their confusions, fill in the gaps. Two, try to get at the cause and help the child to deal with the problem through movement, art and other therapies. In this way, the child's self-confidence is supported. These two aspects need to be united in an individual approach according to the individual pattern of difficulty.

Audrey McAllen:
Thank you very much, Rosemary. That should give us all something to think about.

Rosemary Gebert (now retired) has been a teacher of children with dyslexic difficulties at The Waldorf Institute (Detroit, Michigan, USA), the Elmfield School (U.K.), and the Kings Langley School (UK), and has been responsible for the remedial work at Michael Hall School, Forest Row, Sussex, (UK).

CAUSES OF LEARNING TROUBLES

Else Göttgens

The question often asked today about a child with learning troubles is how one distinguishes the cause in order to find the appropriate treatment? One might find five main causes which class teachers may distinguish, plus an extra one which I'll mention at the end.

I: ORGANIC CAUSES

In the first place, we should always check if there are *organic causes* which may be inhibiting the child's performance in school. As an example of this, I shall never forget the very gifted girl whose receptivity to new subjects suddenly plummeted. It took me some time to tumble onto the fact that because of a change in seating, she was now on my left, and the hearing in her left ear had been greatly impaired by *otitis media* (middle ear inflammation). No more was needed than changing her place to the right and alerting other teachers of this factor. Or, we could have an undiscovered myopic child sitting at the back of the class because that is where his temperament group is sitting. Anemia might be another organic cause and so on. This is where the dialogue between parents, teacher and doctor is so important.

II: LEARNING ABILITY

The child with a 'low ceiling' learning ability or in older terminology, a low IQ, is unable to abstract and apply what (s)he learns. Abstracting is, for instance, the ability to grasp that the letter B that is derived from a picture of the Bear is applicable to all B's. For the child with a 'low ceiling' the 'B' remains a 'bear'. This condition is not recognized so easily in the early classes of a Waldorf school because these children may well be skillful with their hands, be practical, have a sound common sense, and often be socially very able.

Because in Waldorf schools we do not mind if children don't read until early in third grade, the less experienced teacher may not realize a child's actual incapacity in this faculty because he can cope with his classroom situation more ably than many of the 'cleverer' children. The real misery for those children starts halfway through third grade when they and their classmates begin to recognize their problems. The danger is that the harmonious child may become emotionally upset because of the difference of his learning ability as compared with other students' abilities.

Such a child may sometimes be better in a school where the learning tempo is slower and has more repetition than it is possible for the teachers in a Waldorf school to give. These children need more and longer practice in all school subjects — like writing, arithmetic and reading.

In the Dutch Waldorf schools, we have our own circle of educational psychologists who will, among other things, assess at what level of IQ a child with a problem is functioning at a certain given time. They know very well that low functioning may have different causes from the one we have mentioned and accordingly have to be treated differently. Knowing the IQ, as well as other faculties, can help the teacher to distinguish whether the low functioning is due to natural ability or is something temporary. The case history will corroborate the latter (something temporary), so we can take pedagogical steps to help in the classroom.

III: Emotional Disturbances

Quarreling in the home, divorce, a chronically ill sibling, personal appearance (squint, deformed finger, etc.) may upset a child, and an emotionally unbalanced child cannot meet challenges. An experienced class teacher can give great help to improve this condition by choosing exactly the right story for this child, giving him the right part in a play, as well as seeing that he receives artistic or music therapy. If these are not available, play therapy may be indicated.

IV: Excess of Temperament

Any of the four temperaments in the extreme may cause considerable learning disability. An overly melancholic child may be so involved in something he has experienced or in his own misery that he does not heed what is being taught, an extreme sanguine may have concentration problems, the phlegmatic may appear bone-lazy, the choleric can be disinclined to accept any help. The treatment of the temperament is the explicit responsibility and duty of the class teacher.

V: DYSFUNCTION

This is what teaching children with learning difficulties is all about. One of the causes of learning problems in the normal child is connected with the developmental stages of the first seven years, e.g. lack of spatial orientation and/or lack of body geography. When we speak of spatial orientation, we mean the child does not perceive how he moves in space, neither does he recognize his own bodily relationship to it. This can be characterized by his inability to understand the meaning of the preposition, the part of speech which guides us in space. "Go *to* the door." "Put the ball *in* the basket." "Stand *on* the stairs." Inwardly, he cannot connect the movements between himself and his body (body geography). "Touch your head with your right hand" — such a direction then requires thought time before there is a response. Neither can he spontaneously copy (on his own recorder) the movements of the teacher's fingers. To consider this in relation to the heredity body, I would like to direct you particularly to the article, 'Twofold Man as Archetype' in Section I.

KARMA

You may occasionally have a harmonious child who by the middle of fourth grade still does not read. When assessed, he shows no deficiencies in any of the main points. We find that certain rare children claim protection from reading for the first 10 to 11 years. In biographies of certain outstanding people of our century, we do find family situations where the child has not been required to read until he was ready. Field Marshall Lord Alexander and General Smuts are two such people. At the moment, Waldorf schools are the only educational centers where this protection is available. But a conscientious assessment is needed so that we do not mistake this karmic situation for a disability that should have been treated earlier; hence, the need for, at the very least, an Extra Lesson 'spot check' in second grade, and people trained to 'read' them.

Miss Else Göttgens, a Waldorf teacher all her adult life, when she 'retired' became a consultant for Waldorf schools in southern Holland, Belgium, England and the USA.

Observing in the Classroom

Audrey E. McAllen

The classroom teacher who is interested in observing and identifying the children who are likely to have learning problems, as described under *Dysfunction* in the previous article, should watch for the following:

>   a. A child who curls forward over the desk or curls a leg under and sits on it. This is often compensation for retention of immature movement responses (see the following article). He is unable to learn properly if his sitting posture is not corrected.
>   b. A child who does desk work with his head leaning over the paper — eye sight should be checked as well.
>   c. A fidgety child — who rocks on his chair, or taps, is restless and disturbs the class.
>   d. A child who just sits, not paying attention — the head may be turned to one side — a sign that the hearing should be tested.
>   e. A child who looks at his feet all the time, who can't jump from boulder to boulder, or who has to look at his fingers when tying shoelaces or can't talk while tying his shoelaces. This child is using 'splinter skills' (see footnote on page 32). He can only perform one task at a time.

These children have an incomplete cognitive foundation at the sensory motor level.

Things to be aware of when children are writing or when a new child comes into the class:

>   a. Bizarre spelling: the word 'help' becomes 'helg' or 'hegl'; the word 'bread' becomes 'break'; 'the' becomes 'teh'.
>   b. Pressing too hard with the pencil, producing wavy lines —
>
>   HELP

this is a problem of a lack of response by the sense of self-movement; by second grade, Extra Lesson help should be given if the problem has not disappeared.

c. Children who cannot copy more than one letter at a time without looking back at the blackboard. When a child copies each letter separately, then retention of the visual image is a difficulty.

d. Writing such as: *lesson*

shows a continuation of movement — an indication suggesting the astral forces are pushing too hard into etheric and physical body.

e. One letter reversed or complete word reversed, also writing sloping to the left, shows the ego is not penetrating into etheric body properly so the reflection of the visual perception cannot be fully recalled (see article p. 28).

f. Pay particular attention to the bottom of the page of children's work because it is when they are tired that they reveal their problems.

g. The written work of children over ten should be checked for the general characteristics of dyslexia, i.e., reversals of letters in the work, omissions and/or additions of letters: bizarre spelling, made up words, crossing out, correcting on top of errors, indistinct formation of letters, etc.

All these are symptoms of coordination/spatial orientation problems and incomplete development of the stages between birth and seven years; these need immediate attention *before* the secondary psychological reactions set in.

The simplest diagnostic observation that the teacher can make is to notice which children in the class choose their crayon or pencil with the non-dominant hand and then pass it to their dominant hand for use. These children are already in difficulty with their body geography and spatial orientation. They, like the others already mentioned, need immediate help so that the development of their learning faculties can proceed normally.

An Immature Movement Response which Interferes with Reading; the Vertical Midline Barrier

Dee J. Coulter

It has been found that many children with learning difficulties over the age of seven or eight still exhibit signs of incomplete maturation of movement responses. These responses should have been 'integrated' into their central nervous systems as part of their normal maturation in the first seven years. The Asymmetric Tonic Neck Response (ATNR) which can interfere with reading and writing is described in this article.

Asymmetric Tonic Neck Response (ATNR)

Original Function

In newborns/early infants, the head and outstretched arm move as a 'pair'. As the outstretched arm is drawn in toward the head, the opposite arm extends out and the head turns to face the extended arm. This helps the child learn the range of his or her body's territory, and the child begins to learn to coordinate the grasp and to master the linkage of eye with hand that will be so important in life.

Normal Maturation

Crawling on hands and knees integrates this movement response, since the head must turn toward each arm as it reaches forward. This serves to neutralize the ATNR or 'erase' it. If the child doesn't crawl, other movements can also help in the maturation process, but it is more likely that the child will not have overcome the automatic movement repsonse as fully. 'Crawls' that are a seated scooting movement also fail to address the maturation of this response (ATNR).

SIGNS OF ATNR PRESENCE

When the child is jumping on a trampoline or rebounder, rolling hula hoops along the ground or reaching out to move something, the unused arm will reach upward toward the side of the head and the fingers of that hand will curl together.

When the child is on hands and knees and turning the head to one side to see an object placed in that visual field, the other arm will buckle and the fingers of that hand will curl. It is also possible to have a retention of the ATNR on one side of the body, but to have it fully matured on the other side. In this case, to compensate for the problematic side, a child will favor one side of the body over the other in athletic maneuvers and may assume unusual postures while studying.

This movement response (ATNR) can return with whiplash accidents, even in adults, and it will then need to be worked through again with rehabilitation exercises.

HANDICAPPING CONDITION OF ATNR RETENTION

When the child (or adult) is reading, in the typical reading posture with the book centered, the retention of this movement response will cause fatigue within 15 or 20 minutes at the most. Extended seat work or reading will often cause headaches in people with severe ATNR problems. It is very common to have this problem after a closed head injury.

In athletics, the presence of the ATNR may cause 'tennis elbow' from the subtle resistance, by this movement response, to bringing the racket toward the body. The retention of the ATNR may also cause a hook or slice in golf from the tendency to lift the head away from the bent arm; it may lead to erratic breath patterns in swimming from the arm 'violating' the movement response (ATNR) when a breath is to be taken. In basketball, this movement response may interfere with the ability to do front cross dribbling. Finally, a retention of the ATNR may be one cause of 'fender bender' car accidents: the driver has to make a sudden stop, reaches out with the right hand (left hand when car is driven on the left side of the road) to avoid the falling forward of loose items on the front right seat, the head accordingly responds by turning to the right (left) and the left (right) arm by bending. The steering wheel thereby is turned to the right (left) and the car hits another car on the right (left).

Corrective Activities for the ATNR

Begin with activities that are in the horizontal plane, since these are developmentally earlier and simpler exercises. Log rolling games (where the child rolls across the floor or down a small hill with arms either to the sides or stretched above the head) and rolling in a barrel are good beginning exercises. Then, progress to children's games that involve arms swinging across the body; for example, 'London Bridge' (where partners sway arms to toss the captured child back and forth) and any 'tunnel' games where outstretched arms form a tunnel against the wall or with a partner. *Always try to create a game out of the activity to preoccupy the mind, so the body can do the motor activity without cognitive controls.* The goal is to have the movement practice occur in an automating way. If the child always does it under 'cortical' or conscious brain control, it will only create a 'splinter skill' (see note on p. 32) that disappears once the mind attends to something else. Then, the immature movement response (ATNR) will continue to interfere with learning tasks. Your goal is to have the mature motor activity become automatic.[1]

Game Suggestions

1. Do log rolls with children lying on the floor and saying the words, "Rolly, polly, pickety pack, go see what you can see; rolly, polly, pickety, pack, and now come back to me."
2. Stand perpendicular to a wall and lean against it with one extended arm; bend the other arm, placing the hand on the hip, and turn the head toward this bent arm.
3. Roll in a cardboard box or barrel; a barrel with old carpeting inside gives an added tactile experience.
4. Play the game of 'London Bridge'; in the verse "Take the key and lock her up," tossle the 'captured person' back and forth, thus creating shoulder rolls.

Causes of ATNR Retention

Failure to crawl or do other movements that could 'erase' this movement response is thought to contribute to the persistence of the ATNR. Also, there is some indication that yeast allergies, which can arise from overuse of antibiotics, may be a contributing factor. The ATNR can also reappear following a whiplash accident, even in adults. Some bodywork practices work directly with immature movement response maturation as well. The Feldenkrais approach is a good example and might be especially effective with victims of whiplash or older individuals for whom children's games are less appropriate.

THE VERTICAL MIDLINE BARRIER

ORIGINAL FUNCTION

Originally, the vertical midline barrier creates a useful barrier which makes it difficult or impossible for the infant and very young child to use either hand to do tasks on the opposite hand's side of the body. This forces the child to use both hands. Without this barrier, children might grow to rely so heavily on their chosen hand that the other side of the body would not grow into full functioning. The barrier also enhances the capacities of the body to behave in symmetrical ways.

NORMAL MATURATION

This barrier remains active until about age six or seven. It is at this time that handedness is firmly established, and the brain is undergoing a growth spurt that triggers the transformations leading to concrete thinking. The body is readying itself for the vast array of asymmetrical tasks that lie ahead.

Nearly all organized sports activities are basically asymmetrical practices. What one does on one side of the body is not then done on the other side — one learns to kick, throw, catch, or turn one's body emphasizing one side of the body over the other. For that reason, it is inappropriate to introduce these activities until after the vertical midline barrier has been integrated.

SIGNS OF VERTICAL MIDLINE BARRIER PRESENCE

When asked to touch with both hands "head, shoulders, knees, toes, elbows, waist," the child will perform well except for the cue "elbows." At this cue, (s)he will either attempt to curl each hand back toward its own elbow (sign of full presence of the midline barrier) or touch one elbow at a time with the opposite hand (sign of a residual midline barrier which may be fading).

When handprints are placed on the floor in pairs so that alternate pairs are laid out left hand on left side and right hand on right side, and the other pairs are laid out in a crossed pattern, where left hand is on right side and right hand is on left side, the child with a vertical midline barrier will be unable to crawl along the trail of handprints by placing the hands on the proper places across the midline. When encountering the crossed pattern, the child will either turn the hand over so the palm is facing up to match the hand pattern without crossing the midline at all (sign of full presence of the midline barrier) or will do one hand at a time, leaning way over with the body to lessen the crossover (sign of residual midline).

When writing or drawing, the child will lean on one arm and reach out with the other in order to work on the paper which is pushed over to the side, away from the midline. When asked to stand and make small, medium and large arm circles, the large circles won't overlap in front of the body as they should. When doing jigsaw puzzles, the child avoids searching for or selecting pieces that are on the opposite side of the puzzle from where they are to be placed, since that involves crossing the midline.

Handicapping Condition of Midline Barrier

Children who still retain a vertical midline barrier will lose their place easily when reading and when copying from the board or from another piece of paper. This makes them very slow at copying tasks. They will often forget to borrow in arithmetic and to cross t's or dot i's, since these tasks usually involve crossing the midline.

Silent reading comprehension will be poor because the eyes will jerk at the midline causing them to miss those words. With oral reading, however, they may be excellent, because their brains can compensate for this problem by comparing what they say with what makes sense.

They will use visual configuration cues heavily in figuring out words, since phonics decoding strategies demand too much cortically, and they are already very challenged. They will not want to read for pleasure. They will also be poor at dressing themselves since that involves many midline tasks (zippers, buttons, tying shoes, etc.). Later, adult tasks like sawing wood, shuffling cards and striking matches will be difficult as well.

Corrective Activities

All two-handed tasks are excellent practices. Weaving, working with clay, craft work, playing recorder or xylophone or doing mundane tasks like sweeping, raking, or pouring are all valuable exercises. Many game activities are helpful — juggling, blowing party blowers, riding on platter swings with a center rope, playing tether ball, or playing flashlight tag in the dark (while lying on their backs on the floor).

It is also helpful to stimulate the extremities so they become more conscious for the child — wheelbarrow walking, hand or foot massages, going barefoot, wearing wristbands, and Marbles Between Toes Exercise from *The Extra Lesson*.

Causes of Retention of Immature Midline Barrier

Oxygen deprivation at or near birth, poor prenatal diet and birthing that didn't involve pressure to the head (breech births and some C-sections) are thought to be possible causes. Many hospitals send C-section babies home with skull caps to wear for the first 3 months to compensate for this lack of organizing pressure.[2]

Dee Coulter, Ed.D., Phd., is on the faculty at the Naropa Institute, Boulder, Colorado and received her degree in Neurological Studies from the University of Northern Colorado. Dr. Coulter is a nationally known neuro-science educator. She freelances as a consultant and has cassette tapes available on subjects such as: Music Education; Waldorf Education; Montessori Education and Cognitive Development. She also directs her correspondence course **Neurology and Learning***, through the University of Northern Colorado. She may be addressed at Kindling Touch Institute, 4850 Niwot Road, Longmont, Colorado 80503, USA.*

---

1 Rudolf Steiner, *A Modern Art of Education*, Lecture 3.
2 See Elizabeth Hayden, Section II, 'Osteopathy for Children'.

Dominance

Audrey E. McAllen

INTRODUCTION

"Johnny was quite impossible today. I just couldn't do anything with him. It must be the weather or something gone wrong at home."

"Mary's so quiet and slow; she never joins in with the others. I'm sure she could do much better at school, but somehow you can't help her."

Such teacher and parent comments are frequently heard. But are Johnny's reactions to our efforts to educate him entirely caused by our inadequacies, plus weather and possible home circumstances? After all, not everyone was so wild or disturbing in the class: other children may also have home difficulties but their reactions are not so chaotic as his, and they are able to respond to our efforts to bring them into a more concentrated state so that they can take part in the lesson. Mary, on the other hand, disappears from one's consciousness in the classroom; her home is a happy one with parents eager to do all they can to help her.

Educational research has brought to light the fact that 'dominance' plays a great part in behavior and learning difficulties and is a factor which should be taken into account in the home and school life of the child.

Dominance is the preference which we have for using one side of our bodies when reacting to sense perceptions and in making movements.

The normal preference is the right side of the body: right eye, right ear, right hand and right leg. The physiological structure of our bodies makes this the natural preference.[1] Nature is 'right-oriented' in structure, form and movement. Our right side is the active one — we need only to look at musical instruments to see examples of the 'dominance' of the right side of the body: the same can be seen in craft skills.

Nowadays, however, through the avalanche of mechanical, man-made sense impressions which besiege the growing child, the normal preference to adopt the natural structure of our organism is being disturbed. The quiet repetitive routines of life in babyhood are cut short; the child's imitative faculties are no longer rightly engaged in harmonious natural movements of the whole body. Turning switches and twisting knobs, fitting shapes together in games is no substitute for bouncing balls or whipping tops. Neither can bikes and cars be a substitute for the effects of a good long walk.

We are finding that the too early and too complicated activities which are 'demanded' from the senses cause many right-handed children's right eye dominance to shift to their left eye. This is termed a 'cross dominance' between eye and hand. The normal laterality of the body is displaced. Then, too, there are the growing numbers of children who use the left hand while retaining the dominance of the right eye.*

To complicate matters further, the right-handed child may also prefer his left leg for starting movements or supporting himself, thus a zig-zag of dominating members of the body can happen: left eye, right hand, left leg. Some children are able to cope with such a complicated laterality of cross dominances, but experience more and more shows us that this mixture of preferred sides is an important factor behind learning and behavior problems and is one which should not be overlooked in the education of our children in the home and at school.

Children are finding the *compensating movement patterns*, which they have mysteriously adopted, more than they can manage when intricate sense reactions are required in activities such as writing, reading and arithmetic. The strain of this demand can result in chaotic reactions in their general behavior — stubborn immobility, lack of concentration, withdrawal, secret fantasies, social problems — according to the particular temperament or home situation. *Dominance of eye and ear has nothing to do with strength of sight or hearing.* Adding to the complications are a small number of children whose dominant eye is the one with the weaker sight.

---

* 'Left-handedness' due to cross-dominance or lack of established dominance should not be confused with full left dominance which exists in only 2% of the population and for which individual karma is an important factor. (ed)

Simple Dominance Assessment

There are several ways to assess natural or 'simple' dominance:

Eye
1. Observe which eye the child uses to view an object through a pin hole in a piece of paper which is carefully lifted up towards the chosen eye.
2. Place a kaleidoscope in front of the child and ask him/her to look through it and describe what he sees.
3. The teacher can also ask the child to sight an object across the room through a cardboard tube (such as a mailing tube or paper towel core) with both eyes open and tube held at arms length. Keeping the object in sight, he is to bring the tube back to his eye. The teacher observes his choice of hand and to which eye he places the 'scope'; the teacher then asks him to look through the other eye — does he change the hand with which he holds the 'scope'? Does he hold it now with both hands? Can he *find* the other eye, or does he place the 'scope' at the top of his/her nose? Is he able to keep the other eye closed muscularly or does he have to hold it shut when looking through the 'scope'? All this gives us a picture of the complicated adjustments which the child has to make in relation to the sense impressions he receives.

Hand
Notice which hand the child uses to toss up a beanbag and catch it, then to throw it into a basket. Notice the hand which the child uses for the activities of picking up objects, for passing things, or for opening doors. Of course, notice which hand is used for writing or drawing.

Leg
To discover his preference for one leg rather than the other, the teacher asks him to stand on one leg, to kick a ball, to stamp, or to stand on one leg and spin around.

Ear
The child's choice of ear can be discovered by asking him to listen to a shell which he picks up — note which hand it is picked up with.

Also ask him/her to listen to a watch which has been placed on a table, without touching it with his/her hands.

These assessments for 'simple dominance' give us a picture of the developing human being in relation to his day-wake consciousness and sense impressions, but in Steiner's pedagogy the teachers also pay attention to the deeper aspects of human consciousness.

HANDEDNESS PATTERN ASSESSMENT

As the teachers pay attention to the deeper aspects of human consciousness, they take into consideration the threefold physical functioning of the human being — head, rhythmic system, metabolic-limb organization— as the basis of the soul faculties of thinking, feeling, and willing. These soul faculties in their turn have to do with states of consciousness: thinking requires day-wake consciousness; in feeling, the human being has the equivalent of the dreaming state; and in the willing, as far as it is a process, we have sleep. As human beings, we are only aware in our waking-day state of the *results* — not the process — of our willing. So it is true that in the human being the states of day and night consciousness exist simultaneously.

Bringing such concepts to the observations already made can lead teachers to a deeper diagnosis of the trouble and from this to the appropriate help.

Above, the teacher has noted down the child's dominance which he used in his day-wake consciousness. This may be either 'crossed' or 'normal' — right eye and ear, right hand and leg. This *simple dominance* pertains to his reaction to outer stimuli related to sense impressions of things in space; it concerns his head organization and day-wake consciousness. This can be compared with observations the parent has made. The teacher will now see how far the child has mastered his will activity in relation to the day-wake consciousness; has his willing really penetrated its medium, the limb and metabolic system? Is his soul development proceeding with enough harmony to allow him to 'keep awake' in the *results* of his willing; can he get his body to consistently express his experiences in space?

The teacher can find out something about these questions by making what the writer has termed a 'Handedness Pattern Assessment'.[2] Such an assessment enables us to find out all the possible choices of eye, hand and foot when *movements in relation to spatial direction are required*. In some children is found an incredible assortment of interchanges in body sides and movement between left-right, above-below, to and fro, etc. This chaos has its effect in their sleep which in turn plays back into the daytime. The teacher finds that these children have not the stamina to deal with the many and varied sense impressions that surround them and which they are expected to absorb and reproduce at will. These children cannot respond quickly enough with their bodily instrument, and the *flow of the will is interrupted*. This disturbs their natural spontaneous reaction: they become aware of themselves in a wrong way, and their consciousness is deflected from what they intend to do, onto their own self-awareness. This interruption of the will produces reactions of impatience, anger or chaotic restlessness; they lose grip of themselves in relation to the objective contents of space and flit from impression to impression, movement to movement.

If these darting, unconcentrated children are *carefully observed*, the teachers can see how very slow they really are in reacting to what they see and in reproducing it out of themselves. For example, in recorder lessons, these are often the children who cannot follow visually the fingers of the teacher on the recorder and reproduce them easily on their own instruments. (All children who cannot do this are in need of help.) They need an inordinate amount of time for the sense impression or verbal direction to be assimillated and for the right reaction to be reflected in consciousness. The teachers see this same lack of spontaneity in the child who 'never learns' but persistently bangs into things or flings objects around, quite oblivious of what he is doing or of the consequences to himself or to others.

The choices of eye, hand and foot movements in the assessment of the child's 'Handedness Pattern' should then be compared to the previous assessments for 'simple dominance'.[3] Through the 'Handedness Pattern', the writer has observed how the dominance picture *changes* when such a child (as described above) is sitting on the floor, for when one is in this sitting position one has quite a different positional relationship to the 'pattern' from that which one has to oneself when standing. When the normal dominance which is shown when the child is standing (simple dominance) is not maintained when sitting on the floor (horizontal position), this shows that the child has not penetrated through his body — right through his whole body, all the way down to his toes. An example of this is when driving a car; the driver thinks "turn right" and then turns left or when a passenger says "turn right" and the hand gesture will indicate the left. It is the inability of the child to control the horizontal laterality when in the vertical (standing) position that causes the difficulties. This can be expressed in a true picture by saying, "Sleeping man is too strong for waking man," which means that the strong will activity in 'sleeping man' (below the waist) cannot be taken hold of by 'waking man', i.e.,"You haven't got hold through your body — right through your whole body, all the way down through your feet."

Working With Dominance

How can the teacher strengthen the child so that his energies are not involved in a ceaseless battle for supremacy between these 'two men' who live simultaneously in him? Can the teacher free him so that he can use this energy for concentration and learning?

The teacher can help him by guiding the senses of self-movement, balance and sight to come into a harmonious relationship. This will enable the vital lessons of eurythmy and handwork to be increasingly effective, and the classroom behavior and work to consequently improve.

In the early school years (age six to ten), exercises involving all kinds of bodily movements should be practiced regularly by the whole class.[4] The teacher needs to watch for the slow reactors and those who lag behind in order to copy their neighbors. These slow reactors are the ones who need help; they are often the 'poor writers' and the listeners who *may not be able to retell much of the story they hear.*

Nowadays, the teacher can no longer assume that the child will be familiar with his bodily instrument by the time he comes into first grade. The teacher needs to be conscious that the necessary guidance from adults in the child's early years is often lacking or only tentative.

The baby is ambidextrous (mixed laterality of the hands) at birth. He has to work on his brain for its unification. The child does this through movement, imitating movements which he sees around him and responding with inner movement to the objects he perceives.

There is evidence of this through the early drawing of children; it is the flight of the bird which is drawn first, not the visible form of the bird.

As adults we have the responsibility of educating the child to follow nature's pattern rather than one based on momentary expediency. Until between five and seven years of age, nature has put an invisible 'barrier' between the right and left sides of the body, so that if an object is nearest to the left hand, the child will not cross over this central line by using his right hand, but will pick it up with his left hand. This vertical midline barrier enables movement of both his right and his left sides to activate corresponding brain hemispheres. Parents easily take this necessary use of the left hand as an indication that the child is left-handed. For a healthy relationship to the body, parents should see that the young child holds up his right foot first when they put on his socks and shoes, that it is his right arm which goes first into his coat, so that he experiences the movements correctly before he does them himself.

Later on, adults should make sure that the child consistently uses his right hand when playing games like 'Snakes and Ladders' and 'Chinese Chequers', by seeing that he is sitting so that his right hand does not need to cross over. Most children arrange this naturally. Such care also guards against unnecessary imitation of left-handedness in the parent (see Section VIII).

Insufficient guidance in the formative years leaves the child struggling with the mixed laterality of babyhood, often unsuccessfully. Activities with normal right-handed orientation are disappearing in daily living (sweeping, polishing, beating eggs, stirring cake batters). Their substitutes do nothing to educate the child in using his bodily construction in accordance with nature's plan. The result is slowness in developing skills and weakened powers of concentration.

It is important to teach the child his relationship to his body; the national traditional games did this:

> "Here we go looby loo, Here we go looby light.
> Here we go looby loo, all on a Saturday night.
> Put your right hand in,
> Put your right hand out,
> Shake it a little, a little, a little
> And turn yourself about."

What could be better 'bodily education'? It should be all done during the period before the ninth year while the child still experiences himself within the pattern of the world of nature in which he is living.

By the ninth year, all children should be able to *respond to verbal direction independently of their vision*, ceasing to 'mirror' the movements of the adult opposite them. In the ninth year, a wonderful assessment,[5] which is also an exercise showing teachers if the will is fully integrated between the sight and hearing senses, is this:

Facing each other, say and do the following exercise with the child. With hands clenched, and arms crossed at chest height, the teacher says and does:

"Right hand" — Lift hand and arm to the right — away from the body; unclench fist and stretch fingers. Return to first position.

"Left hand" — This hand makes corresponding movement to the left. Return to first position.

"Both and both together" — On the word "Both" the arms uncross, stretch away from the body and the hands open. Return to the first position on the word "and." Repeat the sequence on "both together," returning to first position on "together."

The child is expected to follow the teacher's directions. The teacher and the child should repeat this whole sequence and proceed as in a game, changing arm movements, both arms above the head, then downwards, then alternately — one arm up, the other downwards.

This is an excellent class exercise for developing powers of concentration and bringing order into the unruly situations which can occur when changing lessons, classrooms, or waiting for the teacher.

Finally, in the light of these observations, teachers need to ponder the facts which Rudolf Steiner tells them about the *twofold aspect of all the senses*. By day, their function is to transmit the objective perceptions of the world around to our consciousness. In the night, the senses have the function of directing into the body of the human being the cosmic forces which form the organs and which revivify the life-processes.

1. Alfred Tomatis, *Education and Dyslexia*.
2. Audrey McAllen, *The Extra Lesson*, pp. 42-51.
3. Ibid. pp. 12, 23-25.
4. See Ester Buekers, Section IV, 'Standards of Movement Skills'; Jean Hunt and Mary Nash-Wortham, *Take Time*.
5. A. E. McAllen, *The Extra Lesson*, p. 61.

COMMENTS AND EXTRACTS FROM NEUROPSYCHOLOGICAL FUNDAMENTALS IN LEARNING DISABILITIES

Audrey E. McAllen

Drs. de Quiros and Schrager have lucidly traced the development of the central nervous system and subsequent growth patterns, with particular emphasis on the vestibular mechanisms that organize central processing skills. Throughout their discussion, motor organization is clearly related to perceptual and cognitive development.

Following are a few extracts and comments from *Neuropsychological Fundamentals in Learning Disabilities* by Julio B. De Quiros, MD, Ph.D. and Orlando L. Schrager, MD, in relation to *The Extra Lesson*, prepared by Audrey McAllen:

CHAPTER I — TERMINOLOGY AND CONCEPTS
The fundamentals of human learning are established on symbolic abilities. These abilities demand:
1. sufficient bioneurological development;
2. adequate environmental influences; and
3. non-interference of the body itself on higher cortical levels which is obtained through postural control by lower systems.[1]

CHAPTER II — THE BASIS FOR HUMAN LEARNING DEVELOPMENT
Posture is the reflex activity of the body in relation to space. Posture is based on muscle tonus. It is chiefly related to the body. Equilibrium (balance) is the interplay between various forces, particularly gravity, and the motor (movement) power of the skeletal muscles.[2] Equilibrium is based on:
1. proprioception (deep sensitivity) — (in Spiritual Science this is the sense of self-movement),
2. vestibular function, and
3. vision — the cerebellum being the principal coordinator of this information. Equilibrium is chiefly related to space. The basis

of motor activities (movements, writing, reading) are posture and equilibrium.[3]

"The image of the human body means the picture of our body which we form in our mind . . . The way in which the body appears to ourselves," according to Paul Schilder, neurophysiologist.[4] Purposeful equilibrium, primary body schema (body geography) and integration of the postural system are basic for:

1. the use of instruments or objects,
2. the independence of both halves of the body,
3. the learning of non-conditioned language,
4. the possibility of developing creativity, and
5. the capacity for higher-level learning.

The postural system is established on the interrelationships of primary body schema. It develops toward corporal potentiality. Corporal potentiality is the possibility of excluding body information from higher cortical levels in order to obtain human learning processes.[5]

When higher levels are forced to enter into action in order to maintain posture, learning possibilities decrease. When the cerebral cortex is forcefully employed in maintaining posture, intentional coordinated motor activities or mental actions obviously decrease or fail. Learning processes, therefore, also decrease or fail altogether. It is evident that, in order to apply itself to proper human skills, the cerebral cortex 'transfers' many of its initial motoric responsibilities to automatic levels.* Postural control in humans is produced in a schematic way through a lower level (spine), an intermediate level (brain stem and cerebellum), and a higher level (cerebrum). The postural system begins to act in the child through vestibular - proprioceptive integration.[6]

---

* Thus, the importance of the pupil speaking while doing movement exercises in *The Extra Lesson*, e.g., Ball Twirling, Counting Star, etc. The speaking activity occupies the cerebral cortex so forcing the movements to automatic levels; thus, 'splinter skills' are overcome or avoided. Also, doing the exercises with eyes closed activates the vestibular system inwardly.

Chapter III - Laterality and Human Learning

This chapter contains material on laterality, our right-sided world, right and left, and some developmental aspects and notions of space.

Chapter IV - Motor Activities and Human Learning

Motor activities precede mental actions, then both act together, and finally motor activity is subordinate to mental action.[7]

Researchers working with children and animals agree that knowledge begins through mental activities, but researchers working with human learning processes many times do not consider motor activities to be the basis of knowledge. This fact is due to the transformation of knowledge into motor action; the motor work with concrete objects begins to be used as verifications of hypotheses formulated by mental actions. Such researchers put the cart before the horse.[8]

Chapter V - Posture, Movement, and Learning

It is important to realize that vestibular inputs are extremely closely connected to head position,* and that this is essential if humans are to receive information, to introduce knowledge and certainly *to learn*.[9]

The inner ear in humans has auditory and non-auditory organs. The cochlea is the auditory organ dedicated to hearing while the vestibular apparatus is the non-auditory organ dedicated to posture, equilibrium, muscle tonus, and spatial orientation. Vestibular nerves are related not only to posture and equilibrium, they also control the movements of the eyes and many other functions connected with intentional and coordinated movements.[10]

To achieve postural control is to develop attention span, to open exteroceptors (particularly eyes and ears), and to allow more skilled movements.[11]

---

* Note the importance of sitting position when writing, and reading, as well as investigating the child who sits with the head on one side, or on one leg or twisted in his chair.

Chapter VII — Primary Learning Disabilities

In this chapter, we find the distinction between hyperactivity and restlessness. The former depends on a great amount of motor disinhibition elicited by external stimuli, mainly connected with brain dysfunction. Restlessness depends on a great amount of postural disinhibition elicited by poor body information, connected with vestibular-proprioceptive dissociation.[12]

Glossary

Visceral Input (Sense of Life): Receptors in the internal organs and in major blood vessels provide the brain stem with information needed for bodily health.

Proprioception (Sense of Self-Movement): This is the sensitivity which provides information coming from nerve endings localized in muscles, tendons, and joints related to movement and body position. These nerve endings are arranged in the forms of *spirals* and flower sprays within the muscles and tendons.

Vestibular System (Sense of Balance): The non-auditory organs in the inner ear labyrinth (semi-circular canals, utricle and saccule) respond to the position of the head in relation to gravity, to acceleration and deceleration of movement; these organs also tell us if the head is upright, about our posture, muscle tone, and spatial orientation and *control the movements of our eyes.*

---

1   Julio B. De Quiros and Orlando L. Schrager, *Neuropsychological Fundamentals in Learning Disabilities*, p. 18.
2   Ibid., p. 23.
3   Ibid., p. 24.
4   Ibid., p. 25.
5   Ibid., p. 27.
6   Ibid., pp. 29-30.
7   Ibid., p. 63.
8   Ibid., p. 63.
9   Ibid., p. 66.
10 Ibid., pp. 69-70.

11 Ibid., p. 74.
12 Ibid., p. 111.

Osteopathy for Children

Elizabeth C. Hayden, DO, MRO

This article is not comprehensive, but aims to give some background into the types of problems that we, as osteopaths in England, treat in children and their causes.

Pregnancy, labor and delivery are very physical events for both the mother and child. Osteopathy has enormous potential for helping some of the physical problems associated with these events.

Osteopathy is based on very simple fundamental principles; namely, that if a part of the body is not structurally sound, it cannot function normally; and that given normal health, the body will always work towards self-healing.

Using these very simple basic principles, an osteopath assesses in detail the functioning of the body. He then uses very gentle techniques to correct imbalances and strains, in order to assist the body in its search for health. These techniques are equally applicable to adults and children.

Pregnancy

During the critical nine months of life in the uterus, the baby is totally dependent on its mother to provide a safe, protected environment, and for nutrition. The growing baby may be affected by many different factors:

Illnesses in the Mother

Acute or chronic illnesses in the critical first few weeks can affect the early development of the foetus when the nervous system, organs, and limbs are still forming. The most well known of these is German measles.

After twelve weeks, the foetus is fully formed, but is still very small. The rest of the pregnancy is devoted to growth and maturing, and the baby is then less seriously affected by illness in the mother.

Nutrition and Oxygen

The baby needs a steady and maintained supply of nutrients and oxygen from the mother. For this, the placenta has to be functioning well. Any reduction in the supply of nutrients can lead to a slowed rate of growth for the baby.

Extreme sickness of the mother beyond the normal twelve weeks can have an effect on the available nutrition to the baby.

A sudden reduction in oxygen available to the baby can cause anoxic shock to the developing nervous system, causing delayed development of the baby from then on. This can be caused by oxygen deprivation of the mother, such as an acute asthma attack in pregnancy.

A slower deprivation can be caused by the mother smoking in pregnancy, and this is well known to restrict the growth of the baby.

Drugs

Certain drugs in early pregnancy are known to adversely affect the developing baby, such as well known effects of Thalidomide.

Recreational drugs that directly affect the nervous system of the mother also have the same effect on the nervous system of the child. This is palpable after birth, and can delay development.

Some other drugs can also affect the developing child.

Accidents and Traumas

From mid-pregnancy onwards, the baby is growing in size and may suffer from physical trauma if the mother has an accident such as a fall or impact in the pelvic or abdominal region. The baby may bump against the bony pelvis, and absorb shock or compressive trauma. This may need to be treated after birth.

Emotional Stress

The baby is very sensitive to emotional stress in the mother during pregnancy, particularly when it is affecting her own emotional security as a prospective mother. Stresses can take the form of anxiety about the baby, difficulties in her relationship with her partner, family bereavement or such things as a house move.

In such cases, the baby may be anxious after birth, often insecure and clingy.

Labor

Moulding of the Baby's Head

During normal labor, the infant head is subjected to very large compressive forces. These cause the head to undergo a process of moulding which reduces the size of the head and facilitates the passage through the birth canal. Normally after delivery, the skull re-expands to return to its normal shape.

There are many different factors that can inhibit this unmoulding process, leaving areas of retained compression in the baby's head:

Limitation in the Mother's Pelvis

To help the passage of the head, the three bones of the pelvis separate slightly during labor. A history of trauma to the pelvis such as falls on the sacrum, coccyx, or hips, and some types of whiplash, can limit the ability of one of the parts to separate to its fullest extent. This can restrict the ease of descent of the baby's head during the second stage of labor, and result in specific areas of compression in the infant skull.

Duration of Labor

Slow labor

A labor that is very long exposes the baby's head to large compressive forces for an extended period of time. The amount of moulding in the head is often extreme. Although the head often improves in shape during the first few days of life, in the majority of cases, there are areas of retained compression in parts of the baby's head.

Rapid labor

A very rapid labor can also be very stressful for the baby, since the head does not have time to mould gently and reduce in size. Instead, the compressive forces are very large, and although the baby's head is usually not distorted at birth, in treatment, we find a state of shock and irritation in the delicate and sensitive meninges surrounding the brain. These babies are often extremely restless, fractious, and cry a great deal.

Strength of Contractions

In a rapid labor, the contractions are usually stronger than in a slow steady labor. This subjects the baby's head to greater compressive forces.

Induced labors are often accompanied by very strong contractions, and because the cervix may not be ready to dilate, the labor continues very strongly against resistance. This increases the compressive forces on the baby's head.

A slower steady labor is generally better for the baby.

Size of the Baby's Head/Size of the Birth Canal

In general, the size of the baby's head does not make a great deal of difference to the compressive forces on it, unless the head is very large. Small babies can be as difficult to deliver as large ones!

The size of the birth canal is usually directly related to limitations within the mother's pelvis. Scar tissue from a previous labor can limit the size of the birth canal, but this is usually offset by the fact that the birth canal offers much less resistance to expansion in second or subsequent deliveries.

Use of Analgesic Drugs

Certain analgesic drugs, in particular Pethidine, cause the baby to be born in a drugged or sleepy state. This often persists for several days and interferes with the normal unmoulding process after delivery. The *unmoulding process is assisted by crying, yawning and suckling*, and sleepy babies do not do much of the crying or suckling!

The position of Presentation of the Baby's Head

Normal Presentation

The baby normally presents with its chin tucked well down onto its chest. This offers the smallest diameter of the head to the birth canal.

Unusual/Abnormal Presentations

Sometimes the head is incompletely tucked down, or presenting at a slightly odd angle. This not only slows the labor, but also presents a larger head diameter and results in greater compressive forces being applied to parts of the head that are not well designed to take it.

It may help to imagine that you are pulling on a tight polo neck jumper (turtleneck sweater) and consider which position you would prefer your head to be in.

A common presentation is for the baby to present in a 'posterior position', or 'back to back'. In order to be delivered, these babies have to rotate through 270 degrees within the pelvis. They often get stuck at this stage and need assistance. Inevitably, this rotatory force is absorbed in addition to the normal compressive forces.

The most difficult presentation is a 'face presentation'. The neck is fully extended or tipped back, and the maximum possible diameter of the head is presented. Moulding is extreme, and retained compression is inevitable.

Breech Position

The baby's structure is not designed to come out bottom first, but sometimes they do. In these cases, the head does not get a chance to mould during labor, and is delivered with the forces directed upwards instead of downwards. There are particular patterns of retained compression found in breech babies.

WHETHER THIS IS A FIRST BABY OR NOT

Generally first babies have the hardest time in forcing a way through the mother's pelvis. The cervix of the uterus has not opened up before, the birth canal has not been stretched, nor the parts of the pelvis separated. For these reasons, first labors are usually longer with stronger contractions, and usually carry a greater need for analgesic drugs.

ASSISTED DELIVERIES — FORCEPS OR VACUUM EXTRACTION

When forceps or suction are needed to assist the delivery of a baby, they are used when the baby's head is 'stuck', and under maximum compression. This means that any further compression added to the baby's head is at a time when the baby can least well deal with it.

Forceps and vacuum extraction deliveries are at times life-saving, but they invariably cause increased compression on the baby's head, which rarely releases unaided after the birth.

Prematurity/Postmaturity

The baby's head is designed to best withstand the compressive forces of birth at forty weeks gestation. Earlier than this, the bones are very soft and suffer more from the compressive forces of labor, in spite of the small size of the head. It has been estimated that at thirty-six weeks the baby absorbs four times the compression than it does at full term.

After forty weeks, the bones gradually harden so that they are not able to mould as easily during labor. This means that more of the compression is taken up within and between the bones, and is more difficult to release afterwards.

Anoxia

Babies occasionally suffer anoxia (shortage of oxygen) during labor. This varies in degree from a minor amount of distress, to serious anoxia leading to brain damage.

Anoxia is always accompanied by a degree of shock to the central nervous system (brain) of the baby. It is a major factor in limiting the release of the moulding pressures of birth. It is also true that if the labor has been difficult enough to cause anoxia, it has usually also been physically hard on the baby, with major moulding and compressive forces. These need addressing in their own right, as well as the effect of anoxia on the nervous system.

Caesarian Birth

It may seem that after reading all the above, that every baby should be born by Caesarian section! In some cases, it is a preferable delivery type if the delivery is likely to be very difficult; however, the baby does benefit from the normal birth process. It is a form of 'awakening' for the baby.

In many of the babies that we see who have had a Caesarian birth, there is still much retained compression in their heads. This is particularly true if the Caesarian is performed after a long period of often difficult labor. In addition, the actual delivery by Caesarian may not be easy, especially if the baby's head is wedged deep in the pelvis.

Part of the moulding process and compression of the infant head begins in late pregnancy, so even the babies born by planned Caesarian with no labor at all may have areas of compression.

Emotional Effects of Labor on the Baby

Babies that have had a difficult passage during labor, particularly if they have been 'stuck' at any point, often become very frightened. This can affect them later on, manifesting in a physical way as tension through the diaphragm and chest.

Such babies are clingy and fearful, particularly of new situations, and often need a lot of reassurance from their parents.

Effects on the Baby of Retained Compression from the Birth

Normal Unmoulding

There is usually a gradual reduction in the moulding of the baby's head during the first week of life. This is assisted by the baby crying, suckling and yawning. After this, there is usually little unaided unmoulding of the head.

Many babies have odd-shaped heads. This is invariably due to retained compression from birth; however, they do not have to have an odd shaped head to be suffering from this retained compression. As the child grows, the asymmetry becomes less obvious as they grow hair; however, if untreated, it remains present throughout life — try looking carefully at adult heads and notice signs of asymmetry. Some babies' heads after birth are fairly unmolded, but as they grow in the first six months, asymmetry becomes more obvious. This is because the areas of retained compression from birth are unable to grow freely, so the compressed areas remain small compared with the 'free areas'.

'Compressed Head'

Retained compression from birth causes a very wide variety of problems in the baby. The effects are very individual, and some babies cope better with this than others. In some cases, even quite severe compression may cause no apparent problem as a young baby, but may predispose the child to other problems as they grow up —such as headaches, or an inability to cope well with future trauma.

COMMON SYMPTOMS

Many babies do exhibit signs of retained compression when they are very young. These may include:

CRYING, IRRITABLE BABY

If the retained compression in the baby's head persists, it frequently makes the baby uncomfortable. The baby may have a headache, or simply be restless.

These babies take a long time to settle, and are more comfortable being carried than lying down. They are often fractious babies who cry a lot.

Babies who have had a very rapid labor are often the most fractious, irritable babies.

FEEDING

The nerve to the tongue that is involved in the action of suckling exits from the skull in an area behind the ear. This is the area that takes the maximum compression during the passage down the birth canal. The nerve may be irritated and not functioning easily. This makes suckling difficult.

In addition, moulding of the skull can leave residual stress through the face. This also makes it difficult for the baby to suckle.

The baby may take a long time to feed, and one feed frequently merges into the next. He may fall asleep before he has taken a full feed, and therefore waken hungry after an hour or two. The baby may be a 'windy' feeder.

SICKNESS, COLIC AND WIND

These can be caused by compression in the base of the skull, and also by tension or distortion in the region of the diaphragm.

The nerve to the stomach exits from the skull in the same area as the nerve to the tongue. It is also vulnerable to compression in the same way. This can impair the efficiency of digestion and interfere with the working of the stomach.

Any impairment in the function of the diaphragm will have a major effect on the ability of the stomach to retain and digest its contents. The diaphragm can be affected by stress through the trunk of the baby from its own passage through the birth canal, or from shock from birth. If the umbilical cord has been subjected to tension during delivery, perhaps because it was wrapped around the baby's neck, this can disturb the function of the diaphragm.

Problems in this area will manifest frequently as 'windy' babies, or colic.

The stomach is held shut at its upper end by a muscular sphincter formed by the diaphragm. Stress or distortion in the diaphragm can impede the efficiency of this sphincter and cause the baby to be sick when the stomach is full after feedings. Rarely, this sphincter is structurally deficient, and causes a condition called pyloric stenosis. In this condition, whole feedings are repeatedly regurgitated.

Sleep Disturbances

Where there is retained compression from birth, the baby's system is kept in a persistently alert state. These babies sleep for only short periods at a time, and never seem to fall into a deep sleep. Later in the first year, they are awakened by the slightest noise.

These sleeping patterns gradually become habit forming. If the baby is treated young, then this alone is often sufficient to solve the sleeping problem. After the first year, even after the causative problem of the birth compression has been treated, this habit pattern often needs working on separately by the parents.

Effects of Retained Birth Compression on the Growing Child

Infections

Retained birth moulding compression limits the normal formation and drainage of air sinuses in the head, as well as limiting the venous drainage from the head. This can make the child more vulnerable to infections, particularly ear and sinus infections.

Ear Infections

In the case of the ear, retained birth compression is the major contributing factor to recurrent ear infections and 'glue ear' in children. The middle ear is more likely to become infected when the child has a cold. It does not drain completely afterwards and is therefore even more vulnerable to the next infection. This situation repeats with infections becoming ever more frequent until a persistent hearing loss is suffered, and eventually a sticky residue is left in the middle ear — 'glue ear'.

The auditory or eustachian tube is a tube that connects the middle ear to the back of the throat. It exits from the skull between two bones and is vulnerable to the effects of compression at this point. If this tube is even partially blocked pressure can build up within the ear.

Ear problems in children respond very well to treatment to reduce the retained birth compression, to re-establish efficient drainage of the ear, and to improve the function of the auditory (eustachian) tube.

Sinuses

Children who have retained compression in the nasal sinuses are often mouth breathers. Normal growth and development of the sinuses is impaired, as well as their normal drainage. These are the children with constantly blocked, runny noses.

Behavioral Problems

The pattern started in the early weeks of fractious babies, poor sleeping, and constant need for movement and changes of position changes as the child grows. These children are often much happier once they can move around — they often crawl and walk early.

However, their restlessness may lead to constant fidgeting, difficulty sitting still and concentrating for any length of time, and even to hyperactivity.

This often has implications once the child starts school since they find it very difficult to sit still and stay at any one task for more than short periods. This may slow their rate of learning.

Osteopathic treatment at this stage often helps the child to calm down, sleep better, sit still for longer periods, and therefore improves concentration and learning.

Learning Difficulties

The pattern described above forms the underlying basis for some learning difficulties. If mild, the osteopathic treatment given when the child is as young as possible may be enough to prevent significant learning difficulties.

There is a very close association between difficulties at birth and more severe learning difficulties, including dyslexia. The effects of the birth stresses and ongoing effects of the retained compression may have been sufficient to modify the activity of the brain and alter patterns of learning. In these cases, conventional pedagogical help, to retrain the nervous pathways and assist the learning process, is essential to the child, supported by osteopathic treatment to reduce, as far as possible, the effects of the birth stresses.

CEREBRAL PALSY AND OTHER TYPES OF BRAIN DAMAGE

If the anoxia at birth has been sufficient to cause actual brain damage, it is almost invariably the case that the birth has been difficult, with excessive compressive forces on the baby. The damaged baby is unable to release the moulding effects unaided, so all the above comments apply to these children in the same way as any 'normal' child.

While osteopathic treatment cannot repair the areas of damage to the brain, there is much that can be done in maximizing the potential of the child's development and in making them more comfortable.

HEADACHES AND OTHER ACHES AND PAINS

Contrary to popular belief, many children do suffer from headaches and musculo-skeletal pain in the same way that adults do. This is hardly surprising since the cause is often the same; namely the retained effects of birth trauma.

Headaches often start in children around the age of seven or eight years, which is when the sutures or joints between the bones of the skull form properly. This may be the first sign of retained compression in the child.

Children also suffer from 'growing pains'. These are deep-seated aches in the shafts of long bones, usually in the legs, and are generally worse at night. The cause is stress within the bone that is offering resistance to the laying down of new bone as it grows. The stress may be related to birth or to strains from falls and accidents. It is readily treatable osteopathically.

Other musculo-skeletal aches and pains in the body can arise for similar reasons.

Asthma

There are many causes of asthma, and while it cannot often be eliminated completely, there is much that can be done to help asthma, using the osteopathic approach.

The chest itself becomes very stressed due to the increased muscular effort needed to breath. In more severe cases, this alters the development of the rib cage to a classic 'barrel shape'. Most of the respiratory effort is directed to *breathing in*, and the ability to *breathe out* is often poor. Treatment to render the rib cage more supple and able to breath in and out with less effort, will often ease a chronic asthmatic state.

Asthmatic children often exhibit signs of retained birth compression, are often mouth breathers, and may also have a history of mild anoxia (lack of oxygen at birth). Treatment of these areas as far as possible often reduces the severity of the asthma.

Dental Problems

Dental patterns are often genetically determined and run in families. However, they are also influenced by developmental stresses imposed on the growing face. The same stresses through the base of the skull that limit normal sinus growth and development in children also limit the growth of the face.

This leads to a greater incidence of dental overcrowding, necessitating in some cases dental extraction and orthodontic treatment later on. To prevent this situation as far as possible, treatment of the child is essential as young as possible, but definitely before the age of five years. From age five to ten the face goes through a period of rapid growth. This needs to progress unimpeded to maximize room for the adult teeth.

Other Problems of Childhood

There are many other types of children's problems that are related to birth stresses, and that also respond to osteopathic treatment. The basic principles are the same.

Osteopathic Examination and Treatment

A full and careful case history is first taken, including as much detail about the pregnancy, labor and delivery, and life to date, as possible. This is followed by a detailed osteopathic examination.

Cranial osteopathic treatment techniques[1] are *very gentle*. Specific and gentle pressure is applied to the baby where necessary to *enable the inherent healing ability of the body to effect the release of stresses*.

Children generally enjoy their treatment and often fall asleep during it; however, if compression and stress in the body are extreme, the build up to the release during treatment may be uncomfortable to the child as it focuses them on their 'stressed' areas. This is a temporary situation and soon passes, leaving the child relaxed.

Could There by Any Adverse Reactions?

Reaction to treatment is individual and variable. Usually children are calm and happy after treatment, and symptoms gradually settle over a few days. They are sometimes very tired as their body's energy is redirected towards the healing process. On occasion, children have a burst of energy afterwards, as they enjoy the release of tensions and stresses in their bodies.

Occasionally, children are unsettled after treatment; this is usually when the release of the retained compression has been incomplete. It is not always possible for them to release it all in one session, especially if the compression is severe. These reactions are only temporary.

How Many Treatments Will Be Needed?

This is variable, but on average, four to six treatments are necessary. This varies according to the severity of the problem and the age of the child.

When to Treat

The best time to treat babies is within a few days of their birth. This is when the unmoulding process is naturally at its most active. It is never too soon to treat a baby.

The effects of birth stresses are best treated as young as possible, as the longer they have been there, the longer it takes for the body to release them; however, there is much that can be done particularly under the age of five years.

As osteopaths, we often need to treat the effects of retained birth compression in our adult patients, so it is never too late to treat.

The treatment of babies after birth is of paramount importance in practicing *preventative medicine* and can help both mother and baby recover from one of the most demanding experiences of their lives.

---

1   Adah Strand Sutherland, *With Thinking Fingers;* John E. Upledger, *Your Inner Physician and You.*

Age: 9 years
Laterality: Left;
Ability: Nervous child, (Tiny drawing)

Age: 9 years
Laterality: Right hand,
  undecided eye, right foot
Ability: Unsure, undecided
  child

Sign of Pressure

Sign of Stress

Age: 9 years, 3 months
Laterality: Right

Age: 8 years
Laterality: Right hand, left eye, right foot (cross lateral)
Ability: Poor verbal language, immature articulation, no reading or spelling (Moon/Sun reversed)

GOETHE'S COLOR THEORY APPLIED

Mary Nash-Wortham

Sir Isaac Newton (1642-1727) and Johann Wolfgang von Goethe (1749-1832) failed to agree in at least one major scientific realm, that of color theory and optics. While Newton and his successors based their theory on *excluding* the color-seeing faculty of the eye, Goethe founded his theory on the eye's *experience* of color. Goethe studied color to gain knowledge of objective laws of aesthetics; he concluded that the blue sky was 'illuminated darkness' and that the yellow sun was 'darkened light'. Due to the moisture content of air, the atmosphere lightens the impenetrable darkness of space to create blue and darkens the invisible light of the sun to create yellow/red. Primary polarity is given as *Light* and *Darkness*, and secondary polarity as the colors *yellow* and *blue*.

Goethe's optical investigations showed that the right eye looks out clearly into the world, openly radiating, corresponding in character with the red/yellow colors. The right eye is the 'master' eye, and we know that the right hand is usually the dominant, stronger, more highly coordinated, doing and writing hand; the right foot is normally the better one for kicking, hopping and leading ahead. So we find the right-sided dominant pattern established and linked with the colors red/yellow. The left eye is more receptive and has a 'gentle look' portrayed by great artists as asymmetry (notably in Raphael's *Sistine Madonna*, shown in both mother and child, and in the *Mona Lisa* by Leonardo de Vinci). According to Goethe's findings, the color blue corresponds with the receptiveness of the left eye, so we can see that natural well-ordered laterality shows right as red/yellow and left as blue.[1]

In applying the theory, we accept that all children of seven to fourteen years enjoy drawing and ask the class (7 to 14 $1/2$ age range) to draw in crayon, on a reasonable sized sheet of white paper ($8 1/2$" x 11" is good) — the moon phase is their choice — a *blue moon* and a *red sun*,[2] with the name at the top of the paper. Wrap the request into a story, if it is thought necessary, making sure that every child knows that the drawing is simply to be "a blue moon and a red sun." Collect the results, and after class have a look at the color now related to laterality. Your good all-around pupil with normal laterality and language functions (spoken, written and read) will draw the blue moon firmly on the left-hand side of the paper with a nice red sun on the right. The children in the class who are in need of special aid will reverse the color sequence (red sun on the left, blue moon on the right), or the drawing will be so unlike the concept that you are immediately aware of difficulty! No single indication or 'test' will give us a total picture, diagnosis or therapeutic answer, but the color theory does add an interesting new dimension to our vision.

Some children may have slipped through the early Lower School years with difficulties of undetermined laterality, sometimes, but by no means always, associated with writing and spelling problems, poor vocabulary and verbal expression (stumbling over larger words, reversing spoken or written or even read syllables, using incomplete sentences) and, in general, functioning below apparent ability level. So, it is good to carry out this practical application of Goethe's color theory, and where the results indicate a confusion, take special action.

Mary Nash-Wortham (L.C.S.T MRC SLT (Reg) Teachers Dip. Sp.L.D.) is co-author of Take Time *and also the author of* Phonic Rhyme Time *which describes where sounds are made in the mouth plus gives rhymes for all sounds in initial, medial and final positions. Please feel free to contact: Mrs. Mary Nash-Wortham, 38 Melville Lane, Willingdon Village, Eastbourne, E. Sussex BN20 9EJ, UK, Telephone: 0323-508636, Fax: 01323-508636*

---

1   Ernst Lehrs, *Man or Matter*, chapter 16, part 2.
2   Audrey E. McAllen, *The Extra Lesson*, p. 55 (Eye Color Affinity). Also, see Rudolf Steiner's *Planetary Spheres and Their Influence on Man's Life on Earth and in Spiritual Worlds*, lecture 2 — 'The Cosmic Origin of the Human Form'.

"...the main task of the teacher or educator is to bring up the body to be as healthy as it possibly can be; this means, to use every spiritual measure to ensure that in later life a man's body shall give the least possible hindrance to the will of his spirit. If we make this our purpose in school we can develop powers which lead to education for freedom."

— *Rudolf Steiner*

III

REMEDIATION LESSONS WITH STUDENTS

HAVE YOU SEEN YOUR OWN STAR

Kyle Morton

The time is Advent, the time of the 'Coming'. James is reluctant to face life on earth; our challenge is to gently help him to find his way down.

We may speak to the child about the star above his head, how above every human being shines a star. The child hears of man's guiding star and of how God made man in His own image.

James is becoming separated from and forgetful of the spiritual world; he is beginning to lose touch with his own spiritual being. He is beginning to feel lost. He is in the world, yet is losing his will for life, his feeling for purpose in life.

How can we help the child find himself, find the way to his rightful destiny and the aims that inspired him when he descended on his path toward incarnation? For many years, I worked with Audrey McAllen's exercises in *The Extra Lesson* and came to see clearly how they helped the children day by day. Working with them and pondering on these questions, I began to think about this exercise:

"Have you ever seen your own star?"
"No,.."
"Well, let us look together."

I ask James to lie on his back on the floor, arms and legs outstretched. I ask him which color he likes best and would like to make his star visible in. "Blue." Taking up the ball of blue wool and starting just above his head, I unwind it, first passing it under his right arm, near his shoulder., to his right foot; around the right foot, up under his left leg to his left hand where his outstretched fingers hold the yarn in place. Along his left arm, under his shoulders, straight across to the outstretched fingers of his right hand goes the unravelling ball. And on it goes, under his right leg, down around his left foot and under his left arm, near his shoulder, back to its starting place above his head. As I go, I speak the following verse by Rudolf Steiner:

> From my head to my feet
> I am the image of God.
> From my heart to my hands
> I feel the breath of God.
> When I speak with my mouth
> I follow God's Will.
> When I behold God
> Everywhere, in mother, father,
> In all dear people,
> In beast and flower,
> In tree and stone,
> Nothing brings fear,
> But love to all
> That is around me.[1]

The laying of the form with the wool is timed according to the speaking of the words. I ask James to sit up carefully, then stand. Now, as he turns around, before him lies the image of his own star. There is an atmosphere of reverence and wonder.

I tell James that we are going to learn a verse and speak it as we walk the form of his star. The one I have chosen for him is by Isabel Wyatt:

THE WAY DOWN

He looked down from the sun on high,
And saw Earth, dim and dusty, lie
In a far corner of the sky,
Poor and forlorn.
Said he: "The time has come when I
Must go down and be born."

He stepped beyond the Sun's gold bars:
With Cherubim he trod the track
Of the revolving Zodiac;
Archangels led him on through space,
Towards each planet's resting-place —
Mercury, Venus, Mars;
And Angels welcomed him with grace,
Happy to look upon his face,
In hosts of lesser stars.

Beyond the Moon, he gently drew
Down through a realm of airy blue
To where the coloured flame
Of rainbows like a mantle lay
Round the cold Earth.
Eagerly now he passed through them,
and — last step of his way —
Softly he came
To Bethlehem
And his own birth,
On the first Christmas Day.[2]

Each time we meet, we lay out the star until James can walk the form with assurance and accuracy. As we speak, I walk a similar form backwards so that he may follow my stepping and timing according to the rhythm of the poem. We repeat the exercise time after time, and the poem is learned by heart. When James knows with confidence the form of his own star, we no longer use the visual support of the wool, and in time he can say the poem and walk the form by himself.

With certain children — and James is one — I have taken this poem simultaneously as a painting/writing exercise. On heavy painting paper, he painted very carefully the words of each verse with a very fine brush.[3] It was delicate work, and he paid dedicated attention to the form of each letter. On other sheets, he made appropriate and beautiful paintings to illustrate the book we were making. We used only one side of our 11" x 13" sheets, then covered each with waxed paper, then cellotaped (scotch taped) the appropriate pages back to back so that when we bound the book, all the writing and paintings were protected. We made three small holes on the left-hand side of each double page and bound the book with colored wool so that each page could be opened to lie flat.

There are other children with whom I worked on the star form with another of Isabel Wyatt's poems:

BLUE AND ROSE

Little Son,
Whence comes blue?
It comes when dark is shone into.
Because the Sun's fair golden Light
Shines down into my body's night,
My cloak is blue,
My little Son.

Little Son,
Whence comes rose?
It comes when light through darkness glows.
Because the Sun's fair golden spark
Is shining from my body's dark,
My robe is rose,
My little Son.[4]

This poem is enlivening, bringing to life the colors the child sees in the *Shepherds' Play*[5] and in Christmas pictures, and holding thoughts that may be forever pondered anew and deepened in years to come. *The above exercise has been used with children from grade five up.*

Kyle Morton, Extra Lesson teacher in the Vancouver Waldorf School, (Vancouver, B.C., Canada) first met The Extra Lesson *when the book had just been published in 1974 and has been working with it ever since (ed).*

---

1   Adam Bittleston, *Meditative Prayers for Today.*
2   Isabel Wyatt, *Stars Roundelay.*
3   Audrey E. McAllen, *The Extra Lesson*, pp. 179-180.
4   I. Wyatt, *Stars Roundelay.*
5   *Christmas Plays from Oberufer.*

Variation on the 'Ball Throwing' Exercise

Gaby Wensink

Audrey McAllen:
The times that are available for a child to have lessons for their learning difficulties vary from school to school. How do you work?

Gaby Wensink:
As I am only in the school for four days a week, I take a child every morning, i.e., four times a week for fifteen to twenty minutes. I do the same exercise, or variations of it, every day. For example, Wool Winding and Skein Twisting from *The Extra Lesson* and other fine motor exercises. Then the child may be sent on to curative eurythmy as the need requires. I take a child for a six-week block and after a pause of six weeks, if necessary, I start with him again. In this pause, we can see how the child develops in the class. In some cases, the class teacher also works with the child in the classroom, depending on the problem. In this block period, there are children who can respond quickly, or it may take a long time, according to the problem the child has.

Audrey McAllen:
Have you found any exercise that is particularly effective with specific problems?

Gaby Wensink:
Yes, the Ball Throwing Exercise (*The Extra Lesson*, p. 73 — also done with bean bags) is very beneficial for children with arithmetic problems and for those who cannot wake up. These are the children who cannot reverse the movement in the Ball Throwing Exercise without losing concentration. They start laughing, talking, and show they cannot bring the movement under the control of the will.

So I have developed a variation on the original exercise to reinforce its effectiveness in this situation:

BASIC EXERCISE

PART I
Instead of using balls, the child has a beanbag in each hand.

a. In a small arch, the child throws the beanbag in his *right* hand up so it lands in the *left* hand. At the same time, the left hand 'gives' the left beanbag over to the right hand which is held with palm up. Watch out that a distinction is made between 'throwing' and 'giving' — one hand throws as the other gives. The right hand throws and the left hand gives in this part of the exercise (not like juggling where both hands throw and catch in similar motions). When catching, each hand 'receives' rather than 'grabs' the beanbag.

b. In a small arch, the child throws the beanbag in his *left* hand up to land in the *right* hand, at the same time the right hand 'gives' the other beanbag to the left hand which is held with palm up. This distinction between the motions of right and left hands needs considerable practice as the change over of action often causes problems. The child, however, sees what is happening (for the child needs to concentrate really hard when doing this activity) and must continue practicing until the above exercise has been truly mastered.

PART II
When the child has mastered the above, walking is added:

a. Walk forwards. The *right* beanbag is tossed up every time, and the *left* beanbag is given over simultaneously, as a step is taken. Start walking with the right foot (first throw), 2nd throw left foot, 3rd throw right foot, etc.

b. Walk backwards. Start with the left foot, then right, then left again, etc., as the *left* hand tosses the bean bag up and the right 'gives'.

PART III
When the above (II) is mastered, counting can be added to the movements, first with the walking forwards, then with the walking back-

wards. In this way one starts counting aloud from 1 to 10 or 12, then backwards 12 or 10 to 1. In due course, all the tables can be practiced in this way.

A further variation, using the two-times table (or any other table): step forwards *three steps* as in II(a), while simultaneously counting aloud "2 - 4 - 6" just as the bean bags are tossed/given over (so the number has been spoken by the time the bean bags are caught/received), placing the feet together on the last number, stand still. Continue counting by repeating the last two numbers backwards, as in II (b), while stepping backwards *two steps* — standing still with both feet together between each switch-over. The following may be helpful:

Steps:	Counting Aloud:
3 forwards	2 - 4 - 6
2 backwards	6 - 4
3 forwards	4 - 6 - 8
2 backwards	8 - 6
3 forwards	6 - 8 - 10
2 backwards	10 - 8
3 forwards	8 - 10 - 12 . . . to 24 (12 x 2)
3 backwards	24 - 22 - 20
2 forwards	20 - 22
3 backwards	22 - 20 - 18
2 forwards	18 - 20
3 backwards	20 - 18 - 16 . . . to 0

This exercise could also be done with four steps forwards and three steps backwards, switching after twelve times two (or any other table used) to four backwards and three forwards. With this exercise, where speaking is simultaneous with moving, the will is strongly addressed. In other words, the child is helped to gain control over the will by the heightened concentration. Because the child has to keep changing over, he has to become inwardly mobile. Besides awakening inward mobility in the child, this changing over improves the consciousness of right and left.

Gaby Wensink is a teacher of children with specific learning difficulties at the Eindhoven Waldorf School, Holland.

The Extra Lesson in Triform
an Interview with Janet McGavin

Audrey E. McAllen

Audrey McAllen:
Janet, please tell us about the work that you are doing here at Triform.

Janet McGavin:
Next year, we shall have nineteen students between the ages of seventeen and twenty-six who, for some reason or other, have not been able to find their way in this competitive and demanding world. Some are high school drop-outs, while at least three others have already had jobs and have driven their own cars. All feel dissatisfied with life, have poor self-images, and have difficulty making friends. We have other students who are obviously learning disabled, but otherwise intelligent and able. They all need remedial work at different levels, and what we try to do is cope with their individual needs.

Last year, we had a group of students who during the time they spent with us here, developed a wonderful attitude toward helping each other. I assessed all these students using the assessment[1] from *The Extra Lesson* and found that everyone — younger and older — were lacking, some more, some less, in the spatial orientation and body geography basics which are needed for any learning.

Cheryl Jasock was able to work with four students whom she felt she could help with exercises from *The Extra Lesson*, and I worked with her, helping with the rod exercises and the Grand Crawl.[2] Our community noticed that at least three of these students made quite noticeable improvements.

This next year, we are hoping to work more with the exercises from *The Extra Lesson* and add to our resources with craft therapy, such as pottery and weaving — weaving for developing thinking and pottery for attaining centering. We shall also include woodwork, baking, farming and gardening as part of the curriculum.

At the present time (1987), the day is oriented for work, i.e., housekeeping, farming, gardening and crafts in the morning. In the afternoon, three times a week, we have the educational programs: we use the grade twelve curriculum of the cultural epochs, history ending with the Parsifal period, American history, geometry, eurythmy, singing and painting. The seasonal festivals form a central element, and we prepare these on Sundays; for example, for drama the students worked on and partly wrote together a version of *The Story of the Other Wise Man*,[3] which Channah Seibenburgh produced.

Triform offers a two-year training. Some students need longer, and we do our best to arrange this for them. When they have completed their training, we try to find them work. For example, one local baker took one of our students, another went into hairdressing and has done well, while a third has been taken on by a boatbuilder in Maine. Another is doing lasure housepainting with a small firm. They each soon had earned enough to get a car, a necessity for them since there is inadequate public transportation in this part of the country.

UPDATE 1995

Each year at Triform, the same procedure has been followed with the new students, and they were found to be in a similar condition. Although all these young people had received mainstream remediation, they were unable to meet their responsibilities. This was because the two factors, spatial orientation and body geography, which are essential for self-identity and learning possibilities, were missing.

This again highlights the necessity to see that the senses of balance, self-movement and life are integrated. Without this, tutorial remediation is built on a faulty foundation.

From this and other reports, it is important to note that movement remediation, i.e., *recapitulation of the first seven year development, is possible at any age.*

UPDATE 1996

Seven new co-workers joined the Triform Camphill community. Triform officially launched its apprenticeship program with seven residents. This program meets the changing needs of young adults who have achieved a certain maturity. The program offers extended work training, greater responsibilities within the community, and options for work outside of Triform. The Triform community expanded by adding a three bedroom house for residents. The new house is part of a ten acre acquisition.

Janet McGavin, RN,[4] joined the Camphill Movement in its early days. She followed Mrs. König at Thornbury Camphill School, the first center located in west England. She came to the USA around 1962, with the pioneer group that brought the Camphill movement to the United States. In 1986, she was chosen as 'person of the year' by the Sunshine Foundation for her devoted work with the handicapped person. The forming of the Association for a Healing Education was her inspiration. In the 1980's, she, along with co-workers, again made a new contribution to Camphill's many projects — the helping of learning disabled young adults to find themselves and their place in life at Triform.

On her way to give a course at the Rudolf Steiner Institute[5] in 1987, Audrey McAllen was invited to spend a few days with Janet McGavin at Triform. She had the opportunity to ask Janet to tell her about the aims and the work taking place in this new phase of Triform's development.

        For further information:
        Triform
        Triform Road
        Hudson, NY 12534
        Telephone: (518) 851-9320

---

1   Audrey E. McAllen, *The Extra Lesson*, pp. 27-75.
2   Ibid., pp. 137, 113, 129.
3   Henry van Dyke, *The Story of the Other Wise Man*.
4   Janet McGavin, (1915-1994).
5   For information on these adult summer courses write to: Rudolf Steiner Institute, PO Box. 207, Kensington, MD 20895-0207, USA, Phone/Fax 301-946-2099.

The Extra Lesson for Children in an EBD School in England

John Marking

In 1984, I took on a newly formed class six at Philpots Manor School, for 'maladjusted children' in East Sussex, England. Terminology has changed and it is now called a school for children with emotional and behavioral difficulties, an EBD school. I had just spent three weeks at Audrey McAllen's course, which inspired me to hold this group together. During the three years to class eight, it grew from eight to twelve children, and I always brought to them as many exercises from *The Extra Lesson* as possible.

Every morning, after saying the school verse together, we did the Mirroring Exercise[1] and a Bothmer Gym exercise. Then 'questions and comments'; three or four hands would go up. All had the same question in mind, "Please can I go in the study?" What is the 'study'? It arose from a conversation with Audrey. She told me of experiences in classes where the teachers had a 'quiet corner' — with cushions, playthings, etc., often shielded from the others. I happened to have a puppet theatre ready for disposal. I quickly adapted it, called it the study, and introduced it to the class beforehand; then, one day, it was there with a desk and a chair inside. Every day from then on it was occupied for at least an hour; it was the same with several other classes I had after this group. Children who normally did three or four lines of writing produced a couple of pages in 'the study'. It can also be used in a different way. These disturbed or maladjusted children are always so restless from overstimulation of the senses; and they easily infect each other until one or the other of them cannot stand the restless working in themselves and 'lashes out', causing a rumpus in the class. The children know in themselves when this point is coming, and the 'study' gives them the quiet they need to overcome it.

After this came the painting exercises.[2] We started the whole series again after every holiday. First, we did the Red-Blue Spiral Exercise, one to three weeks, depending on how many repeats I felt they needed. Next, the Sun in the Blue Sky motif — again one to three weeks. Then, the Secondary Colour Exercise. Eventually I included the Blue-Red Perspective Exercise. Sometimes the results were poor or deliberately spoiled. Often a joyful experience arose. One girl who was a poor painter and who once painted the sky vertically up one side of the paper just took to the Blue-Red Perspective, and even on a very chaotic morning with water, paint and boys flying around, she sat calmly filling a larger than usual paper with the red and blue strokes. One boy said of painting the secondary colors, "I like this painting." They hardly ever showed boredom. Painting was followed by individual verses, a poem recited as a class, tables, (yes, still in class eight). The last five or ten minutes of main lesson time was for recorders — every day — another recommendation of Audrey's.

In that class, I had four children who could not read, so when I introduced English comprehension, those four, in pairs, did the Three-Fold Spiral and Copper Ball Exercises.[3] After a few repetitions, these non-readers could repeat the exercises correctly. Some of the others asked if they could do them, too. We had a new boy join at the beginning of class eight; he was a real tough and noisy one. After a couple of weeks, he asked to do the Copper Ball Exercise, and lay there performing the movements of the exercise for fifteen minutes, while another played a glockenspiel up and down the scale. This is why I originally wrote this article — it's the *extraordinary response the children have to these exercises.*

Another example is with the blue and red beans (Hand, Eye and Speech Coordination[4]). I would pour the mixed beans onto one child's desk and he would sort them out. "Can I do that next?" another called. As Audrey says, what appears simple to us is enjoyed by them, because they have missed out on such things in early childhood.

Yet, another example is the students' homework. One term, I changed one of the five exercises for homework to a 'special'. I happened to let slip to them that I was preparing it, before I had cleared it with the house parents, but the students were so enthusiastic that I had to give it out straight away. Each child had his own list of six to ten activities from *The Extra Lesson* which their house parents or another child helped them with, for example Balancing Lemniscate,[5] Interpenetrating Triangles,[6] blue and red balls to bring awareness to left and right, Bouncing Balls Exercise[7] (large), stilts, 'five stones' (jacks —often only two are used), writing on backs, writing with pencil between toes, and Marbles Between Toes Exercise.[8]

On three mornings while I was checking homework, each student did a special drawing, for example Counting Star,[9] hexagon patterns with a compass, and Scribbled Whirl[10] — repeating these day after day.

I also had special activities lessons in the class with one child doing the ball throwing,[11] or Ball Twirling,[12] or ball-under-leg catching,[13] etc., while the others watched, and almost all wanted their turn; we did similar things outside. When working in pairs, they had five minutes at each activity and then moved on. These exercises give the children essential experiences of self-movement and balance, coordinating above to below, left to right, forward and backward. If we leave it to the children's play, those movements, which they need most, are often neglected. A movement assessment from *The Extra Lesson* is needed to direct them to their particular exercises. And it needs the authority of the class teacher to ensure that they are carried out.

UPDATE 1995

After another six years of working like this, I was relieved of class teaching to be able to do individual Movement Therapy lessons using exercises from *The Extra Lesson*. Student teachers, parents and inspectors of OFSTED (Governmental Inspectorate of Schools) are very interested to see the work.

---

1   Audrey E. McAllen, *The Extra Lesson*, pp. 61-62.
2   Ibid., p. 159.
3   Ibid., pp. 122-127.
4   Ibid., pp. 40-41.
5   Ibid., pp. 144-145.
6   Ibid., pp. 154-155; Rudolf Steiner, *A Modern Art of Education*, "Through form drawing you so prepare the etheric body during the waking hours, that during sleep it continues to pulsate. But within these movements or pulsations there will be a greater degree of perfection than in what was done while awake."
7   Ibid., p. 136.
8   Ibid., pp. 103-104.

9   Ibid., pp. 150-153; see also Keith Critchlow, *Time Stands Still*, p. 53.
10 Ibid., p. 141.
11 Ibid., pp. 74-75.
12 Ibid., p. 126.
13 Ibid., pp. 106-107.

INTO THE FUTURE HERE I GO

Kyle Morton

Adam Bittleston was the source of inspiration with this meditative prayer:

AGAINST FEAR

May the events that seek me
Come unto me:
May I receive them
With a quiet mind
Through the Father's ground of peace
On which we walk.

May the people who seek me
Come unto me:
May I receive them
With an understanding heart
Through the Christ's stream of love
In which we live.

May the spirits which seek me
Come unto me:
May I receive them
With a clear soul
Through the healing Spirit's light
By which we see.[1]

The Mirroring Exercise[2] brings awareness of the dimensions of left and right; the following exercise fosters awareness of before and behind. It was developed through observing the reluctance, or hesitation, of some of the children to go forward and meet what comes toward them in life, and of others who tend to rush forward, unheeding the effects they leave behind. Between the two lies one's center from where one can step forward into the future and backwards into the listening, reflecting space behind us.

Like many of the exercises in <u>The Extra Lesson</u>, the exercise I shall describe encourages spatial awareness and the flexibility to move, adapt and to look at things from different perspectives. Whereas with the Mirroring Exercise one works with the physical and etheric streams, flowing from left and right respectively,[3] with the following exercise described here one is working with the streams of the sentient body and the sentient soul.

To introduce the exercise, we begin with this sequence of movements:

Right foot forward	(return to center)
Left foot back	(return to center)
Right foot forward	(return to center)
Left foot back	(return to center)

Facing Forward:

Jump	right foot forward	left foot back
Jump	left foot forward	right foot back
Jump	right foot forward	left foot back
Jump	astride (left and right)	
Jump	Together (feet together in the center)	

When we have done these movements a few times, we add movement with the arms (to shoulder height), as described below, *looking down the arm to the extended hand and finger tips*. The movement sequence is essentially the same (changing slightly when there is a 'Jump') and is accompanied by the spoken verse:

"Into the future here I go," with right arm (at shoulder height) and foot forward (gaze to the north). *Return to center.*

"Remembering those who love me so," with left arm (shoulder height) and foot back (eyes again look down the arm to the fingertips; gaze to the south). *Return to center.*

"Into the forest down the straight and narrow way," right arm and foot forward as before (gaze to the north). *Return to center.*

"With love and gratitude each day," left arm and foot back as before (gaze to the south). *Return to center.*

"Ready to greet," jump 90° to the left, arms and legs astride (gaze to the east).

"With steady feet," jump 180° to the right, arms and legs astride (gaze to the west).

"Everything," jump 180° to the left, arms and legs astride (gaze to the east).

"That I," jump 90° to the right, arms and legs astride (facing the original direction — north).

"Must meet," jump feet together, arms by one's side (gaze to the north).

---

1   Adam Bittleston, *Meditative Prayers for Today.*
2   Audrey E. McAllen, *The Extra Lesson,* p. 61-62.
3   Rudolf Steiner, *A Psychology of Body, Soul, and Spirit.*

Tutorial Lessons for Children with Specific Learning Difficulties

Mary Jo Oresti

I work with two children individually and with three children together. I have them for two lessons each week — one lesson is devoted primarily to healing movement from *The Extra Lesson*[1] and Jean Hunt's Bean Bag Exercises from *Take Time*.[2] The other lesson focuses on Language Arts, including a little speech work.

With language arts, I use a variety of activities to bring the children into an experience of a story. Usually, I tell them the story or read to them, then we work artistically: we act out the story, create music for it, use beeswax for modeling, or paint a scene. Then they dictate to me and write the story. Following this, we read their compositions. Some phonics work or other language skills can then come from this. Sometimes we create an experience, such as a nature walk instead of a story, and then write about it. It is important that the work is done carefully.

There are many activities and games to support the necessary repetition for skills: writing on the back or in sand trays, walking while reading, dictations with foot writing, spelling with wet sponges, treasure hunts, etc.

Writing with a wet sponge can be helpful with reinforcement or practice activities. Have a child stand with you or by himself alongside a wide clean blackboard. You write a word with a damp sponge in large letters and separate the phonemes, such as PR OU D LY. Use whatever board space you have. Then, "Ready, set, go." Now the child moves *quickly* along in front of the board saying the sound for each letter or letters as he moves in front of them and repeats the phonemes quickly, saying them over and over until finally he stops at a predetermined spot in the room — perhaps at the end of the board or at his desk. As soon as he reaches the spot, he is to say the word.[3] Try to write the word just damp enough so that it will dry and disappear about the time the child reaches the spot where he must say the word.

This game works well with those who need practice reading from left to right, those who are not synthesizing sounds into words, and those who just must be moving physically. It is understood that these children also need to build other faculties. This activity with a damp sponge is used when progress has begun, and they are expressing a wish to read and synthesize. The wet sponge technique can also be used for memory games with forms, spelling, or for teaching syllables. This exercise is a variation from Magda Lissau.

The following lesson plan arose while I was working with a group of three seventh graders. It became apparent that their knowledge of grammar would almost disappear soon after each block. The challenge was to approach grammar in a living way which they could embrace and so retain it for recall; their program was arranged so that they did the required movement exercises from *The Extra Lesson* for spatial development and body geography on a once a week basis, while the other weekly lesson was devoted to a tutorial class in English.

Through various sources, a lesson plan arose which combined Waldorf methods of language teaching, color and gesture, some of Chomsky's principles of language, the rich moral fables of Tolstoy and indications by Rudolf Steiner.[4]

First, we read the fable *The Three Questions* by Tolstoy and discussed how the hermit, out of his own being, created an experience for the King. We consolidated the story into one paragraph, and then into just one sentence: "The hermit gave the King advice." Next, we looked at the story as an act of creation: 'hermit' was identified as the creator; 'gave' was the act of creation; 'the King' received the creation act; and 'advice' was what the hermit created. Following this, we acted out the sentence in gesture (mainly each child taking a turn to gesture every word). Then, we wrote the sentence in color ('hermit' in blue, 'gave' in red, etc.) At last, we could name our work as scholars do: subject, predicate, indirect object, direct object. Finally, we made up additional sentences that followed this pattern. We did two other Tolstoy fables, *Esarhaddon* and *The Just Judge*, in this same way; the children never tired of doing this. We then experimented with different sentence structures and added other parts of speech. This completed our grammar block, and we went on to another block.

The children retained the grammar quite successfully. At the end of the first year, without benefit of review, they were given a quiz of ten questions and each child had eight or nine correct answers.

This block was a special one for the children and became a model for further teaching. This lesson is being shared to help towards answering questions that have been expressed from those who do tutorial work in addition to Extra Lesson exercises. I hope this gives these teachers ideas when creating their lessons.

---

1   Audrey E. McAllen, *The Extra Lesson*.
2   Mary Nash-Wortham and Jean Hunt, *Take Time*.
3   Rudolf Steiner, *Practical Advice to Teachers*, Lecture 5; "Spelling lessons must run parallel with developing the children's feeling of respect and esteem for what their predecessors have established."
4   Rudolf Steiner, *Balance in Teaching*.

Strengthening the Reading Process

Mary Jo Oresti

The exercises listed below can assist in adding variety to the reading process. They do not include specific activities for those who need healing of the senses or strengthening of their inner constitution; but once these areas are strengthened, the teacher will find the following activities helpful. Reading, of course, does not stand alone but is part of a full 'language arts' program, including writing, drama and speech.

1. In reading, as in all learning, the movement system and the senses must be brought into joyful and balanced activity. Children should read from their own stories of experience and dramatizations. The teacher can tell (read) a group of children a simple story (such as a fable) which they then act out. During the acting out, the teacher can write down the exact words as spoken by each character. This dialogue becomes the text of a 'play' which they later copy into their main lesson books; this provides a familiar text from which they can later read.

2. Be mindful of children who easily tire when reading and then begin to make errors. Switch to another activity when the reading process begins to break down, *before* they feel unsuccessful.

3. Some children may be visually overwhelmed by the words on a page. Make a 'window' for them, so they have to concentrate on one or two words at a time. Cut a piece of paper into a shape (rectangular or oval) — 2 inches by 4 inches. Then cut a rectangular opening (as the 'window') in the center. The child can slide the paper along the line of print allowing them only to focus on a word — the one word showing through the 'window'.

4. Read together, all voices in unison (choral reading).

5. You read, then they read (echo reading).

6. Look for word patterns (such as band, grand, sand).

7. Play "I spy" (e.g., "Find the word in line four which means the opposite of 'jagged'").

8. Read while walking. Read one word as a step is taken, pause at commas, turn or jump at periods. This helps the less awakened child and improves the memory for reading. This technique can be used for small groups or individuals. It is excellent for observing how a child relates to the musical, flowing element of language. You can also do different gestures for the various punctuation marks. Select the material carefully and keep the time for this practice limited.

9. Assign ahead. Give a copy of a designated selection to a slower reader for overnight practice.

10. For the older student who is stuck in poor reading habits:
    a. read as different people and use different tones, accents, styles, etc. How would an old person read who was very wise. How would a nervous, quick person read, or a haughty person. This helps the child become less self-conscious and helps change inappropriate reading styles. This is especially good for the older student; it has initiated giggles, enthusiasm and fuller breathing.
    b. Read in different speeds. Read as quickly as possible, no matter how many mistakes, or read very slowly. Use this as 'gymnastics', but use sparingly and select the passage carefully.

11. Write practice words on the student's back or on the top of the hand, letter by letter, as you say each sound. The student immediately repeats each sound. Monitor your pressure, children who have a sensitive or undeveloped sense of touch need a firm touch. As a variation the child then writes the word, sound by sound, in a sand tray or on large paper. This is a favorite and is excellent for the kinesthetic learner as well as for those with auditory processing difficulties.

12. 'Move' the word by having the child walk the letter shapes on the floor (as with form drawing).

13. The student walks forward and backwards while spelling the word forward and backward. The student takes one step for each letter.

14. The 'Jewel' game: Hide words on cards in designated areas. These are the 'jewels' which the children hunt for. They then read

the words to you. Beginning readers will feel more comfortable with pattern words, for example: tall, fall, call.

15. Cut a piece of window screen (about 4 inches by 6 inches) and tape the edges with masking tape. Lay a piece of paper over it and write the word to be learned with a crayon. This will give a 'nubby', raised texture. The child can then trace with the finger tips and feel the word as they sound it out.

16. Many children respond well to singing. Sing the vowels in order ă ā ē ŏ ōō. Then add a beginning sound, such as 'L', to each vowel as you sing, Lă, Lā, Lē, Lŏ, Lōō. Finally, add an ending sound, for example, Lăt, Lāt, Lēt, Lŏt, Lōōt.

17. Introduce new vocabulary carefully — with a story, in colors, using synonyms and antonyms, act them out, etc.

I would like to thank Audrey McAllen, Rosemary Gebert, Molly van Heider and other colleagues for inspiring these techniques.

Mary Jo Oresti, remedial teacher since 1979 in the Detroit Waldorf School, a member of the College of Teachers, and since 1992, co-director of The Waldorf Education Remedial Program (see p. 282).

Exercises Researched by the Dutch Remedial Group

Joep Eikenboom

Remedial teachers in Waldorf schools have been receiving reports of children's lack of response to the archetypal element of form. This would seem to be a new stage showing a deterioration of the spiritual capacity of the eyes; a divorce from the connection between eye and ego. This is, no doubt, the culminating effect of TV and other electronic devices, as well as of the 'blank' looking at nature and our surroundings.

Audrey McAllen and this writer had the opportunity of meeting Liane Collot d'Herbois[1] and presented this problem to her. She made the following suggestion which I have been carrying out with my pupils. Audrey McAllen also used it with a group of artistic therapists at the Tobias Artistic Therapy Training Course, UK. She reported that the reaction of the therapists was appreciative, the mood quiet, concentrated, and that they said they felt enlivened and 'rested' afterwards.

Exercises

1. Use a large sheet of water color paper — moisten the paper with longest side vertical. Colors: *viridian green*[2] and *magenta*[3]. Mix the pigment with water to paint a light viridian wash from the top to about *three quarters* down the paper. Paint with long, *unbroken brush strokes,* from *left to right,* horizontally. The veil of viridian green *must give the impression of light.* This color helps the ego to penetrate the organism. Finish the remainder of the paper in the same way with magenta. This ending brings about a balance to the concentration of the ego activity into the etheric forces. Use Winsor and Newton artists' water color paint for the viridian green or Grumbacher Academy water color #A232. For the magenta, use Winsor and Newton Permanent Magenta Series SA #0102-489. This painting exercise should be done with children only after secondary colors have been introduced in class.

2. The writer has also used these two colors for the Interpenetrating Triangles Exercise[4] using blue-green and red-violet beeswax stick crayons (Stockmar). The upper triangle: viridian green (blue-green crayon), lower triangle: magenta (red-violet crayon).

3. Rudolf Steiner spoke to teachers about 'Color Perspective as an aid to reading'.[5] This can be achieved by augmenting the 'Sun in Blue Sky Painting'[6] by using a lemon yellow for the center of the sun, deepening to the outside with a warmer golden yellow. Use cobalt blue for the sky and deepen the outer edges with ultramarine. (The above indication on the painting of yellow, given by L. C. d'Herbois, is based on a lecture by Rudolf Steiner, July 5, 1921, Dornach, Switzerland.)

Joep Eikenboom, a Waldorf teacher since 1980, met Audrey McAllen in 1984 and studied extensively with her. For 8 years a remedial teacher at several Waldorf schools, he is currently a class teacher and teaches in remedial training courses in Holland, Germany, USA, and Norway.

---

1   Liane Collot d'Herbois was born 1907 near Tintagel, Cornwall, England. Her artistic studies in England led her to Rudolf Steiner's Anthroposophy through which she developed a painting therapy based on the origination of color through the forces of darkness and of light. For information about studying this painting therapy, write to: Emerald Foundation, Nassau Dillenburgstraat 13, 25 96 AB, The Hague, Holland, Telephone 70-324-0554.
2   Liane Collot d'Herbois, Light, *Darkness and Colour in Painting Therapy*, p. 150.
3   Ibid., p. 70.
4   Audrey E. McAllen, *The Extra Lesson*, pp. 154-155.
5   Rudolf Steiner, *The Child's Changing Consciousness and Waldorf Education*, Lecture 4 (Formerly called 'The Swiss Teachers' Course').
6   A. E. McAllen, *The Extra Lesson*, pp. 160-161.

Three Dimensions of Space Around Me

Marieke Lofvers

Use a copper ball and enough space for movement for both teacher and child. Teacher and child stand opposite to each other, approximately three yards/meters between them. Feet firmly on the floor, a little apart. Copper ball in the right hand, the left hand giving support under the right hand. Hands in front of the solar plexus.

Under — Above Vertical

Stretch your right arm across your body to the left side holding the copper ball on the palm of your hand. Move the copper ball slowly downward — arm stretched — in a large circular movement, bending to be able to touch your feet; continue the movement until your arm comes back to the right side — standing upright. During the movement, follow the copper ball with your eyes saying, "All this is under me."

Bring hand and ball back to the starting position in front of the solar plexus. Give the copper ball to your left hand. Holding the copper ball, stretch your arm across the body to the far right side. Move the copper ball slowly in a circular movement above the head — arm stretched — to the far left side, following the copper ball with your eyes saying, "All this is above me." Bring hands (with the copper ball) back to the starting position.

In Front — Behind Horizontal

Give the copper ball to your right hand. Stretch your right arm holding the copper ball across your body to the left side. Move the copper ball slowly with arm stretched in a large circular movement through the space in front of you from the left to the right side. Throughout the movement, follow the copper ball with your eyes saying, "All this is in front of me." Return to starting position.

Give the copper ball to your left hand. Holding the copper ball stretch your arm behind your back (difficult!) as far as possible to the right side (hand holding the copper ball to protect it from falling). Move the copper ball in a horizontal line returning it to your left side. Try to follow the movement with your eyes (in an inward gesture — not moving your body) saying, "All this is behind me." Return to starting position.

LEFT — RIGHT HORIZONTAL

Give the copper ball to your *writing* hand. Holding the copper ball, stretch your arm directly in front of you. Move the stretched arm in a circular movement all around that side of your body which this arm belongs to — to exactly behind you. Follow the movement with your eyes saying, "All this is on my right (left) hand side." Return to starting position.

Give the copper ball to other hand. Holding the copper ball, stretch your arm directly in front of you. Move the stretched arm in a circular movement all the way around — exactly behind you. Follow the movement with your eyes saying, "All this is on my left (right) hand side." Return to starting position with hands together in front of the solar plexus.

After helping the children with exercises with bean bags in all directions, the above exercise brings peace and concentration. I love doing this exercise with the children.

MY OWN FOOTPRINTS

For this next lesson, ask the child in advance to be ready to take off her shoes and socks. The teacher stands opposite the child. The child stands with bare feet in front of a tray with sand in it (enough sand to make good prints).

We will call this child Rose Marie Smith. Ask her to step with her right foot into the sand saying the first part of her name, "Rose." Stepping and speaking should be synchronized. The left foot follows with the second part of her name, "Marie." Ask her to give full weight into the feet so that they make strong prints. (When the child is called "John" just have him say "John" while stepping with each foot.)

Let Rose Marie step carefully backward out of the tray and we look together at her footprints. We talk about their size, form, sharpness, etc.; they are so special!

Now we ask her to jump with *both* feet together into her footprints saying her last name "Smith." For safety, stand opposite to her and hold her hands.

This experience of calling her name while making her footprints is most wonderful. Most children like the challenge of this exercise.

I find 'footprints' good for starting an Extra Lesson session. At the very moment you notice she has made progress in her process of incarnation, she will succeed in jumping exactly into her footprints.

This exercise is helpful for a weak incarnation process, lack of self-confidence, too little courage, too much uncontrolled moving, or being too eager to make plans before starting something.

THE THREEFOLD SPIRAL EXERCISE

When there is no longer any confusion in doing the Threefold Spiral Exercise as described by Audrey McAllen in *The Extra Lesson*, we can bring the child immediately after this exercise to the blackboard. Place chalk into his writing hand. Ask him to draw what his hand has just done in the spiral form. After doing this, let him step backward and 'see' if he has done well compared with the form used for the Threefold Spiral Exercise (that is still there on the floor). *No comments are made by the teacher.*

Now bring him to a tray (on the floor) with enough sand to leave a form after tracing it in the sand. Ask him to make with his right foot the same form he had made on the blackboard. Do the same with the left foot. Have him look at both forms afterwards. If needed, you can hold his hand for balance while he is doing this.

By adding this drawing on the vertical blackboard and the footwork in a horizontal sand tray, we add the postural system to the exercise and the memory of the moving system as well.

Aaron's Story
A Third Grade Student

Mary Ellen Willby

Third grader Aaron was brought to me because he was still not learning to read. He came from a family where all siblings were in the Waldorf school and there was no TV at home; he had started kindergarten at four years. He was gifted in drawing, extremely musical and good at mathematics. He had an exuberant personality; he was very skilled in athletic activities, but clumsy in his feet. His mother reported that his had been a quick birth; as a newborn, his left pupil was dilated and he had tremors on the right side.

Extra Lesson Assessment

During the assessment procedure, Aaron's lack of spatial orientation[1] was revealed especially in the Handedness Pattern - Relationship to Three-Dimensional Space.[2] In the Weight-Lifting Exercise,[3] all fingers on Aaron's right hand pulled out and his left hand clenched into a fist. This showed that the acute sensitivity to sense impressions had spilled over from the receiving sense organs into the 'stretching' muscles.[4] When the impact is so strong, the perceiving sense of self-movement is overwhelmed. If overwhelmed enough, the soul finds no anchorage and begins spiraling out uncontrolled, as in Aaron's case. 'Simple Dominance' was right hand, right foot, right ear, and left eye.[5] In the Eye-Color Affinity drawing,[6] Aaron drew a blue moon on the left and on the right a large orange sun with rays over the entire page — orange indicating the problems stemmed from his heredity body which he had not been able to overcome. His Person-House-Tree picture[7] confirmed this in showing a healthy soul (person) with problems in the house (heredity body).

EXTRA LESSON DEVELOPMENTAL PROGRAM

In the course of thirty-eight hourly lessons, once a week during term time, Aaron did the following exercises from *The Extra Lesson*: Rod Rolling,[8] Ball Throwing, Wool Winding, Skein Twisting, Flower-Rod (until done properly), Copper Ball followed by Moving Straight Line and Lemniscate, Counting Star (with blue lens for the left eye), the Exercise for Establishing Dominance on the right (or left) side of the body (for children between 6 and 11 years of age),[9] and the Blue-Red Spiral Painting as well as tasks in shaded drawing for homework.

His social acceptance improved; he now met challenges where formerly his feelings of being overwhelmed and frustrated had spilled over into social difficulties. From the boy who fell out of his chair at least once a day in second grade, he became quite poised with no sign of clumsiness and developed a good self-image. It was heart-warming to see Aaron at the same subject level as his peers and an avid reader.

---

1. Audrey E. McAllen, *The Extra Lesson*, Chapter Four.
2. Ibid., pp. 42-51.
3. Ibid., pp. 135-136.
4. See A. E. McAllen, Section I, 'Twofold Man as Archetype'.
5. A. E. McAllen, *The Extra Lesson*, pp. 35-40.
6. See Mary Nash-Wortham, Section II, 'Goethe's Color Theory Applied'; A. E. McAllen, *The Extra Lesson*, pp. 55-61.
7. Ibid., pp. 75-87.
8. Hand hammered copper rods and balls were used. Contact Rudolf Steiner College Bookstore regarding purchasing.
9. A. E. McAllen, *The Extra Lesson*, p. 130.

ANDREW AND HIS SENSE OF TOUCH

Mary Jo Oresti

A child in our school who was making little progress visited a Sensory Integration[1] clinic; the assessment found that he had 'tactile defensiveness', i.e., he had a disturbed sense of touch. As this was a new experience for me, it is shared in the hope that it may shed some light for other teachers.

This child — we shall call him Andrew — was a transfer student and was presented two years previously by the class teacher for a child study because of constant inattentiveness, talkativeness, poor academic skills (his relation to the world of ideas), inability to sit in a chair, clumsiness, poor handwriting. He preferred to play with younger students and had a delightful, but bizarre habit of sitting in the waste basket.[2] He was also presented as being intelligent, perceptive, and a voracious reader, but poor in arithmetic. He received special lessons for some time and progress was made, but in grade six all the problems escalated, especially the constant chatter. His family was asked to take him for further testing at a Sensory Integration clinic, but they chose a psychological-educational assessment which did not prove effective. Finally, he went to the local Sensory Integration clinic, was found to be tactile defensive, and received treatment.

Andrew demonstrated several manifestations of tactile defensiveness. He resisted the rule of no outside jackets in class, talked constantly, avoided eye contact, and found odors 'disgusting' (especially the blue paint which seems to go 'sour' quickly). Fortunately, he did not manifest any signs of aggression and did not physically lash out. The mother shared that he had always been irritable when touched and found certain textures unbearable. We were informed that these are signs of tactile defensiveness. The clinician explained that touch alerts what occupational therapists call the 'fight or flight' system, and consequently children with tactile defensiveness do not discriminate between threatening and friendly contact. When touched, they might strike back forcefully. The sense of smell is often affected and is then very sensitive. Also, these children often have difficulty discriminating between foreground and background noises or are very sensitive to sound, so they talk incessantly as a way to control the sound environment. We were warned that he might exhibit some erratic emotional reactions and may appear to be getting worse for a while. This is because the sense of touch affects the limbic or emotional area of the brain. We were also advised to firmly touch his shoulder and make eye contact when giving instructions.

Andrew also had other difficulties. He had visual motor difficulty, trouble with his sense of balance (equilibrium), and difficulty learning new movement exercises. He rushed through most activities. He received help for these problems at school, as well as his weekly visits to the clinic.

The clinic, which Andrew visited weekly, prescribed the following: at home he was given a special type of massage down each limb (a technique called 'brushing' which ended with pressure on the shoulders and on the head), stamping on the way to bed and a heavy blanket for sleeping.

When the above program had been in effect for six months, we began to see improvement in all areas of previous difficulties. Andrew became quieter in class and more aware of his physical boundaries. His mother came to us with gratitude for our persistence. "He's not afraid of the dark — I didn't believe these things would change." Andrew, himself, saw his improvement, "I'm glad I'm not such a pain to others."

Andrew participated in both mainstream activities and those that arose out of Waldorf pedagogy. With most children, the Waldorf pedagogical methods can be sufficient, but sometimes it is necessary to seek outside resources. However, we should never just 'hand over' the children entirely, but carefully determine what resources we can provide, build a relationship with the therapists to help them to be awake to our intentions, and balance mainstream work with related arts.

As we know, the sense of touch is a fundamental sense, penetrating our earth experience along with our sense of life, sense of self-movement and sense of balance. These senses are nurtured and developed in the first seven years and are the basis for developing higher faculties. Often with the children of today these senses are not sufficiently developed, so we must consciously help the children to develop them. Without the full development of these senses, the teacher does not have access to the rhythmic system which is the basis for Waldorf school pedagogy in classes one through eight.

The sense of touch has many characteristics, but simply put, we can think of it as the sense that brings the feeling of separation of self from the world. "This is me, that is the world." The sense of touch[3] is also related to the sense or ability to perceive another's ego.

With all this in mind, we reviewed Andrew's child study concerns and decided to add some activities to his school program. More beeswax and sandtray work in math was emphasized. In form drawing, he was directed to hold the crayon at its tip so that his fingertips could feel the paper. We also were attentive to getting eye contact and to using a firm touch on the shoulder before giving instructions. I hope this picture might help other teachers in their observations.

Note: When the sense of touch is not integrated, a child does not accomplish bilateral integration. This can be seen in the Handedness Pattern-Relationship to Three-Dimensional Space.[4] Such a child may seek a protected personal space (may not want to be touched). Be sure to use a firm, caring touch that doesn't trigger a startle response when you do touch the child who can be easily overstimulated by too much 'levity' or light touch, by too much humor, or too much physical levity from bouncing, swinging, jumping and tickling. The child can be calmed down by experiencing 'gravity' or firm touch, i.e., from a low, serious voice and the physical gravity that comes from feeling firm pressure against the skin (clothing that fits firmly and calm, firm hugs). He himself will try to experience gravity by falling to the ground, lying down or getting sat on by peers (it may look like the child is trying to start a fight, but the child is mostly seeking the firm pressure that comes with it).

The two systems of touch (light and firm) are regulated by different parts of the autonomic nervous system; firm touch calms and organizes; it overrides light touch because its messages reach the brain first when both stimuli are present.[5]

1. A. Jean Ayres, *Sensory Integration and the Child*.
2. Andrew liked 'pressure' around his body; this is why he sat in the waste basket and asked the younger children to jump on top of him. Regarding the relation between the sense of balance and pressure, see Rudolf Steiner, *A Psychology of Body, Soul and Spirit*, lecture 2, pp. 25-27.
3. Rudolf Steiner, *A Psychology of Body, Soul, and Spirit*, lecture 2.
4. A. E. McAllen, *The Extra Lesson*, pp. 42-51.
5. See Dee J. Coulter, Section II, 'An Immature Movement Response which Interferes with Reading'.

Laura's Story
A High School Student

Mary Ellen Willby

Laura was in grade eleven when she was referred to me by her teachers. She had always been in a Waldorf school. There did not seem to be any problems during the class teaching period (first through eighth grade), although her mother had always had to help her with homework that had required the grasping of thoughts/concepts.

When in high school, Laura would often raise her hand to answer a question, but when she stood up to answer, she couldn't find her way to speak out what she had thought. When her mother realized she still needed help with her homework, a meeting with the teachers was arranged, and a decision was made for Laura to have an Extra Lesson assessment.

The Extra Lesson assessment is based on the principles of a main lesson. The children are asked to do different activities so that we can see if the movement skills, feeling and inner visualization have been attained which are normal for a child from the age of seven.

In the book *The Extra Lesson* are the instructions and explanations needed to understand why Laura was asked to do such a simple thing as draw a line down the center of a sheet of paper and put a cross on one side of it. She placed her cross (a St. George type)[1] on the right side of the line. I asked her to draw a blue moon and a red sun.[2] This was reversed — the red sun drawn on the left instead of the right. This reversal showed that her will forces were too deeply engaged in her organism, so that her formative forces, which should have been released by age seven, were not freed for their thinking/conceptual function. The type of cross and its placement gave the same picture.

We then did the movement exercises from *The Extra Lesson*; ball throwing, ball bouncing, wool winding, etc. I noted how in such activities Laura's left arm remained uncommonly passive. The tension in her body when doing these exercises revealed an obstruction in the correct flow of movement. I suspected cross dominance which was confirmed by the appropriate tests.

The results of the Handedness Pattern-Relationship to Three-Dimensional Space assessment,[3] confirmed and enlarged what had already been revealed in her movements; namely, the astral body (soul body) was too strongly united with the etheric/physical forces which accounted for her difficulty in grasping thoughts/concepts.

To complete the assessment, I asked her to do the clapping, jumping routine and then draw a 'Person, House, Tree' picture.[4] For a girl of seventeen years, the drawing was very immature. There was no sun or blue sky. The person was placed between the tree and house which gave an impression that she was not centered in her physical body (the house). The tree was sturdy with roots and many branches, but the foliage was just a scribble over the branches. The person had no hands or feet, no features in the face (which would have been there if the development of the first seven years had been completed), and the head was pressed into the shoulders.

After a few lessons, I observed that Laura did not have a natural way of moving her neck. I reported this to her parents and they sent Laura to a chiropractor (a parent at the school), who confirmed the need of his therapy which she received. During this treatment, we continued with the exercises in order that the release from the constrictions causing her neck problems could be integrated into her bodily coordination. The Right-Angled Triangle Exercise[5] and homework were also part of her remediation program.

Laura made considerable improvement in the short time of only fifteen lessons. This she showed in the freedom of movement in her neck, and in the ease of correctly accomplishing previous exercises that she had found difficult.

After a number of lessons with pupils, I have them repeat the Eye Color Affinity drawing. In Laura's case, it was drawn correctly in the tenth lesson and remained so through the rest of the course of work with me. Similarly, I insert into a lesson a 'Person, House, Tree' drawing at suitable intervals. After five lessons, Laura's second picture showed that she had made considerable changes. The foreground was artistically drawn and the home was on a hill with flowers on either side. The person was still in the center, the head turned toward the tree. The neck, although not delineated, showed movement awareness, but there were still no hands or feet. The branches of the tree were now formed, and it was full of red apples, already ripe and fallen onto the grass — drawn so they formed a triangle. The foliage of the tree was rhythmically spiraling round the branches instead of just being scribbled over them. A radiant sun shone over the house, and a blue bird was flying toward it, although the sky was still empty.

Her final picture was a delight. In the center was a maiden in a blue pinafore dress, a white blouse and a necklace — sturdy legs with shoes — in one hand a bunch of red and blue flowers, in the other a basket. The radiant sun shone in a blue sky on the right in which the bird was now flying with a worm in its mouth to feed the three little blue baby birds in the nest. The mother bird drawn in red was perched on a little tree house with a ladder[6] from it to the earth. The apples were brown and many had fallen. All around the tree were red, blue and magenta flowers.

During the time Laura had been coming for lessons, the difficulty she had experienced with her menses corrected itself, and she could answer questions and contribute her thoughts in class.

---

1   This is 'flat mirroring'. See Audrey E. McAllen, Section I, 'The Mirroring Process in Relation to Two- and Three-Dimensional Space'.
2   A. E. McAllen, *The Extra Lesson* (Eye-Color Affinity); see also Mary Nash-Wortham, Section II, 'Goethe's Color Theory Applied'.
3   A. E. McAllen, *The Extra Lesson*, pp.42-51.
4   Ibid., pp. 75-87.
5   Ibid., Rudolf Steiner, *Foundations of Esotericism*, Lecture XII (Berlin October 7, 1905), Simon Singh, *Fermat's Last Theorem*.
6   Michaela Strauss, *Understanding Children's Drawings*.

David's Story
A High School Student

Lalage Craig

Sixteen year old David was brought to me because of his stuttering which had started in pre-school. His motivation to work was poor, his reading below age level, and he was left-handed.

Personal History

The mother had hepatitis from February through April and became pregnant in June of that year. At this time, the mother's father was terminally ill. The family moved to a different house early in the pregnancy. The mother was always tired and lethargic throughout pregnancy.

Birth was induced and took place within three hours.

David was breast fed for six months.

Both grandparents died when David was nine months and ten months old respectively.

He sat at 9 1/2 months, crawled at 10 1/2 months, stood at 10 1/2 months, walked at 13 months and talked at two years.

In David's fourth year, his problems started; he began stuttering, showed no tendency toward a dominant hand, and his behavior was extremely disruptive.

An older child in the family had speech therapy.

Extra Lesson Assessment

David was referred to The Dural Extra Lesson and Therapy Centre by an educational psychologist.

A tall thin boy, David was very pale when he came for the assessment. He stood badly, poking his head forward; there was very little eye contact and he had poor social skills. His balance was very poor. He also used a computer at home excessively.

Abberrant Primal Reflexes (immature movement responses):[1] the Asymmetrical Tonic Neck Reflex (ATNR) was significantly retained and was impeding his handwriting.[2]

The Symmetrical Tonic Neck Reflex was significantly retained.[3]
Landau reflex was not a problem.[4]

Moro reflex was also quite strongly retained, causing him to be anxious and withdrawn.

HANDEDNESS PATTERN-
RELATIONSHIP TO THREE-DIMENSIONAL SPACE[5]

On the vertical chart where the instructions were to "use two limbs together," David traced the forms simultaneously, i.e., with the left foot on the left side and right hand on the right side of the center line.

The horizontal forms were traced in the same way.

Where one hand was used, David chose the *right hand*.

HEARING

He was more left-eared than right-eared. When a child is left-eared, there is a 5 - 9 micro second delay in what is heard and this shows there is an auditory processing problem. These children may hear the first and last spoken sentence, but will not hear the rest. So if they are given a list of things to do they will only be able to remember the first or last thing on the list.

CROSS TEST,[6] FLOWER-ROD,[7] READING

David drew a line across the original vertical line.
Flower-Rod was done correctly.
His reading age was 12.10 on the basic Schonell reading test.

PICTURE DIAGNOSIS[8]

The person, the house and the tree were all separated by a line between them down the page in spite of instructions to draw a lovely picture with those items in it. The head was outlined in black with a black top knot (showing cranial pressure) and the neck was all black. The tree showed a lack of full breathing, had no roots and was barely on the ground. The house was drawn on the left side with only part of it on the paper, and the windows without the usual 'St. George' cross. The roof was in black and covered in black tiles. There was no ground under the person or house.

Extra Lesson Movement Program

David was given all the floor exercises to aid the integration of primal reflexes (immature movement responses) and a series of homolateral movements leading up to cross-lateral movements, including the Grand Crawl.[9]

These were given between February 2nd and February 21st.

On February 14th, I introduced the Right-Angled Triangle Exercise,[10] (the forms for the *left* side because he used his left hand). David did this at home twice a week for two weeks, and then in the following weeks, he did this exercise three times a week.

In the lessons at the clinic, he painted the Sun in the Blue Sky Exercise.[11] I then followed this with the Moral Colour Exercises.[12]

All the bean bag exercises were done by David during the lessons.

Concentration exercises — with rods — throwing, passing, catching, walking, and speaking a tongue twister backwards and forwards were done.

The Counting Star Exercise was introduced February 21st.

On May 2nd, David's mother reported that his concentration had improved, his memory was better, he was reading more, and his comprehension of what he read had improved.

On May 23rd, she reported that David was getting good results on his tests at his school, he was more motivated, and his organizational skills had improved.

As we worked, it was fascinating for me to see, how after doing the correct archetypal movements for three months, he wanted to become right-handed. He demanded to do the Right-Angled Triangle Exercise for the *right* side and the Threefold Spiral Exercise. Both of these were done daily for six weeks. Only after David had done the above for six weeks, did I suggest he practice writing a little bit at home every day with his right hand until he felt confident to do it at school.

By July 27th, his reading had improved — in fact it was up to his chronological age.

David's attitude at school was much better, and his grades at school had come up so far that we ended the lessons. He continued with the Right-Angled Triangle Exercise and the Threefold Spiral Exercise for another month at home.

David now stood upright with good eye contact and revealed he had a good sense of humor!

He was passing all his exams at school, and his social skills had improved.

I telephoned his mother three months later to make sure there had been no backsliding; she reported that he was continuing to improve, and she was very grateful for the work David had done with us at the Centre.

The children sent to our centre all have one hour sessions. We see two children at a time. One has massage for one half hour while the other is having Extra Lesson Exercises with me. Before beginning the second half of the lesson, the two children have 'bean bag' exercises together.

David did not come from a Rudolf Steiner school. When children come from other than Steiner/Waldorf schools, they are given an intensive crash course. Then parents, are instructed what to help them with at home, and they return at the parents discretion. When children come from a Rudolf Steiner school, they receive a one-hour lesson each week for one to two years.

Lalage Craig is a U.K. trained teacher. She taught in various schools before becoming a class teacher at Glenaeon Rudolf Steiner School in Sydney, Australia, where she taught for 17 years. Lalage is a trained Neuro-Developmental Therapist (NIPP) and studied The Extra Lesson with Audrey McAllen. She is currently doing research in her second year of a Masters of Education (Hons) Degree at the University of New England. She has been in private practice for ten years and runs The Dural Extra Lesson™ and Therapy Centre where 40-50 children attend each week. She is also a director of The Institute for Learning Difficulties, Pty. Ltd., through which she runs the Graduate Diploma in Educational Studies, Extra Lesson.™ This is an accredited 3 year part time course through The New South Wales Higher Education Board, in Australia. This course is currently being run in Sydney and Perth, Australia, and since the year 2000 it has been run in New Zealand.

1. See Dee J. Coulter, Section II, 'An Immature Movement Pattern which Interferes with Reading'.
2. Jane Field, *Talking to Teachers*.
3. Peter Blythe and Jane Field, *Towards Developmental Re-Education*.
4. Ibid.
5. A. E. McAllen, *The Extra Lesson*, pp. 42-51.
6. Ibid., pp. 28-32.
7. Ibid., pp. 51-54.
8. Ibid., pp. 75-87.
9. Ibid., pp. 113-114.
10. Ibid., pp. 130-134; Rudolf Steiner, *Foundations of Esotericism*, Lecture VII.
11. A. E. McAllen, *The Extra Lesson*, pp. 160-161.
12. A. E. McAllen, *Sleep*, pp. 32-45.

Nancy's Story
A University Student

Lalage Craig

Nineteen year old Nancy was brought to me because she was not doing well at the university. She was having difficulty organizing her time; she was handing in her assignments late, was getting very emotional, and was thinking of dropping out.

Personal History

Her mother was not very happy at becoming pregnant with Nancy, for she already had three older children. The eldest was six years old. The pregnancy was uneventful, although they moved when she was six months pregnant. The birth was a planned induction. The mother had an epidural anesthesia. The labor was quick — four to five hours.

Nancy was breast fed for 2 - 3 months; her mother was tired and depressed, and there was little joy.

The developmental milestones were a little delayed. Nancy's mother could not remember when Nancy began to crawl, but did remember that Nancy crawled properly on all fours and was walking at fourteen months.

Nancy was a clumsy child. When running, she would easily trip and fall.

She had a ruptured eardrum in her seventh year.

Nancy's siblings had learning difficulties.

Extra Lesson Assessment

Nancy came to the clinic because her younger brother had followed our program with success.

A well built girl with good colour, she was friendly and eager to talk.

Aberrant Primitive Reflexes (immature movement responses): Assymetrical Tonic Neck Reflex (ATNR) was significantly retained and generally impeding all eye-hand coordination. Symmetrical Tonic Neck Reflex was also retained. Spinal Galant Reflex was retained enough for her to find sitting still through lectures difficult and tiring. The Moro Reflex— the flight or fight reflex — was causing her a lot of anxiety and making her very emotional.

Vestibular (balance) sense: this was very poor; she could not maintain her balance while standing on one foot with her eyes closed.

Handedness Pattern—
Relationship to Three-Dimensional Space

On the vertical chart where instruction was to "trace the forms with both hands (or both feet) together," Nancy traced the forms with the left limb on the left of the vertical line and the right limb on the right side of the vertical line, moving the limbs simultaneously — consistently from the inside to the outside of the forms. The horizontal forms were done in the same fashion.

When the instruction was "one foot, one hand," the use of left and right was completely mixed. She had strongly retained the vertical midline barrier. Her hearing did not appear to be a problem.

Cross Test

She drew a line down the page as instructed and put a 'St. George' cross on the right hand side of the vertical line.

Picture Diagnosis

The house dominated the picture; the roof was not drawn as an archetypal triangle and there was a veranda with an awning. The windows did not have the cross through them. The tree was on the left side of the page and was leaning over towards the house and covering some of the roof. The person was on the left of the house and was well drawn.

Extra Lesson Developmental Program

Nancy started lessons with me on March 25th. For homework she was given the Right-Angled Triangle Exercise for the right side with some floor exercises to increase muscle tone and inhibit the primitive reflexes. She had a specific exercise to inhibit the Moro Reflex. Nancy telephoned regularly (in tears to begin with). She could not keep several appointments, but continued with her home program. August 28th, she was very tearful and still having trouble with organization. By November 17th, Nancy was keeping up with her work, and she reported that her friends were amazed at how she had handled a potentially emotional situation in her life. Nancy thinks she is better and received a 'credit' for one of her assignments — the first time she had received such a high mark.

The following year, Nancy returned on February 14th to our clinic. The following is her list of everything which had improved: she organized her time better; she allowed herself time to express her feelings, all her marks had improved, and she either had 'credits' or just one mark off 'credits'. She kept the Right-Angled Triangle Exercise forms behind the door of her room and did them every time she felt herself becoming stressed.

At the time of this writing, Nancy has her degree and is holding down a demanding job.

EXERCISE QUICK REFERENCE GUIDE
from *The Extra Lesson*, 6th Edition

First Educational Support Lesson
Cross Assessment 29-32
Writing 32-35
"Simple" Dominance 35-40
  Hand Dominance Check 36
  Eye Dominance Check 37
  Ear Dominance Check 38
  Foot Dominance Check 39
Hand-Eye-Speech Coordination 40-42
Handedness Pattern 42-51
Flower Rod (Concave-Convex) 51-55
Eye Color Affinity 55-61
Mirroring 61-62
Early Movement Patterns—Senses of
  Touch, Life, Self Movement, Balance 63-68
Midline Barriers 68-72
Eye Movement 72-73
Bean Bag or Ball Throwing:
  Above-Below Integration 73-74
  Left-Right Integration 74-75
Person-House-Tree Drawing 75-87
Spot Check for Whole Class 87-88
School Entry 88-90
Reassessing Children in the Class 91

Extra Lesson Exercises
Body Geography:
  Grades 1-3 (age 7-10) 96-97
  11 Years on 98
  Tracing, Coloring Hands 98
  Cubes between Fingers 99
  Beeswax Ball Rolling 99
  Fingers Walking on Rod 100
  Wool Winding 100
  Skein Twisting 102
  Marbles between Toes 103
  Copper Ball Spiral 104
  Bean Counting 105
Spatial Orientation
  Left-Right Ball Exercise 105
  Above-Below Ball Exercises 106
  Forward-Back Rod Exercise 108
  Whole Body Exercise 109
Integrating Early Movement Patterns
  Fish, Seal, Lizard, Eagle, Crab,
    Roly-poly, Wheelbarrow 110

Creeping like Stalking Cat 111
Caterpillar Crawl 112
Grand Crawl 112
Wrestle 113
Integrating Horizontal Midline Barrier 114
Integrating Vertical Midline Barrier 114
Development of Senses 116-118
Eye-Finger Exercise 119
Eye-Hand Coordination:
  Extra Lesson Exercises 120
  Childhood Activities 121
Rhythm, Body Space, Breathing:
  Copper Ball Exercise 122
  Ball Twirling Exercise 125
  Threefold Spiral 127
  Triangle Rod Exercise 128
Establishing Dominance
  Dominance Form 130
  Right-angled Triangle 130
Stretching and Lifting
  Lifting One's Weight 135
  Bouncing Ball Exercise 136
  Rod Rolling Exercise 137
Drawing
  Positions for writing and 138
  Release arm-hand tension 140
  Continuous Pattern Exercises 142
  Vertical & Horizontal Mirroring 143
  Lemniscates 144, 146
  Moving Line & Lemniscate 147
  Thumb Twirling 147
  Counting Star 150
  Interpenetrating Triangles 154
  Geometry of Hexagon 155
  Shaded Drawing 158
  Palindrome and Area 203
  Triangle Expansion & Contraction 196
  Counting Triangle 197
Painting
  Sun in the Blue Sky 160
  Blue and Red Spiral 161
  Secondary Color Exercise 165
  Blue-Red Perspective 168
  Painted Lemniscate 170
  Eye-Hand Exercise 171
  Magenta & Viridian 172

IV

Questions and Answers

Audrey E. McAllen

To fulfill the need for a teachers' forum, as stated in the first issue of the Bulletin of the Remedial Research Group, the following questions which were asked by teachers were kindly answered by Audrey McAllen.

Visual Sense Impressions

Question: For someone who can blend sounds but not retain memory of *simple* words from one line to the next (usually a difficult word in context will be remembered), what exercises would be suitable?

Answer: This is a matter of the visual sense impressions (which are taken up by the sentient soul) not being able to be impressed into the etheric and physical bodies by the Ego. We need to bring the Ego more strongly into connection with the physical, etheric and astral bodies. This is done by walking and stepping on each word that is read, pausing at commas, turning round at periods and walking in the opposite direction. It is very important that each spoken word is said aloud clearly, and that the step coincides with the spoken word. The next stage is eye-and-hand activity. Write a short sentence on the blackboard, then let the child trace each word of the sentence in the air with his eyes closely following his tracing finger. Now, with both eyes closed, have the child's eyes trace each word of the sentence — the teacher must watch and see that the child's eyeballs move underneath the closed eyelids. You may find that, rather than moving the eyeballs because the muscles around the eyes are poorly organized and/or weak, the child's head tends to move with the eye tracking. This often means the vestibular (balance) system is not functioning freely, which would have to be investigated. Now rub out the sentence and let the child write it. Don't let him hesitate. Get him to write in a flow, even if it means leaving out a word; he can make another line for the missing word. These words can then be written in his hand (with his vision occluded), or on his back, so that again he has to inwardly visualize and connect up the sequence of letters into a concept. Exercises of this kind have to be practiced *daily* — which is the *rhythm of the Ego* — and *over a number of weeks.*

We have now worked from the body on to the soul by calling on the will in which the Ego is embedded at this stage of man's development. Now we will help from the other side: we will engage the soul directly through painting.[1] Steiner gives two painting exercises for memory: One for children who are 'stuck' in their sense impressions, and one where the child is 'like a sieve' and everything drains away. The latter is the case with this child. Such a child should do a form of 'drawing-painting', i.e., painting forms in the colors that are near each other, like green, yellow, orange, or blue, purple, red in loop-like forms.[2]

Tension while Writing

Question: A right-handed child in my second grade holds the pencil between the index finger and thumb and presses so hard that the upper arm muscles are hardened. The child refuses to correct the hold. Can you suggest something?

Answer: Try to release the tension and bring about movement by working with the right foot. The child should *write* his name and address each day *with the foot*, then a short sentence (the same sentence for a week). If the class is too large for the teacher to provide this help, then the mother should supervise the child doing this every evening. It must be done on a *daily* basis. The principle underlying the exercise: work with the feet, if the hand is unskilled; work with the hand, if the foot is clumsy.[3]

Writing with the Foot

Question: How can you write with the foot with classes of twenty-four children and over?

Answer: Put the children in pairs. Let one child hold the paper on the floor while the other sits and writes. They can draw a geometrical form or some mirror drawing they are working at. This child can sign his name. Then, turn the paper over and the partner writes the word to be learned in spelling or the form drawing or mirror drawing, and he can write the date. Next day, the first child can write the date and the other sign his name. Don't forget the many ways the date can be written! It is the *variety* of doing the *same* thing that works into the will.

If teachers will do such an activity for at least six weeks of each term during grades one and two, they will find that the mildly hyperactive or clumsy children will benefit enormously, the integrated children grow strong and skillful, and those with real problems stand out so that they can be spotted and receive one-to-one help in time. Remember *the rhythm for the Ego is a daily one; for the astral body, a week; for the etheric body, at least a month, and for the physical body, a year. Doing such an activity for a few days has little benefit.*

Person - House - Tree Picture[4]

Question: What does it mean when children draw a child on a swing in their Person-House-Tree pictures during an assessment?

Answer: Children on swings in pictures is a motif appearing from age five to six and a half and shows that their middle system is still working. By six and a half onwards, a swing appears in pictures with no child on it, showing development is completed. If swings are drawn much later, it could be a 'repetitional' picture motif, but usually it means that the etheric body — formative forces — have not detached themselves from organic activity; therefore, forces are not free for use in thinking pictorially.

Copper Ball Exercise

Question: Regarding the Copper Ball Exercise in *The Extra Lesson*, should the child balance the ball on the palm of the hand, or cup the hand loosely holding the ball?

Answer: Most children choose the latter way, but there are some who balance it on the palm of the hand. Perhaps, it is best not to alter this as it seems the soul is articulating its problem to itself and expressing this in the movement, and often it will alter. The Copper Ball Exercise is an activity for balancing seeing and hearing man.[5] This exercise can be done following the nine-year change, that is, on an individual basis. With a group, it is done only after major and minor has been given the class by the Eurythmist. (For hand-hammered copper balls for this exercise, contact Rudolf Steiner College Bookstore.)

Lyre with the Copper Ball Exercise

Question: When playing the lyre for the Copper Ball Exercise, should the music scale upwards until the child's hand is on the floor behind the head, and scale downward for the return of the arm to the floor?

Answer: The scale is played until the child's arm is resting on the floor. Remember to keep in time to the child's movement. If one runs out of notes before the child's arm is comfortably settled on the floor above the head, one can play the last note of the scale several times. Play the scale downward as the child returns the arm to the floor beside the body.

Lying and Stealing

Question: Why is the painting of a Sun in the Blue Sky recommended for children with a tendency to lie and steal?[6]

Answer: Let us consider the colors themselves first. The properties of blue: It encloses, surrounds and yet draws one out into far distances. Yellow radiates; it wants to expand and fly away. It is light in the soul realm, whereas blue is representative of the darkness. We have here two prime or archetypal colors. They are also the colors in which the child between one and seven lives, the colors in which his formative forces are weaving.

If a child lies and steals, he has in effect lost his way. Lying means a losing of the connection with the up-building powers of the etheric body. Stealing means the soul enters too intensely with its astral forces into the sense world. Both activities point to a hollowing out of the soul, inner emptiness.

Working with these two colors helps the soul to start an inner breathing within the life processes; a task in remolding and making the heredity body his own if this has not been properly accomplished. These colors can set activity in this region into motion —there have been pupils who, during this painting sequence, have produced for themselves one or other of the childhood illnesses at a time when no one, either at home, school, or friends, has had it.

From another aspect, the 'picture' these two colors make has a moral, admonishing aspect in relation to the antisocial nature of lying and stealing. The Grimm's story *The Sun Reveals All* takes up this theme, as does Tolstoy in one of his short stories.

Working with these colors helps the soul to become strong enough to stand before his true being in his sleep life and receive healing.

The *constant repetition of the motif* and the weekly addition of objects in the picture allow the child to picture forth his problem and its resolution. In this way, the etheric body is cleansed and the astral body brought into a right relationship with the world of sense impressions.

Artistic Element in Lessons

Question: Where is the artistic element when teaching the Extra Lesson with children?

Answer: The artistic element is between the child and the teacher. The teacher's observation and inner work is required to understand where the child's particular difficulty lies, and the teacher's inner artistic 'feel' is required to arrange the lesson structure in such a way that the soul of the child can assimilate the processes involved. The artistic element is also in how the teacher sequences the exercises — for example, having the child play on the lyre after an exercise — or in how the teacher builds up the lesson artistically as a whole. The forms of the individual exercises and the activities themselves awaken a mood of wonder in the child's soul. This atmosphere of wonder and surprise during the lesson works on the soul life. These various elements, woven into the lesson, all combine to make the Extra Lesson with children an artistic activity.

It is important that every teacher know that each lesson should be conceived as a concentrated meditation on the archetypal form of the physical body's coordination aspect; that is, the interaction of nerves, muscles and bones. Each lesson is an organism: living, sounding, light-filled movement, music, form drawing, and painting. All this is arranged in such a way that an artistic experience of time within the lesson, and of the soul living in its own element of in-breathing and out-breathing, is created.

Blue and Red

Question: Please write something about blue and red.

Answer: Blue and red, how can we think of them? The little child loves red — the color of sympathy. The little child will stretch his will forces into this color. The stretching element is called forth with red. Blue takes the child into the periphery and calls upon consciousness to bring over what has been achieved in the past. The Extra Lesson painting exercises[7] address the soul — a statement to the soul, a soul meditation in color and movement. These are an extra dimension — a picture of how the Ego incarnates.

Strengthening Memory

Question: For children who can't remember arithmetic, how do we strengthen the memory?

One Answer: In Waldorf schools we are so strong on the verbal activity in learning that we may not give enough visual help. Here is one suggestion:

Employ as many senses as possible, i.e.:
Give each multiplication table a different color;
Give each multiplication table a different melody;
Give each multiplication table a different interval;
Also see Section III, Variation on the Ball Throwing Exercise.

Memory Problem

Question: Can you suggest something for a child who cannot remember what he has done?

Answer: One can help with the following: on the first day the child is told what to do. The child does it, e.g., "Go to the center of the room, take the jug out of the cupboard, and fill it at the tap (faucet)." The second day the child does the same thing and says what he is doing *while doing it.* The third day ask the child what he did the day before. The fourth day the child writes down what he told on the third day.

Writing on the Blackboard

Question: How long should a teacher in a Waldorf school continue to write on the blackboard for copying?

Answer: Generally, copying from the blackboard goes on too long in many classes. Children in class one can copy until words are known/learned. By end of class one, children can be writing short sentences and can help the teacher to write the story. By class two, put the essay or story which is thus composed jointly by the students and teachers on the blackboard. Begin simple dictation by class three or end of class two — write words they will need on the blackboard during the dictation. First, read the story through; then, dictate it. Allow them time to write it correctly. Next time, clean the blackboard and write the same words again in front of them — always let the children experience your 'doing'. In classes two, three and four both copying from the board and writing on their own is done. In class five, well prepared before writing, the children can write their own work. In class six, children should be able to compose and write by themselves with support from the teacher for spelling complicated words and for organizing the material. Copying does not bring forth from the child his own work. Avoid poor spelling by working on seeing and hearing first. Until class seven, writing should always be connected with what a child has experienced in class. Then, the child can begin to create out of himself without so much guidance.

PICTURES ON THE BLACKBOARD

Question: How 'perfect' should the pictures be that a teacher draws on the blackboard?

Answer: Too perfect and complete pictures on blackboards are stultifying to the children. The teacher must leave enough for the imaginations of the children to complete — but keep variety. Maybe begin a new main lesson block with a complete picture. Note: It is important that the children see the activity partially done in front of them as the teacher draws while they watch, so the children complete the pictures with their own inner activity (inwardly). Rudolf Steiner indicated that hanging a picture in the back of the room is of importance — there is a connection between what the teacher is seeing and what the children know is behind them. (This latter comment was made in connection with a second grade and concerns paintings or prints connected with the curriculum.)

RESTLESSNESS IN CLASS TWO

Question: Why are children so restless or more active in class two?

Answer: This is a time when the astral body is breathed in and touches the border of the physical/etheric — one could say the children feel an inward 'tickling' from this process. Form drawing is a way to get them comfortable in their bodies, but do not let them color in their form drawing for this destroys the working back on to the physical/etheric bodies of the dynamic that is working in the form (Frohlich,[8] Kirchner[9] and Kutzli[10]). They need the activity of going into the flat, two-dimensional space. Note: This restlessness in class two is not the same as hyperactivity. Hyperactivity is already apparent in class one. For hyperactive children, a 'sheltered corner' can be prepared with a table, chair, reading books and many cushions. When a student begins to be too hyperactive, he can be asked if he would like to go to 'the study' to listen to the lesson or have a conversation with his angel? This 'quiet corner' can be there from class one through class eight.[11]

THREE DIMENSIONS OF SPACE

Question: Can you refer me to Steiner's lectures where he gave information about our relationship to the three dimensions of space?

Answer: A very important lecture cycle is: *Mystery of the Universe: The Human Being, Image of Creation.*[12] The themes elaborated in great detail in these lectures may be summed up as the search for concrete, realistic knowledge of the whole being of man and the position he occupies in the universe. It is *essential that man shall experience his own relationship to the three dimensions of space* in a concrete way, realizing the difference in *quality* between them. Without such concrete understanding of the dimensions, man cannot define his position in the great cosmic process, "... the organic structure and activities of the human being are considered in intimate detail, but also the expressions of his life of soul...." The whole course of the wide range of themes presented in this volume, all demanding strictly logical and bias-free thought, leads finally to the coming of Christianity, the Mystery of Golgotha and the limitless effects of those events.

THE SCRIBBLED WHIRL

Question: Can you say more about the 'scribbled whirl'?[13]

Answer: The time when children scribble is when they leave the ambidextrous stage. If they haven't done enough scribbling and if sidedness is weak, this exercise helps. If there are blocks from this time, this helps to release them. This 'scribbled whirl' should be done in a one-to-one lesson for the period of time that one sees it brings release and enjoyment. The teacher should note the amount of pressure the child uses and zest with which he scribbles — this will indicate the need or otherwise.

One teacher shared that his children found more enjoyment with the 'scribbled whirl' after he gave them the imagination of making a bird's nest, suggesting an eagle's nest for those who needed encouragement to make larger movements.

OLDER CHILDREN WITH LEARNING DIFFICULTIES

Question: When older children are having learning difficulties, how have their needs been met?

Answer: Parents came to the Care Group in one school saying, "My child needs help and we cannot pay for additional lessons." This was presented to the board and parents as a pedagogical situation. It is known that if learning disabilities are present, writing in other languages should not be attempted until after remediation and until their own language has been established sufficiently. As the child was of the age when writing in his foreign language lesson was required, it was decided that the child should be taken out of his twice-weekly foreign language lessons for an Extra Lesson session and a tutorial lesson in his own language.

LENS MIRRORING[14]

Question: How is 'lens mirroring' addressed in Waldorf education?

Answer: Circle games help children develop a facility in lens mirroring. In class one, the circle games are continued from Kindergarten. In class two, games are played where there are two lines with the children facing each other. Here, the children begin to learn the cross-over of lens mirroring. This lens mirroring capacity should be there by age seven because spatial orientation should be accomplished by this age. One might say, that through the games which the children are practicing/learning, this lens mirroring capacity will rise as a more conscious capacity following the nine-year change.

1. Rudolf Steiner, *Spiritual Ground of Education*, Lecture 8. (also known as 'The Oxford Course').
2. Audrey E. McAllen, *Teaching Children Handwriting*.
3. R. Steiner, *Conferences with the Teachers of the Waldorf School in Stuttgart*, Vol. 1, June 14, 1920, pp. 86-87; Kingdom of Childhood, Lecture 5.
4. A. E. McAllen, *The Extra Lesson*, pp. 75-87.
5. R. Steiner, *Balance in Teaching*, Lecture 3.
6. A. E. McAllen, *The Extra Lesson*, pp. 160-161.
7. A. E. McAllen, *The Extra Lesson*, pp. 160-172.
8. Margaret Frohlich, *Form Drawing*.
9. Hermann Kirchner, *Dynamic Drawing, Its Therapeutic Aspect*.
10. Rudolf Kutzli, *Creative Form Drawing Workbook 1, 2, and 3*.
11. See John Marking, Section III, 'The Extra Lesson for Maladjusted Children in England'.
12. Formerly published under the title *Man: Hieroglyph of the Universe*.
13. A. E. McAllen, *The Extra Lesson*, p. 141.
14. Ibid., Chapter One; see A. E. McAllen, Section I, 'The Mirroring Process in Relation to Two-and Three-Dimensional Space'.

Vertical, I Walk a Horizontal Line

Vertical, I walk a horizontal path
to meet the Christ at point of the right angle.
At the diagonal, his shielding blessing
creates a temple for encounter in the eye,
a seven pointed star in dodecahedron,
- time embraced in space in revelation.

Always the form beneath such revelation:
in triangles borne by and bearing the cross,
at every angle, vertical I may meet
the Christ approaching me on the horizon.

So I am: so center, so connect with stars:
constellation weaving into constellation
streaking lemniscates of light through skies of time
within the offering (the sacrifice) of Christ.

— *Daisy Aldan*

V

Exercises for Classes

Standards of Movement Skills Grades One through Four

Ester Buekers

All these skills should be acquired by third grade. We must be strict in demanding attainment of these skills by each child in the class. They are incarnating body schema and equilibrium skills necessary for integration of the senses and for learning abilities.

First Grade Skills
1. Throwing balls up and catching balls (or beanbags).
2. Throwing balls or beanbags to *each* other — after the age of seven.
3. Singing and action games.
4. Clapping above and below the legs, while sitting, standing, and walking. Make sure the children lift the legs up with the back straight rather than bending the trunk down.
5. Jumping — with rope (feet together).
6. Running and skipping, joyful skipping along the road, is essential for a first grader.
7. Good body geography. (See Ingun Schneider, Section V, 'Body Geography through the Grades'.)
8. Writing with the foot of the dominant side (should be legible by the end of second grade).

Second Grade Skills
1. Clapping in front of and behind the body.
2. Catching a ball with different parts of the body (under the chin, between the legs, below the arm).
3. Balancing on a balance beam.
4. Walking by stepping from one brick to another (combine with a verse).
5. Walking a line on the floor with something on the head (e.g., rod or beanbag).
6. See-sawing together (place a frightened child in the middle to begin with).
7. Playing aiming games (balls into buckets, rings onto sticks, etc.).
8. Exact rhythmic clapping (by the end of first grade — latest by the end of first term of second grade).
9. Playing hopscotch, playing with hoops and tops.
10. Double skipping with rope.
11. Doing vowels with the legs (check with a eurythmist).
12. Picking up acorns with the toes of the foot of the dominant side and putting them in a bucket (could be done as a race).
13. Standing on one leg (like a stork) while doing something else (e.g., clapping games).
14. Writing with foot (which should now become legible).
15. Walking in a straight line (as if on a tightrope) with toes touching heels.
16. Jumping over a horizontal rope held at increasingly higher levels.
17. Elastic rope jumping (see directions at the end of this article).

Third and Fourth Grade Skills
1. Walking on a bridge or balance beam with something on the head (e.g., rod or beanbag).
2. Passing each other on a log (a felled trunk of a tree) without pushing each other off.
3. Walking on stilts.
4. Skipping in sequences (skip, stop, twirl around, etc.).
5. Clapping complicated patterns.
6. Singing songs of the various trades.
7. Playing team games: passing a ball between the legs to the end

of a line or passing a ball over the head to the child behind, or alternating over the head and between the legs to the end of the line.

8. Doing the 'crab walk' from one side of the room to the other. (To do the crab walk, ask the child to squat down, reach backward and put both hands on the floor behind him *without sitting down*. Have him walk or run in this position. He should keep his head, neck and body *in a straight line*.)

PROFICIENCY REQUIREMENTS

In first grade — all children *must join in*.

In second grade — all children *must do the skills well in small groups*.

In third grade — each child *must be able to do them properly on his own*.

In fourth grade — each child must know and do and *be accustomed to doing them individually in front of the class* so that they are encouraged to emulate each other.

In these days of TV watching and listening to the radio (and maybe too many stories in the lower grades), passivity is encouraged. Too much listening leads to laziness and inertia. The body becomes too heavy and passive for the soul to carry. When puberty comes, the body has to be carried by the soul's activity and initiative; the body is then experienced by the soul as a clumsy obstacle, something too heavy to be moved. Even by seventh grade, we often have to urge the children to go out at break-time (recess) and encourage them to move about.

In Rudolf Steiner/Waldorf schools, there is the danger that children may get too many stories in the early years during main lesson, religion lessons, language lessons, sometimes handwork lessons, and lessons given by substitute teachers.[1] Please note Lecture 4 in Steiner's *Balance In Teaching* where the effects of subjects are enumerated: storytelling and drawing are activities which can easily lift the ego out of the body. In these early grades, the *natural need and love of movement* should be educated; then, when puberty comes with its soul lethargy, the body of itself will demand movement *because of the good movement skills which have been laid into the physical/etheric bodies — into the habit life — in the early years*. The foundation for movement, exercise, gymnastics, and games should be established in the first four grades so that the body itself will make demands on the soul for movement.

ELASTIC ROPE JUMPING

(also known as 'French rope jumping' in the UK and 'Chinese rope jumping' in the US.)

Use one yard or one meter of elastic or rubber bands, knotted to form a circle. Three people are required, two standing facing each other with the elastic rope on or near the ground around their ankles, their feet holding it apart and open. The child whose turn it is:

1. stands with feet apart on the outside of the elastic;
2. jumps up, lands with one foot inside the elastic, one outside;
3. then jumps up, lands after swapping position to the other foot inside the elastic and the first one outside; this sideways jump is repeated a total of four times; speed increases with practice;
4. jumps landing with feet together inside the elastic;
5. jumps landing with feet apart outside the elastic; this in-out jump is repeated four times, gradually increasing the speed;
6. jumps and places both feet onto both sides of the elastic, so holding it down, jumps in; jumps outside sideways with feet together.

Repeat this sequence, increasing the speed as it is practiced.

When the child gets the sequence and rhythm of this jumping really rapidly, the game includes repeating the sequences with the elastic raised a little off the ground, progressively higher.

These movement skills are compiled from the work of Ester Buekers, retired class teacher and consultant for Waldorf schools in the north of Holland, and in collaboration with the Dutch Teachers Consultant Group (ed).

---

1   Rudolf Steiner, *The Kingdom of Childhood*, Lecture 4.

EXERCISES FOR CHILDREN WITH LEARNING DIFFICULTIES

Else Göttgens

Out of experience as a class teacher, remedial teacher, and now a school consultant, my first and foremost advice to class teachers on incorporating special exercises in their classes is: "Learn to observe your children." In that way, you will find their talents, obstructions, temperament, and whatever they bring from heredity and environment or from each individual past. While observing the individual children, it is equally necessary to observe the character of the class as a whole, as different classes will have different characters. Some classes have quicker or slower development than parallel classes, even in the same school. But in every class, there are similar problems because the children have been born in the second half of the twentieth century. Those of us who are older teachers will have noticed how memory has deteriorated, how, partly through technology, children are incredibly clumsy compared with those of forty years ago.

While at the beginning of the century Rudolf Steiner recommended a great number of individual exercises to strengthen diverse faculties, we may now perceive that generally we can hardly expect the fundamental faculties to develop fully of their own accord. Unless class teachers take action, they will find a huge percentage of their classes developing writing, reading, and arithmetic difficulties, poor orientation in time and space, and associated problems.

One may well ask, "Are there exercises to counteract these problems that are suitable for whole classes?" The answer is, "Yes, there are."

In the first place, there are the direct exercises: speech, body geography, form drawing, and walking while speaking as the pupil steps forward and backward. Although these exercises are not as generally practiced as they were in earlier years, we may consider them as well known in most Steiner/Waldorf schools. But now we find that a number of children cannot even begin to do these exercises properly.

There are instances where having to do them over and over again causes discouragement to the child because he just cannot do them. For instance, we may find that a child is unable to aim, to direct his gaze. The gaze is constantly shifting in all directions, but with most of these children you will not notice anything special. In reading from the blackboard, however, they may skip words, land on the wrong line, etc. A very simple devise is to practice aiming daily for a long time. For this, for instance, classes two and three might have a basket in which each child should have a tennis ball with his or her name on it. Before the usual counting/number work with balls, each child should be able to catch his ball as the teacher throws it to him, and at the end of the ball exercises, the children could practice throwing the ball back into the basket and in this way get their daily dose of aiming practice.

Another condition is obstruction to the flow of movement; for example, a child writes only as far as his wrist or elbow, or he walks only as far up as his hips and the rest of the body is not involved. For this condition the Rod-Rolling Exercise[1] will help. (See Section V, 'From the Classroom'.)

For six weeks, after morning verse, we have a circle of pairs of children standing opposite one another and they do this exercise while humming a song where the giving and taking of the copper rod takes as many beats as the rolling up and down of the rod. After having hummed the song once, the inner circle may move to the next partner. The effect of this exercise is that it helps in very diverse conditions — as in the given examples. Then, there are many children who cannot make a connection with their fellow beings; in severe cases of this kind, the class teacher, Extra Lesson teacher, or curative eurythmist may have to do this exercise with the child alone for a while. If it is done with the whole class, it helps the connections between all the children in the class.

This exercise was inspired by a child's condition which is now being recognized in an increasing number of children: that seeing and hearing do not connect up. When we read, we make inwardly audible to ourselves what we see. In writing, the opposite happens; we make visible what we hear inwardly. One of the now generally recognized forms of dyslexia springs from this weakness between seeing and hearing. The Rod-Rolling Exercise (with a copper rod) has improved this condition in many cases that I know of. The connection of the visual and audial occurs in the rhythmic system.[2] I think that is the reason why this rhythmic exercise is so helpful.

1 Audrey E. McAllen, *The Extra Lesson*, pp. 137-138. For hand hammered copper rods and balls write to Rudolf Steiner College Bookstore.
2 Rudolf Steiner, *Balance in Teaching*.

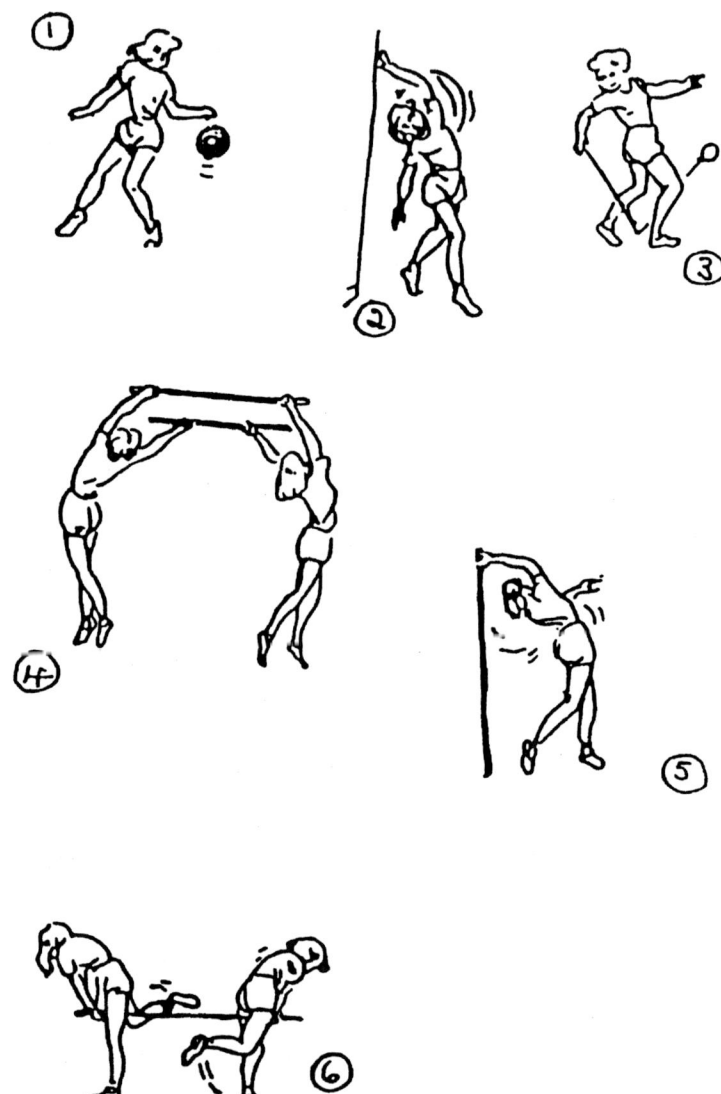

Exercises Suitable for Groups and Individual Children

compiled by Gymnasts

Collected from gymnasts for freeing the gym exercises from mechanized, stereotyped movements and for encouraging children to work on their own. (See illustrations opposite this page.)

1. Standing feet apart, bounce a large ball and catch it on the *palm* of the hand. In this way, bounce the ball on the floor from front — to side — to behind the back. After bouncing the ball behind the back, quickly twist around the other way *without moving the feet* and catch the ball on the palm of the *other hand*. Repeat the same going around the other direction — from front — to side — to back. (Use for older children, especially those who have to turn themselves to their side to stand up after the Copper Ball Exercise.[1])

2. Stand with left or right side toward a wall with the arm which is away from the wall held above the head with fingers touching the wall. Twist continuously under the arm, fingers continuing to touch the wall. Later lower the fingers gradually as low as possible on the wall. Turn around and change arms. (This exercise brings about interplay between stretching and lifting muscles[2] and is a supplementary exercise to Skein Twisting Exercise[3] for older children.) Note: Turn both clock — and counterclockwise under each arm.

3. Stand with the feet apart, holding a ball in one hand. Keeping the eyes on the ball, twist the torso, to bounce the ball from behind between the legs so that it rises up from between them to be caught in front of the body. Catch with both hands when bilateral integration is weak. (Variation — use hands alternately.) Bounce and catch with same hand only on the side for which you are confirming dominance.

4. Two wooden dowels are required. In two's, stand feet apart facing partner, both holding one end of a wooden dowel in *each* hand; turning in circles, both turn under the dowels. This stimulates the lymphatic system and opens up arms and shoulders.

5. Standing, hold (with one hand) a wooden dowel vertical with one end touching the floor — twist under — keeping the dowel end on the floor. (More difficult variation of number two above.)

6. In two's, hold a broomstick or a wooden dowel at each end with each foot step over the stick. From this position (dowel behind you), lift the dowel up as you twist under it until starting position is reached. This exercise helps the sense of balance and breathing.

---

1 Audrey E. McAllen, *The Extra Lesson*, pp. 122-126.
2 See A. E. McAllen, Section I, 'Twofold Man as Archetype'.
3 A. E. McAllen, *The Extra Lesson*, pp. 102-103.

Pioneering The Extra Lesson in a Waldorf School

Howard Schrager

This year, 1985-86, I am fortunate to be working as a full-time Extra Lesson teacher at the Santa Cruz Waldorf School. Fortunate because at this time, few Waldorf schools can afford a teacher who can focus on this work full-time. Our faculty thought it would be fruitful to gain a deeper understanding of the work of Audrey McAllen and to incorporate more of *The Extra Lesson* exercises into the classrooms. As I had had prior experience with the Extra Lesson and had just graduated an eighth grade class, we applied for and received a grant for developing an Extra Lesson program. I would like to share what we have done in hopes that it will promote the development of this much needed work.

I began in September by assessing children in five classes, grades 2, 3, 4, 5, 6, and 7. The next step was to meet with the class teachers and to share my findings with them, and for them to share their insights about the children with me. Then, we determined which children I would work with on a regular one-to-one basis. As it turned out, we chose three from each class. An unforeseen positive effect, from initially having assessed so many children, was that exercises could be incorporated into their weekly class activities to help them. For example, children with midline difficulties were given two-handed tasks like sweeping and raking. Any discussion we had concerning a child invariably was helpful. Throughout the year, we continued our talks on the children's progress, and this increased the awareness of the special needs of many children.

As I already mentioned, a primary thrust in my working this year has been in the direction of teacher education. This has been carried out in three ways: first, by meeting individually with class teachers; second, in faculty meetings through demonstrating exercises and studying pertinent material such as *Sleep* by Audrey McAllen; and third, by entering into the classroom for approximately one half of one main lesson period in each class each week.

There were several benefits to my having gone into the classrooms. Seeing me do the exercises in class has given the teachers a clear picture of how the exercises are to be done. By having me lead the class, the class teacher was freed to fully observe his children in movement, to note their strengths and weaknesses, and even to observe class dynamics in a more detached way than usual. Meanwhile, both of us could check to make sure the movements were done properly, and we could check each other as well, something which is called for at first in such working. Also, in working together we came up with new ideas, variations and imaginations in which to clothe the exercises. Finally, the classroom sessions have given the fifteen children I worked with individually that much more Extra Lesson time to their benefit.

In all classes, my first step was to introduce Jean Hunt's bean bag exercises, numbers one through eight.[1] The class teachers carried on with these exercises several times a week. Incidentally, we found practicing these exercises in our faculty meetings to be very enlivening! We then went on with various other bean bag exercises (tennis balls can be substituted), Rod-Rolling and Wool-Winding (a small ball of red and one of blue yarn for each child). We scoured the tennis courts for tennis balls so that the children could do Ball-Twirling to such varied verses as "Jabberwocky" and "Song of Hiawatha". These are among the Extra Lesson exercises involving movement.

Working with the upper grades has been particularly challenging. There I began interspersing gymnastic movements between Extra Lesson exercises, especially those pertaining to balance and flexibility, in order to sufficiently challenge them. The Interpenetrating Triangles drawing exercise was very effective in grades six and seven as a help in overcoming problems associated with puberty..

Each term, along with the movement activities, the children did a painting sequence. For five weeks of the first term, all classes did the Blue-Red Spiral painting sequence. This was repeated second term in grades two and three. Fourth grade went on with the Secondary Color painting exercise while the upper grades did the Blue-Red Perspective painting. The next term, they did the Moral Color painting exercises[2] while the lower grades did the Sun in the Blue Sky painting series.

One experiment I did with four third graders proved successful and, I feel, holds great promise in working with children who are new to the school, as indeed these were. This entailed doing a traditional Waldorf first grade introduction to multiplication, which all were struggling with, and included stories and a systematic visual build-up of the times tables. Good results were shown after only a few sessions. The next project is to do a similar introduction of the alphabet through pictures.

The presence of the Extra Lesson activities has had a health bringing effect on our school. A further benefit of the work has been to share my experience with Audrey McAllen, Mary Ellen Willby, Ingun Schneider, and Monica Ellis during and following West Coast Teacher Conferences. This collegial working has provided me with much support and deepening for my work, and our joint working has led to new insights for all of us.

UPDATE 1997

Following the year of Extra Lesson teaching, I went on to teach a class, taking them from first through eighth grade. During the first four years, I especially made a point of bringing Extra Lesson activities to the children.

At the present time, the writer just embarked on a new round of teaching, having taken another first grade class at the Santa Cruz Waldorf School.

---

1   Mary Nash-Wortham and Jean Hunt, *Take Time*. See p. 198 for verses for the Move in Time exercises.
2   Audrey E. McAllen, *Sleep*.

How Many Feet Are You?

Ester Buekers

Teachers often find that children's feet are too fixed, rigid and unsupple; they ask what are the causes and what can give help to this condition? Children like to walk, yet when they, as toddlers, are learning this vital stage of development, our households are not always a suitable place to practice this activity. Some parents feel forced to put their children in playpens. They then hang over its sides and stand too much instead of using the legs and feet to experience the floor, the stairs, and the way from one room to another. They do not have enough experience of walking a few steps and then finding their legs give way so that they plump down on their bottoms and have to lean forward and push themselves up again. This is a vital activity — the plunge into gravity and the 'lifting-will' effort to raise themselves out of it.

When the mother goes out, she puts the child into a push chair (stroller). So many of the modern ones are with the child facing away from the mother, so the child is exposed to the rush and noise of traffic; above all, mother and child are not able to talk to each other as they go along. Often you see the mother lost in her own thoughts and the child sitting or slipping into positions which are not good for the growth of the spine nor for the position of the head. Also the mother's shoes are sometimes not suitable for walking, so she does not enjoy it; consequently, she avoids walking with her children as a pleasurable activity.

Our feet must be used. They want to be used when we are children for playing, balancing, or walking on stilts. When you are living in your 'make believe world of play', then the feet carry you, and you put your intelligence into them as you hop, skip and play leapfrog. Feet are cleverer than brains. They know what to do if they are not interfered with by consciousness. They are aware of the rough ground and can adjust to it, and that is why it is good to go without shoes in nature. If the floor of the house is concrete, the feet need protection. They should not be stamping on concrete, as the jolting is felt all the way up to the head. If the adult notices on a walk that the child is tired, let him take off his shoes, and the variety of sensations that he receives from the earth as his feet come into contact with it revive his forces because his interest is awakened.

If you watch a child who is overactive in his movements, you will often see that he cannot do things instinctively with his feet. To help this condition, he needs to learn to jump over a rope. Leave him free to do this as he likes in class one, but later he must practice all different ways: standing and jumping over it, running and jumping, and so on. Feet that have problems being 'conscious' need to pick up acorns and drop them into baskets, or 'marbles between toes' races — an Extra Lesson exercise.[1] It is also beneficial to have a child on his own and let him walk slowly over the prepared smooth sand in a sand pit. Let him walk a form and then look back over it, how his feet have made a pattern, then he can draw the form he has walked. This helps the child to place himself in his organism.

In class three, when measuring is introduced, we again have the opportunity to be interested in our feet and what they can do. Have the children in pairs. One lies on the floor and his partner marks the place where his head and feet reach. He gets up and draws a line to join them and then with his feet measures it toe-to-heel and sees how many times his feet fit into the line. Then, the same procedure is done with his partner. When I first did this, there were two girls in my class, great friends, one at least a head taller than the other. But when they measured their length with their feet, the number was exactly the same for each of them. In a misguided moment, I asked the children why this was so, as I was trying to establish an average measurement from their work. There was a long mystified silence, then one boy put up his hand and said, "I know, it's because they are friends." Luckily I had enough common sense to say, "Yes, that must be it," and quickly went on to something else.

The next year, in class four, when we were doing fractions and more measurement, I reminded them of this problem; I had immediate response, "Because they had different sized feet." This is a good example of the difference between the thinking of the pre-ninth year child and the birth of the logical thinking that comes afterwards.

Class teachers can awaken children's interest in feet so they are ready for the handwork teacher when slipper making is introduced (class six). In class five, they may have had the story of Nala and Damyanti, where Nala has to recognize which of the travelers is her lover. So hang a curtain from the top of the open door so that it is a few inches above the floor, send half the class outside and let them walk, barefoot, one by one across the open doorway. The children inside have to recognize to whom the pair of feet belongs.

At the right time another enjoyable activity is making 'ink prints' of one's feet before making the pattern for the slipper. The 'pairs of feet' can be hung up and the children asked to recognize their owners.

With such things you can also interest the parents in the importance of feet. After all, they carry us to our destiny — something many people can recognize from their own experience. Healthy feet are essential to life.

Ester Buekers is a retired class teacher, grandmother, and consultant for schools in the north of Holland.

1   Audrey E. McAllen, *The Extra Lesson*, pp. 103-104.

Body Geography
through the Grades

Ingun Schneider

One of the great benefits of being a Waldorf teacher is the opportunity to develop a theme through the grades, to see how the students' capacities evolve in a certain area. One such theme in the movement sphere is body geography exercises through the grades, starting with Audrey McAllen's indications given in *The Extra Lesson*.

In the 'Ilkley Course',[1] Rudolf Steiner suggested using body geography exercises as a strengthening activity for the nervous system — the child quickly lets his thoughts flow into his movements which helps him make a connection between concepts and impressions. Dr. Steiner describes how these exercises help the child "... become skilled and mobile in his pictorial imaginative thinking." He adds that when a child learns to do these exercises "... in a quick and alert manner ... when he is about eight years old they will teach him to think for his whole life.... If he has to do actions with his own body which need great alertness in carrying out and which need to be thought over first, then later on he will be wise and prudent in the affairs of his life."[2]

Body geography exercises are particularly important for today's students, since so many of them have an incompletely developed imprinting of the physical body into the etheric.[3] This imprinting of the 'map of the body' is normally completed by the time the child is seven. The main 'surveying instrument' for creating this map is the sense of self-movement; the senses of touch, life and balance are also important. These 'instruments' are 'tuned' and brought forth by the child's movement system. If unhindered, the young (birth to 7 years) child's organism (guided by the ego-organization and astral body) gives the child the urge to repeatedly seek movement experiences which gradually are performed with less and less conscious attention of the astral body. When the movements can be performed subconsciously without the slightest intellectual involvement, they are fully imprinted into the etheric body, having become habit.[4] This means they can be performed while the child is speaking or mentally engaged with something else (e.g., the child can continue talking to you while tying his/her shoe laces). The child needs this 'map of his internal landscape', as a foundation from which to orient himself, for the unhindered development of the skills of writing, reading, and mathematics.

When doing the following exercises with a class, it is suggested that the teacher give the instructions without doing the exercises to begin with only 'helping out' by demonstrating after the students have had a chance to figure it out on their own. When the teacher does do the motions, (s)he can stand in front of the class to one side, *back turned toward the students*. [If you face the students while performing the movements they get confused; if you choose to use the opposite side of your body so they can mirror your movements, you aren't doing the movements correctly according to your own instructions (i.e., for "right" you use left), and that's confusing, too.]

Grade One

Fall Semester

Use the right hand to touch parts of the body on the right or in the middle.

Examples:

Touch your nose with your right hand.
Touch your right hand to your right shoulder.
Touch your right eyebrow with your right thumb.
Touch your right index finger ('pointer') to your right big toe.

Spring Semester

Use right hand to touch parts of the body on the right or in the middle, left hand to touch parts on the left or in the middle.

Examples:

Touch your right cheek with your right ring finger.
Touch the back of your neck with your right hand.
Touch your left index finger ('pointer') to your left ear.

Grade Two

Continue using each side separately, but gradually switch instructions more rapidly and/or give two instructions at a time. Also, bring in 'new' parts of the body.
Examples:
> Touch your right heel with your right hand and touch your left hand to your left ankle.
>
> Gently touch the fourth finger of your right hand to your right eyelid and touch your back with your left hand.
>
> Touch your forehead with your right hand and your chin with your left hand; switch hands. (Switching of hands only if both hands are touching the body in the middle.)

Grade Three

To Begin With
Move hands (and feet) to cross over the midline and touch parts of the body on the other side. (This does not mean that the students shouldn't have crossed the midline before this time, quite the contrary. Only now this is done more consciously by the teacher's naming the parts of the body across the midline.)
Examples:
Touch your right index finger to your left knee.
Touch your left hand to your right thigh.
Let your right little finger touch your left earlobe.

Later On
Once the students are comfortable with one 'across the midline' instruction at a time, give two instructions at a time and/or switch positions.
Examples:
> Touch your right palm to your left knee and your left thumb to your left cheek.
>
> Touch your right upper arm with your left second finger ('long finger') and your right heel to your left knee.

Touch your right ankle with your left hand and your left heel with your right hand; switch; switch again; and again.

Fourth and Fifth Grade

Continue as at the end of third grade, naming specific fingers, top of the hand, wrist, and other parts of the body (e.g., calves and shins), picking up speed as the students get better.

Sixth Grade

To challenge this age group, and to bring in a social element, you ask the students to face their desk partners. They are then asked to touch the specified parts of the body on their partner with their own named body part. This always ends up being an enlivening and fun session. It's good to mix boys and girls to help them interact naturally with each other. Each student has to help the partner identify the correct body sides; it's a cooperative effort.

Examples:

Touch your partner's right shoulder with your left hand; touch your partner's left elbow with your right hand.

From that position proceed, without moving anything until the next request.

Touch your partner's right knee with your right hand, then your partner's right shin with your left hand; touch your right hand to your partner's right big toe, then your left hand to your partner's left ankle.

Seventh Grade

As the class teacher introduces experiments with mirrors in physics, have the students perform a mirroring variation of the body geography exercises. Here, individual students take the lead, and that is appreciated. The desk partners face each other; to begin with one student imitates what the partner does by completely mirroring the movements, as if looking in a mirror. At a certain point (may be decided by the students themselves or by the teacher), the other partner takes over the lead; the first 'leader' now imitates. The 'leader' students are encouraged to move arms and legs into different positions, either in a flowing, continually changing way or from one stationary position to the other. Later, the exercises can be done as cross-mirroring exercises where the imitating student uses the same body side as the 'leader' student.

Grade Eight

As the students learn the anatomical parts during the anatomy block, it's fun to return to the body geography exercises, but with a new twist.
 Examples:
  Touch your right ulna to your left radius.
  Touch your left humerus with your right carpal bones.
  Touch your second right phalanx to your left patella.
  Touch your right tibia with your left fibula.

Summary

In this way, each student keeps 'in touch' with his/her internal map through the grades, getting a chance to complete it or revise it, as necessary. If these exercises are done for a block at a time, the students don't tire of them; they should enjoy the challenge the exercises present. Many times we ended these exercises with something that was fun.

Example I
 In the lower grades, you could end with the right hand on top of the head and the left on the stomach. Then, it's time to: 1: pat the head while stroking the stomach, 2: stroke the head while patting the stomach, 3: switch hands, and 4: repeat 1 and 2.

Example II
 In grades six, seven, eight you might end with the instruction to touch the right palm to the partner's left palm; then, proceed with a hand clapping game (an 'old' one from the younger grades, or a new one — maybe in a foreign language).

EXAMPLE III

In the upper grades, you can also end by having the partners touch each other's right palms, ending the exercise with a handshake.

Enjoy coming up with even more ideas to enliven this important exercise theme through the grades!

After taking a class through eight grades at the Sacramento Waldorf School and working with The Extra Lesson for thirteen years, Ingun has become a consultant and teacher advisor to Waldorf schools. She is a part-time faculty member and coordinator of the third three-year Remedial Education Program at Rudolf Steiner College in Fair Oaks, California. Originally a physical therapist and Lamaze childbirth educator, she has specialized in the work based on the Extra Lesson approach. She has spent the past two years visiting Waldorf schools in California, Mexico, Israel, and Europe, advising teachers, giving teacher and parent workshops on learning difficulties issues and child development, as well as assessing children with learning and/or behavior difficulties. She also maintains a private practice for children with learning difficulties.

---

1   Rudolf Steiner, *A Modern Art of Education*, lectures 11 and 12.
2   Rudolf Steiner, *The Kingdom of Childhood*, lecture 4.
3   See Audrey E. McAllen, Section I, 'On the Imprinting of Man's Structural Physical Body's Spiritual Archetype into the Ethereal Body of the Earth'.
4   Rudolf Steiner, *A Modern Art of Education*, lecture 3.

From the Classroom

Mary Ellen Willby

While working with teachers at conferences, the question was asked: "Can we deal with children who have learning difficulties in the classroom situation?" The following exercises have been proven in classroom groups and contribute toward answering this question.

Grade One

To establish dominance: Right handers do the exercise with right foot and right hand; left handers with left hand and left foot. Children face one another:

> I step into the path of light.
>   (step with right foot)
> This the foot that guides me right.
>   (point with right hand to right foot)
> This hand greets friend,
>   (children shake right hands)
> And vanquishes foes;
>   (bring right fists together, bumping fists
>   to feign battle)
> This hand shall point the way I go.
>   (right hand pointing straight ahead.)

Rope jumping: every day, even if only for five minutes. Teacher on one end of rope (turning counterclockwise so that the child with his right hand turns clockwise): develop a pattern such as the rope is to slap the ground once only between one child leaving and another running/jumping in or the child jumping three times after entry, then jumping out. Use this for a will and concentration movement exercise by having the children be very quiet so they can concentrate to be able to come in with the pattern developed. This exercise can be used to learn times tables. (Begin jumping with feet together.)

Rod-rolling Exercise:[1] Use an imagination such as: "Make your arms like an oaken bridge." One could give the picture of drawbridges to castles as a background to this. Children face each other, arms held forward, palms uppermost, fingertips touching, copper rod across the hands of the child who received it from the teacher. Raising his arms, the child rolls the copper rod back over his arms until the rod touches his throat. The arms are then lowered to carefully roll the rod back down the upper arms, forearms, wrists, and hands, then onto the outstretched hands of the partner who has copied the first child's movements. The arms of the child mirroring the movement should also curve slightly. The first child now mirrors the second child's arms moving up and down with the rod, then receives the rod again. All children have arms going up and down together. A verse to do with this exercise:

Watchful we will work together (up, down)
Wander wide in windy weather (up, down)

This verse is particularly beneficial because of the "w's" which have a calming and harmonizing effect while the exercise itself releases tensions. It may be repeated several times so the children move their arms up and down more than twice.

GRADES ONE AND TWO

Balance beam (4x4, 12 ft. long): A picture is given first that they are crossing a bridge from the outside world to 'our' room, a very special place where we do special things. All are silent as they wait their turn — must sit down if they disturb — a dishonor not to cross the bridge — story first of feet connected to the earth and head to the stars. The teacher touches with a finger the top of the hair as the child crosses the beam or holds a strand of hair "like a gold thread to the child's star." The order for learning to walk over the bridge:

Eyes open — forward, then backwards; later with a bean bag on the head.

Eyes closed — forward, then later backwards.

Rhythmic Exercises: Feet slightly apart, standing very straight, moving forward while stepping with each word. Make fists and bring together first in front, then second behind and third overhead — in that order. Do three times, saying all three times:

Come King (in front), conquer with courage (in back),
Quell the cool quarrel (above head).

Follow this verse with: moving forward while stamping and clapping with each emphasized syllable.

Sub<u>d</u>ue the <u>d</u>readful <u>d</u>ragon
<u>D</u>own in the <u>d</u>eep <u>d</u>ungeon.

Grade Three

Rod-passing Exercise: This rod-passing exercise immediately addresses the older students' growing need for social interaction, and in unison with the entire class, it brings about social cohesiveness. It also meets the need for more challenging physical activity by requiring simultaneous passing and receiving of the copper rods.

Standing in a circle, the children face the center, each child holding a copper rod. The rods are passed clockwise for the first verse, counterclockwise for the second verse, clockwise for the third verse. The rhythm is: short, short, long. The rod is passed (and received) on the 'long', and with 'short, short' both hands are on the rod and it is moved vertically twice at the center of the body.

1. We are straight, we are strong,
   We are valiant and bold,
   For the sun fills our hearts
   With its life-giving gold.

2. We are truthful and helpful
   And loving in trust,
   For the sun in our hearts
   Glows so brightly in us.

3. We will open our hearts
   To the sunbeams so bright,
   And will fill all the world
   With our heart's inner light.

Crossing a balance beam with rods:

Copper rod on top of the head, eyes open, forward, later backward.

Copper rod on top of the head, eyes closed, forward, later backward.

Copper rod on top of the head, eyes open, turn 360 degrees in the middle of the beam, continue to the end.

Copper rod on top of the head, eyes closed, turn 360 degrees in the middle of the beam, continue to the end.

1   See Else Göttgens, Section V, 'Remedial Exercises'. For hand hammered copper rods write to Rudolf Steiner College Bookstore.

CHILDREN'S GAMES

Susan Goldstein

One of the objectives of the Remedial Research Group was the support of the renewal of the culture of early childhood in the form of the children's games which in the past contributed to the development of faculty. The following is a *childhood game*, submitted by class teacher Susan Goldstein at Santa Cruz Waldorf School, California. Originally, it was played with a small rubber ball. It was adapted for use with a bean bag:

> To the tune of "A Tisket, A Tasket" (loosely):
>
> A mimsy (throw bean bag up and catch it)
> A clapsy (throw bean bag up and clap, then catch it)
> I twirl my hands (throw bean bag up and twirl hands, then catch it)
> To my babsy (throw bean bag up and touch shoulders and catch it)
> My right hand (throw and catch with right hand)
> My left hand (throw and catch with left hand)
>
> (the following verse is done as a chant)
> High as the sky (throw high up into air and catch it)
> Low as the sea (throw up only a little and catch it)
> Touch my knee (throw up and touch knee and catch it)
> Touch my toe (throw up and touch toe and catch it)
> And under we go (toss under right leg for right handers and catch it)

When children are skilled with the bean bags, take this game outside and play it with balls.

Note: Make sure the *action* and *word* are performed simultaneously. "High" — throw on this word, "low" — throw on this word, "touch" — move as you speak the word, etc. *Creating a game* and *coupling the movement simultaneously with language* are two ways to guarantee that the child won't use 'cortical' efforts to perform the movement. This is because speaking places a 'cortical demand' on the child so the movement is then processed at lower centers in the brain (which is what is wanted). For when the movement goes into the subconscious, it becomes faculty.[1]

This exercise also works well for learning body geography. After "Touch my toe," you can add "Touch my ear, nose, right eye, etc." in the form of an echo. The children love this part! Always end with, "And under we go!"

---

1   Rudolf Steiner, *A Modern Art of Education*, lecture 3; also footnote p. 32

Stacking Sticks

Howard Schrager

Teacher says:		**Movement:**
1) *Thin sticks, thick sticks,* *Let's stack sticks.*		Alternate crossing little fingers and thumbs

2) *A thin stick stack,*
    A middle-sized stick stack,
    A thick stick stack,
    A mixed stick stack.
	(Little fingers)
	(Index fingers)
	(Thumbs)
	(All 3)*
		Cross little fingers, switching position on 'stick stack'. Same with index fingers and finally with thumbs. Keep hands in front of you.

3) *A small stack of thin sticks,*
    A small stack of middle-
    sized sticks,
    A small stack of
    thick sticks,
    A small stack of
    mixed sticks.
	(Little fingers)
	
	(Index fingers)
	
	(Thumbs)
	
	(all 3)*
		Hands below waist level. Continue crossing fingers as indicated.

4) *A middle-sized stack of*
    thin sticks,
    A middle-sized stack of
    middle-sized sticks,
    A middle-sized stack of
    thick sticks,
    A middle-sized stack of
    mixed sticks.
	
	(Little fingers)
	
	(Index fingers)
	
	(Thumbs)
	
	(all 3)*
		Hands and arms out in front.

* Stay with thin, middle-sized and thick sticks at first, and add 'mixed sticks' for a treat after they've mastered the others. One beat with each of the three fingers — index, little fingers and thumbs.[1]

5) *Thin sticks stacked tall,*   (Little fingers)   Hand and arms
   Middle-sized sticks   up high.
       stacked tall,   (Index fingers)
   Thick sticks stacked tall,   (Thumbs)
   Mixed sticks stacked tall   (All 3)

6) *A small stack of thin sticks,*   (Little fingers) Raise arms through
   A middle-sized stack of   all 3 positions.
       middle-sized sticks,   (Index fingers)
   A tall stack of thick sticks,   (Thumbs)
   A mixed stack of
       mixed sticks   (All 3)   Move arms through
                                                       all 3 positions,
                                                       ending above head.

7) *Thin sticks, thick sticks,*   Alternate little
   We've just stacked sticks.   fingers and thumbs
                                                       as initially.

---

1   Rudolf Steiner, *Kingdom of Childhood*, Lecture 4.

Jean Hunt's Bean Bag Exercises in the Morning Circle

Patrick Marooney

As a class teacher in first grade, I experienced great frustration with an abundance of children in my class who had letter reversals. In second grade, I began using the first four of Jean Hunt's bean bag exercises.[1] Every morning, as part of the rhythmical aspect, the children went through these exercises, to verses[2] and counting by two's, three's, and so on. Without fail, every morning we carried on. The reversals began to disappear in two weeks, and in two months were completely gone, with the exception of two children who had deep physiological difficulties.

After three months when I stopped the exercises at various times for various reasons, some reversals would reappear. So I would do the exercises again, and the reversals would vanish. By third grade, we had learned to do all eight of the bean bag exercises and all the reversals had completely disappeared.

The first four exercises I named 'giving and receiving', 'ring-around-the-waist', 'rainbow', and 'waterfall' (in that order). These exercises metamorphosed into circle exercises (social aspect) which I carried on through third grade. They brought a social harmony to the class that was quite apparent. I went on and developed many variations of the circle exercises, and the children have become, as a class, a unified organism, working together.

As children experienced the 'separation' in their ninth or tenth year[3] during third grade, these social/circle exercises helped them socially.

---

1   Mary Nash-Wortham and Jean Hunt, *Take Time*.
2   Rudolf Steiner, *A Modern Art of Education*, lecture 3; see footnote p. 32.
3   See James A. Dyson, Section II, 'Nine-Year Change'.

Care of Desks and Exercises

Daena Ross

Care of Desks

For each of the children starting first grade, have a carpenter carefully make all the pieces for the desks and drill screw holes. Then, have the child who will be using the desk and the parent assemble and varnish the desk. Each desk must have adjustable legs so that it becomes the child's desk through all eight grades.

The care of the desk becomes the responsibility of the parent and child, and periodically the desk is renewed by sanding and varnishing (approximately every three years). Through this activity, the child has a far greater feeling of responsibility for his desk and truly 'takes care of it'.

Exercises

Exercises can help the whole class, especially with senses of touch, balance and self-movement. The first three exercises may be done together.

1. **Fell the Trees.** The children make a line. When the child comes to the front of the line, the child turns his/her back to the teacher. The child falls backwards into the teachers' arms and the class says, "Timber." The teacher slowly lowers the child to the floor.

2. **Log Rolling.** The log (the child) rolls across the floor. Improvement may be seen when the child can roll straight, initiating the roll with the head and shoulders.

3. **Sawing Wood.** The children stand with one foot in front of the other, cross arms, and hold onto partner's wrists. They then begin to move back and forth with arms in a sawing motion. They should also move downward by bending the knees as they saw. Say the following verse:

To and fro, to and fro
See the saw so smoothly go,
Little saw, do not tire
Cut the wood for winter's fire,
Cut the logs, one by one
Till the pile is all done,
To and fro, to and fro
See the saw so smoothly go.

4. **Skein Twisting.**[1] This can be done regularly by the handwork teacher, or have four to six children do it each morning as you start the day, letting each child have a turn once a week for a month.

5. **Leap Frog.**

6. **Wheelbarrow.**

7. **Game for quiet corner** to be done individually. Have one each of the following items in two separate bags so there are identical items in each bag. It is important to have a variety of textures, e.g.,

    an acorn
    a shell
    wooden buttons
    a quartz crystal
    iron pyrite pieces, etc.

Have the child put a hand into each bag and find the same item. No peeking till you bring the hands out of the bag with an object in each hand.

8. **Caterpillar Crawl Exercise.**[2] This is a wonderful activity for rainy days at recess time. Young children enjoy making a 'caterpillar parade'. Older children like 'caterpillar relays'.

9. **Working with above and below:** a) Hold a rope so lightly between the fingers, that if it is bumped, it falls to the ground. Then have children *jump* over the rope that is about 6" above the ground. Move it up higher several more times, sensing the ability of the children. b) Have the

children go under a rope held about shoulder height. Next, lower to mid-chest, then waist, then knees. If done inside, in the classroom or gym, the lowest one can be so low that the children must either roll or crawl under the rope.

---

1   Audrey E. McAllen, *The Extra Lesson*, pp. 102-103.
2   Ibid., p. 113.

CLASSROOM EXERCISES FOR HELPING EYE MOVEMENT IN RELATION TO WRITING AND READING

Audrey E. McAllen

Using ultramarine blue and carmine red watercolors calls the soul into activity through the eye. These colors stimulate the physiological activity of the eye to produce the complimentary colors so that the child inwardly experiences the total rainbow.

Paint a paper with unbroken brush strokes across the page *from left to right* — with each brush stroke of the same color slightly overlapping the previous one, for the first three of the following exercises. (Dry paper of less than painting paper quality is fine, as long as it is pure white to allow the color red and blue to shine — the white paper acts as the light.)

Painting Exercises:

1st	—	only blue to cover the page
2nd	—	only red
3rd	—	blue on the upper half, red for the bottom half
4th	—	Begin with one blue brush stroke straight across, then one red brush stroke straight across not overlapping and continue to fill the page.
5th	—	Begin with one blue brush stroke straight across, then one red wavy brush stroke; not overlapping, continue alternating, filling the page.
6th	—	Begin with one blue wavy brush stroke, then one red brush stroke straight across, continue alternating, filling the page.

This helps to coordinate eye and hand and concentrates the eye movements. The movements of the eye involve the whole body; the above exercises are based on indications by Rudolf Steiner given in the Ilkley[1] and Oxford[2] courses to teachers on the preparation of the hand for writing and the eye for reading.[3]

Due to car rides, radio, TV, etc., the child's relationship to his/her body is disrupted in today's world. The soul/spirit of the child is not able to remain in harmonious connection with the physical/life bodies first thing in the morning. Teachers can help the children to overcome this by doing something *before* the morning circle. For example, cover a paper with one color — the brush strokes going across the page from left to right — choice of color as the teacher feels they need. In this way, the teacher can prepare the children to receive their lessons. Ten to fifteen minutes spent in such activity is a real economy in teaching. First grade teachers please note that an exercise using one color brings over what the children have done in the kindergarten by practicing it in a more formal way — the discipline of the brush stroke from left to right is now added.

For children of eleven years and older, grades six, seven, and eight: On Mondays at the beginning of main lesson, the sequence of the Moral Color[4] exercises can be used. This will concentrate the children after the weekend activities.

---

1   Rudolf Steiner, *A Modern Art of Education*.
2   R. Steiner, *Spiritual Ground of Education*, p. 156.
3   See Joep Eikenboom, Section III, 'Exercises Researched by the Dutch Remedial Group'.
4   Audrey E. McAllen, *Sleep*, chapters 7 and 8.

Exercises with a Sixth Grade Class

Patrick Wakeford-Evans

In class six, I had the children paint first thing when they arrived in the morning because so many of them had long car rides to school, and because of the general destructive sanguinity of the class.

The students covered a paper with color, brush strokes using left to right movements; choice of color as I felt that they needed. Later ,they painted the Blue-Red Perspective Exercise 'L' version[1] for four weeks — each Monday and Thursday. For economy, I used butcher paper as large as the desk. If their paints dripped, this was pointed out to them. The hardest thing was to watch that they painted correctly, i.e., in the proper directions. I made a list of those students who might have trouble and watched those first. Gradually, children began to help by noticing those who were painting in the wrong direction. Blue-Red Perspective Painting Exercise is to be done after the children have turned eleven years old.

Later, the Moral Color exercises were done twice a week in main lesson time.[2]

I also did the Copper Ball Exercise with eight children at a time, once a week, following this exercise with the Moving Straight Line and Lemniscate drawing exercise.[3]

---

[1] Audrey E. McAllen, *The Extra Lesson*, pp. 167-169.
[2] A. E. McAllen, *Sleep*, Chapters Seven and Eight.
[3] A. E. McAllen, *The Extra Lesson*, pp. 147-150.

Bean Bags in First Grade

Jackie Treinen

After working for many years with learning disabled and socially/emotionally dysfunctioning children, I was well aware of the importance of movement to the learning process — in both the academic and social realms. But I wasn't quite sure how to integrate my experiences as I made the transition to Waldorf teaching. With the help of my class of 27 first graders and Jean Hunt's beanbag exercises,[1] I began developing the foundation for a movement program. I found that Waldorf children are very active and need many opportunities to move their limbs. I also found, as I did in my previous teaching experiences, that a movement program will only succeed if the children learn to bring their movements under control; thus, we led into Jean Hunt's beanbag sequence with a song and verse (moving all the time in various ways) that took us from the periphery to a more centered state of standing straight and strong (using another verse for imagery), with each child ready to catch a beanbag and to place it on his/her head. When each beanbag was balanced (this in itself is an acquired skill), the beanbag sequence was begun, each accompanied with a verse (nursery rhymes, verses I have written and those from other teachers). As the children became more proficient in following the teacher's carefully executed movement, more accurate and beautiful movement was called forth from each child (according to his/her ability), giving imaginations as needed to bring chaotic movement into balance and form. Doing daily movement activities in the class offers the teacher the opportunity to observe the movements of the children, discerning the need to incorporate more skipping, balancing, log rolling, backward stepping, etc., into the movement program. Of course, certain children require longer to achieve such beautiful movements and may need individual curative eurythmy and/or Extra Lesson exercises to develop integrated bodily movements.

The children take pride in mastering the movement skills and in gaining control over their bodies as they move with more certainty through space, while (unknown to them) developing those faculties that will aid them in writing, reading and thinking. In my first grade, we did Jean Hunt's beanbag activities twice a week and other movement activities (rope jumping, skipping, hopping, rhythm, balancing, tumbling) the other three days. I have found that the children's enthusiasm remained constant for the beanbag activities, and they developed those skills necessary for controlled bodily movements. Working with the children has allowed me the opportunity to work on my own movements — to be more aware of how I must move in order to bring about beautiful and rhythmical movements in the children. We have fun together while developing those skills that are no longer a part of our sedentary daily lives.

Verses for Jean Hunt's beanbag exercises number seven and eight:[2]

7. Hummingbird, hummingbird, whizzing and whirling,
   Fast as fire your wings are twirling,
   Flitting to branches so fragrant and sweet,
   Your wings hum a song as you eat.
   Sipping sweet nectar through beak oh so long,
   Sun radiant colors flash and you are gone.

8. Down in the bottom of a lake I found
   A big gold fish swimming around.
   Up we swam the fish and I,
   Round and round 'till we saw the sky.
   Then down to the bottom of the lake so deep,
   The fish swimming merrily around my feet.
   Then up we swam, I needed some air.
   As for the fish, it didn't care,
   It flipped its tail and down it swam,
   Around and around and around again.
   Then up we swam, round and round,
   I and the goldfish that I found.

---

[1] Mary Nash-Wortham and Jean Hunt, *Take Time*.
[2] Ibid.

Verses for Jean Hunt's Bean Bag Exercises

The verses below are from various Waldorf class teachers which they used to accompany the bean bag exercises developed by curative eurythmist Jean Hunt. (The exercises, with diagrams, are in the book *Take Time* by Mary Nash-Wortham and Jean Hunt.)

Traditional Childhood Rhymes

Verse for Exercise 1.

Cross patch,
Draw the latch,
Sit by the fire and spin.
Take a cup,
And fill it up,
And ask the neighbors in.

Verse for Exercise 2.

Whisky Frisky,
Hippity hop,
Up he goes
To the tree top.
Whirly Twirly,
Round and round,
Down he scampers
To the ground.
Furly-curly,
What a tail!
Tall as a feather,
Broad as a sail.
Where's his supper?
In the shell,
Snappy Cracky,
Out it fell.

VERSE FOR EXERCISE 5.

Jack be nimble,
Jack be quick,
Jack jump over
The candlestick.

VERSE FOR EXERCISE 6.

Cushy cow bonnie,
Let down thy milk,
And I will give thee
A gown of silk,
A gown of silk
And a silver 'T',
If thou will let down thy
Milk to me.

VERSE FOR EXERCISE 7.

Wee Willie Winkie runs through the town,
Upstairs and downstairs in his nightgown,
Rapping at the windows, crying through the locks,
"Are the children all in bed, for now it's eight o'clock?"

by Howard Schrager

VERSE FOR EXERCISE 3.

Did you ever see a rainbow
On a lovely sunny day,
After it's been raining
In the magic month of May?
Out of a cloud it comes,
And there it's gone.

VERSE FOR EXERCISE 4.

Waterfall, waterfall
Down you fall,
Down you fall,
Like a veil.
Do you ever stop falling,
Waterfall?

by Patrick Wakeford-Evans

VERSE FOR EXERCISE 1.

Two birds did play,
A game one day,
One flew up high,
The other low,
The high one dropped
A seed below.
The low one caught
The seed and flew
From there above,
And dropped it, too.
The other caught
It underneath,
And sang because
He was so pleased.
The other sang,
Let's play again,
And so they played
Until the end.

VERSE FOR EXERCISE 2.

Two squirrels did run around a tree,
They chased their tails most merrily.
Round and round the tree they ran,
The squirrels scurried swift and then,
They chased until they were a blur,
Whose tail was whose, they were not sure!

VERSE FOR EXERCISE 3.

The butterfly flew on the rainbow
After the weather cleared,
But he could not decipher
Which color he preferred.
Should he race along the red,
Or drift along the blue?
Should he charge along the orange,
Or walk the purple hue?
Should he dance the yellow sheen,
Or drift within the pleasant green?
No, he said, I love them all,
I'll arc each one till darkness falls.

VERSE FOR EXERCISE 4.

Down the waterfall,
Down from farthest heights,
Down o'er slippery stone,
Down with watery might,
Dash on down the stone,
Splash the water's foam,
Crash the waters home,
Flash the water's gone.

VERSE FOR EXERCISE 5.

Under and over, the gnomes in the clover,
The roots are entwining and vining below.
Over and under they slide in the clutter
Of pebbles and water and compost and mold.
Under and over and deeper and bolder,
The earth turns both drier and dark.
Over and under give way to the plunder
Of gnomes heading straight for their mark.

VERSE FOR EXERCISE 7.

While high in the sky
And below on the ground,
The birds they fly upward,
The beasts they look down.
As eagles will soar,
And bright fishes swim,
Our Spirits reach upward,
Our feet feel the ground.
The bees buzz by brightly,
The ducklings dive down.
The lambs all leap lightly,
The cattle graze slow.
In starlight the owls fly,
The mice darting home,
We dream with the angels,
And work with the gnomes.

VERSE FOR EXERCISE 8.

Spin me a cloak of fine gold,
Gold from my neck to my toes,
Ring it about with bright thread,
Hem all its borders in red,
Clasp it with jewels of blue,
Line it that no light shows through,
Press it and brush it, then place it on me,
For I on the morrow shall meet my true queen.

by Will Crane

VERSE FOR EXERCISE 5.

Proud, prancing ponies,
Parade in a line,
Not hurried,
Not worried,
Each stepping in time.
Their heads,
They hold proudly,
Their backs,
Straight and strong,
Each stepping,
So lively,
As they march along.

by Ingun Schneider

VERSE FOR EXERCISE 3.

Lovely rainbow, hung so high,
Glistening 'cross the clearing sky.
Red and orange, yellow and green,
Shining colors brightly gleam.
Blue and indigo, purple so fine,
Rainbow colors softly shine.
Pots of gold may there be found
As the colors meet the ground.

by Esther Centers

VERSE FOR EXERCISE 7.

Busy bee
Busy bee
Buzzing buzzing
'Round the tree.

'Round you go
Not so slow
Down and up
And to and fro.

To the heights,
To the side,
Flower sweetest
Be my guide.

Bee so tiny
Be my guest,
Busy bee
Now be at rest.

VERSE FOR EXERCISE 8.

The bell chimes one
We're ready for fun
From up at the top
We can't let it drop.

The bell chimes two
Now see what we do
We bring it around
Ringing lightly the sound.

The bell chimes three
And what do we see,
Dancing up in a cloud
The bell chimes oh so loud!

The bell chimes four
There isn't much more
The bell's soft ring will now
Inwardly sing.

"The most important, the very most important of developments for the future will not occur through institutions, will not occur through all kinds of establishments, despite today's belief in institutions and establishments as the only panacea. Instead, the most important of developments for the future will occur through the initiative of the single, human individual. This initiative of the single, human individual will, however, arise only out of a true, genuine trust in an inexhaustible source of divine strength in the human soul."

— *Rudolf Steiner*

VI

GUIDANCE FOR CLASSROOM TEACHERS

GUIDANCE FOR NEW TEACHERS

Else Göttgens

In Holland, I had the responsibility of advising new teachers in schools that were often just beginning. There are certain teaching habits that should be avoided at all costs. Also, I see some things many teachers are doing which could be improved upon.

There are very different levels on which things have to be learned or unlearned (discarded). Some of the things may seem to be rather superficial; for instance, the teacher looks over the heads of the children, or looks at the floor, or simply does not look anywhere while teaching; however, you can always find that such things are an expression of an inner attitude towards oneself or towards the children. The person looking at the floor may turn out to lack self-confidence or ego strength to really meet the children, whereas the person looking heavenward may be so preoccupied with his ideas that he may be unable to see the real children in front of him with their very real destiny problems.

When a class becomes unruly, some inexperienced teachers will advance towards the children, go to a particular child to 'tell it off' or calm it. The rest of the class will oppose this intrusion into its body and will 'spurt out', the same way a lump of butter will spurt out through your fingers if you try to squeeze it. This kind of teacher will do better to take a small step back and experience his own verticality. Other teachers will recede when the class gets difficult, and you may be sure that undesired elemental beings will happily fill the space thus vacated. Here, too, the teacher's experience of his verticality may bring peace and quiet.

Another cause of unrest in classes is the pitch of the teacher's voice. Desperate young teachers find out with relief what happens when they learn to drop their voices into a much lower, warmer pitch. The voice should come from the region of the heart and will, not from the head. The previously mentioned factors and many more of this kind have an immediate effect on the comfort of the children and the teacher.

We now come to a realm of pedagogy that has a deeper and long lasting effect even on the health of the children and the class as a unity. Imagine an excellent teacher who gives the most exciting lessons to the children. He tells wonderful stories, teaches the children all the skills they need in imaginative and exact ways. His store of songs and poems and games is *in* inexhaustible, and still it may happen that a class becomes restless, dissatisfied, nervous, and pale. What is the matter? When we look how the teacher builds up his lesson, we may find that too little or nothing of yesterday's lesson comes back today. What the children take in on one particular day is worked over in sleep. When the child wakes up the next day, (s)he has the desire to do something with the now matured content of yesterday's lesson. But instead of getting the opportunity to do something with yesterday's content, the teacher only pours in new material. Today, tomorrow and the day after the same happens, and by then the children are 'fit to burst' and 'burst' they do, to the teacher's despair and astonishment. But even if the teacher lets one of the children retell yesterday's story, practice yesterday's newly learned type of sum, or work hard at yesterday's song, he may still find that the children are not really satisfied.

What has he done wrong now? If we see the content of the main lesson, we shall find that the children have been guided quite effectively in everything they have done. They have, for instance, been told not only what to draw from yesterday's story, but also how to draw it. This, of course, is needed to teach the children skills, but they have another need which is often not recognized. They have the desire to bring out in *their very own way* something they have absorbed yesterday and digested during sleep.

Insert in every main lesson seven to fifteen minutes during which the children can choose whether to draw, model, write or make a collage from one small item — chosen by the teacher — out of yesterday's lesson in their own way ('free rendering'). At first, one might offer the children a number of suggestions, but very soon that will prove unnecessary. One will see how contentment, rosier cheeks, and gratitude take hold in that class.

Note: Of course these are only a very few suggestions and someone whose work is consulting could write five books on this subject.

Child Study and Assessment

Audrey E. McAllen

The teachers in Waldorf school faculty meetings try to build up together a picture of the *soul content* which each child is bringing with him into the present incarnation. The teachers bring together all the different facets of the child's character and abilities which are revealed to them in their daily contact with the child in the classroom and on the playground, and the child's responses to the individuality of the different teachers.

The teachers observe first the child's physical appearance: the size and shape of his head, neck, trunk and limbs; his sitting and standing posture, the coloring of his skin, eyes and hair; how he uses his hands, how he places his feet when walking and running, where his movements are initiated. These observations show how the soul-spirit is working in relationship to the heredity factors and to the imitation of his environment.

Then, the teachers note how his general body health (constitution) speaks to them. Is he pale or flushed, are his hands hot and dry or sticky, cold and clammy? Has he cold feet, does exertion make him breathless, does he gobble his food, is he sleepy in lessons? Here are factors where the teachers need to turn to the doctor for advice. Maybe there is the need of a supporting medicament or for curative eurythmy to help the soul-spirit to grasp and penetrate a particular organ or life-process. There are, of course, the children with specific constitutional problems — asthma, bed-wetting, hysteric soul conditions, all needing long-term medical help.

The 'child study' is not complete without descriptions of his class work. Which subjects does he enjoy most, with which has he difficulties? A teacher may describe a pupil's enthusiasm for geography, and how the child produces two main lesson books full of pictures and descriptions far beyond the subject matter of the actual main lesson. Another teacher may recall what Rudolf Steiner has said about the subject geography leading to sanguinity and scattering of soul forces and how to balance this. Rudolf Steiner said the teacher should set this particular pupil tasks relating to the geometric-mathematical element in geography, in making contour maps and the like. A discussion would follow as to whether this would be necessary in this particular instance.

Probably the class teacher would end by describing the moral qualities the child has brought with him: fearlessness, truthfulness, friendship, or the soul weaknesses that lead to specific therapeutic help in painting, modeling or speech. These moral qualities can be summed up in the 'report verse' written by the class teacher as a strengthening verse for the child.

In such a study, the teachers make an imaginative picture of the content from the spiritual world which the soul has worked upon there and which now has to pour itself into the soul powers of thinking, feeling, and willing as they develop during the class teaching period, ready to be taken up into ego consciousness in the upper school and adult life.

This content, however, requires a receptacle, a 'cup', into which it can be poured. This cup is the heredity body which is transformed into a soul-image of the individuality during the first seven years. But besides the image of itself which the soul imprints into this vessel are the universal factors which make this vessel a 'cup' — something able to receive the imprint of the soul. It is an archetypal factor that — whether we are an Eskimo in the far north or an Aborigine in the center of Australia — the body is capable of being upright. It is a body shaped and formed to bear an ego; this is what was accomplished by the end of the Old Saturn evolution.[1] A sensory body of warmth was formed, its "ego-hood capacity" manifesting outwardly in the cosmos, inwardly as smell percept. This *cup* for the eventual content of an ego, this *physical body* Steiner defines as the *sum total of the senses* in its present manifestation, "an echo of the zodiac."[2]

To this was added 'life' on Old Sun and 'activity' on Old Moon. When the child stands upright, he manifests the archetypal accomplishments of the Hierarchies of Old Saturn evolution; that he lives and breathes and moves is a manifestation of Old Sun and Old Moon evolutions. This archetypal structure of the 'cup for the ego' is alike for all humanity. A Japanese has the same nervous system (astral organ from Old Moon) as an American. A skeleton and a muscular system are the same in Holland or in China; there are the same number of bones and they are in the same positions; the muscles control the bones in the same way. If everyone were as unique as his individuality, there would be no surgery possible! Even in the organs' form and number are objective factors: four chambers of the heart, two lobes of the left lung, three of the right lung. *How* we use them depends on the soul content which is being poured into this 'cup' of the physical body.

It is the *education of the archetypal physical body which is the task of the kindergarten teachers.*[3] They continue on earth, day by day in physical reality, the work of the Hierarchies so that, by the change of teeth, the soul will have a receptacle to receive its content. The unification of the archetypal image (that has been learned from the Hierarchies during the ego's sojourn in the spiritual world) with the model image that the heredity body provides is the work of the Spirit in man. The ego lifts its organism into uprightness and to standing freely in space, becoming able to differentiate left and right, up and down to move forward and back. This is the outcome, the gift of the Spirits of the Hierarchies to man, from the developments of Old Saturn, Old Sun, and Old Moon evolutions.

The physical body which we care for and protect during the first seven years of life is the organic basis for the Consciousness Soul. The Consciousness Soul is that soul member which the ego needs as its organ to perceive itself as a spirit and to recognize that the same spirit is working in the outer world around him. This archetypal structure is, on the other side of the 'threshold', an organism of moral forces, those forces from the highest spiritual world which underlie the structure of the Earth. Is it any wonder that Rudolf Steiner required that the teacher of the pre-school child should be one in whom an earnest striving for moral development — for the *good* — is present?

This physical body — an architectural, spatial movement organism (see Section I) — is also the basis for those human powers which separate us from the animal and unite us into a whole. These human powers are revealed in the capacities we require from the human body for the education of the human spirit to write, to read and to calculate. *If these do not spring up as the fruit of the development of the body during the first seven years, all class and upper school teachers are thwarted in their educational work for the soul of man.*

Because we have a bone-muscle-nerve organization in common, we can ask all incarnating souls the same question in the same, yet manifold ways, namely, "How is it with your incarnation? Can you move freely in space; is it at your command outwardly, inwardly, can you coordinate above to below, left to right? Are you so centered that you can move freely forward and back? Are you in command of the senses of self-movement and balance; has your life sense, concept sense been damaged?"

These are the ever constant questions which an assessment on the basis of *The Extra Lesson* asks of the soul-spirit. From the answers which the body of the child gives in response, we can anticipate how the learning faculties of writing, reading, and arithmetic will develop and whether we need to give help so that frustration does not fetter the soul to the organism and lead to psychological complications.

The curriculum is there to serve and *save the soul*. To *save the spirit*, that is, to prevent the organ of the spirit from being disrupted between one and seven years, is the aim of the kindergarten movement. *The incidence of learning problems shows that the adversary forces know where to attack so that man shall be deprived of consciousness of his spiritual origin.*

---

1   Rudolf Steiner, *An Outline of Esoteric Science.*
2   Ibid.
3   See Section VII.

Suggestions from Else Göttgens

Ingun Schneider

Miss Else Göttgens is a consultant for Waldorf schools in England, Holland, Belgium and the United States. The teachers in the different grade levels have found her insights to be very helpful in observation of children, circle work, curriculum development and practical teaching skills. The classes to which Miss Göttgen's suggestions were directed are indicated in parenthesis although there will be much which is applicable to other grades as well. The following suggestions were given by 'word of mouth' and are shared here:

Main Lesson

For the class teacher from Easter of first grade through second grade: *anything done with the whole class (in circle or otherwise) can be done individually as well.* However, this can be accomplished gradually by decreasing the number of children at one time, i.e., one day ask for six volunteers. All the other children watch. Then, the next day, choose one child who does it well and one child who is not so good at it (good and poor together). Give other children the task of watching and then ask, "which of the children lifted the feet higher?" Ask something different each time. This makes it possible for all to participate and develops discrimination. These years are not the right time to call upon judgment, but it is good to develop discrimination which will be needed after puberty. (Grades 1 - 3)

The children benefit more from writing 'on their own' in their main lesson books. This applies right at the beginning, in first grade. They can begin by composing together with the teacher at the end of first grade, and in second grade, part of the time, they can compose their writing in small groups. By grade three, composing can be done partly on their own, composing with the teacher or in small groups continues; avoid too much copying off the board. (Grades 1 - 3)

Use good images addressing the senses of sight, smell, taste, hearing, touch, etc., when telling stories. Give brief, clear pictures with interesting and varied adjectives to describe them. The child's imagination needs enlivening. (Grades 1 - 3)

In your storytelling introduce two new vocabulary words daily. Use them over and over again. (All grades)

The retelling of the main lesson story can be done in a variety of ways. After the kindergarten years, the retelling can be different from the telling. The story can be acted out by the teacher, and the children can join in as they recall different parts of the story. Or tell the story on the first day in the mood of one temperament and, on the second day, in the opposite temperament. (Grades 1- 8)

Retell the story by having the children create their own drawing, cut-out, glued tissue paper, painting, modeling (clay, plasticine or beeswax), or writing about an episode in the story from the previous day — 'free rendering'. (Grades 1- 8)

Before recess, if the children have been very incarnated, tell a little story or otherwise loosen them (excarnate) so they will not be too physically aggressive on the play yard. (All grades)

LANGUAGE ARTS

Use a free flowing pencil for writing — or even a (narrow tipped) felt tip pen. Do *not* use a beeswax crayon for writing; they are too 'sticky' and give too much resistance. The writing and form drawing needs to flow, so the children don't have to hold the writing implement with such tension in their fingers. (Grades 1 - 3)

Lines for guiding the writing are not important. Let the children write as big or as small as they want. (Grades 1 & 2)

Do more speech work! Use report verses and expect the children to speak them well with good enunciation, projection and intonation. (Grades 1- 8)

In speech work, do not let the children get into a 'sing-song' rhythm. Especially with poetry, avoid getting them into a 'drone'. (Grades 1- 8)

Practice every day, but vary the speaking: use high-pitched and low voices; quick and slow; quiet and loud; have small groups and individuals speaking (parts of) the poem or verse. (Grades 1- 8)

Use a bean bag for the child to throw while speaking a line from a poem or verse. Use, for instance, the image of a bird flying into its nest while throwing the bean bag with the last word in the line. (Grades 1 - 6)

Individualize speech exercises more. Already in first grade, start having 'strong' children recite a class poem alone. You may want to start with small groups and work toward individuals. (Grades 1- 8)

By second grade, make sure all children are reciting individually — even the melancholics (with prior preparation). (Grades 2 - 8)

Include the greatest poets for class poems, such as Shakespeare, Wordsworth, etc. (Grades 2 - 8)

The children's first 'readers' can be made up of verses and songs that they already know. The teacher writes the words— the children do the art work. (Grade 2)

Teach phonics from memorized verses.[1] (Grades 2 & 3)

Schedule a reading block during Advent. (Grade 2)

Have a class library in the room for those who want to read; a quiet, separated-off corner with cushions and mats as well as a single desk and chair, is especially appreciated (Grades 1- 8)

Spelling may be done individually with a card (business-card size) and box (large match boxes work well). The teacher writes the word beautifully and the child keeps the card in his box to look at 10 times that day. The teacher may ask the child to write the word on the board or in his practice book the next day — until he gets it correct. (This method may also be used for math problems). (Grades 2 - 6)

Do more prepared dictation — it helps their memories. To begin with dictate passages which are already familiar to the students. (Grades 3 - 8)

READING EXERCISES

A way to tell whether children are slow readers or just cannot 'flow' is: point out a word quickly on a page then cover it. If the child can see and read it that quickly, they are not slow but need to practice the 'flow'. This is done by having them follow your reading with their finger (hesitating when you hesitate, moving quickly when you move more quickly). Practice this for about six weeks. (Grades 3 - 8)

Here is one imagination: 'the eagle hunts for the rabbit'. The teacher chooses a word on the page and speaks the word, telling the student that the 'rabbit' is the chosen word. The child, as the 'eagle', hunts for the word by 'circling' with his eyes (not skimming or scanning) letting the eyes bounce around on the page or area of page until the word is spotted. 'Hunt' for three or four words every day.

Point to a word and immediately cover it. The child must 'guess', not read, what the word is. Do this three or four words every day.

The student slides along the text with his finger (not pointing at each word) as you and/or he reads. He must keep up and not go ahead. The teacher reads with expression at different paces. Content must be something the student wants to read. Practice five to fifteen minutes every day.

Take turns reading aloud. Require reading with expression (student reads to himself until all words are recognized, then reads the sentence aloud). Practice five to fifteen minutes every day.

MATH

Expect something great of their memories for numbers beginning in first grade. They must know the simple number combinations in addition and subtraction (up to 12) by heart, without using fingers: 9-5=4, 6+5=11, 12-3=9, etc.

If the memory is cultivated in the early classes (one and two), they can do it so much easier! (Grades 1 & 2)

Expect the students to know all twelve tables and to be able to do them individually, forward and backward — in sequence — by the end of second grade. (Grade 2)

By the end of third grade, expect them to be able to answer a problem from the tables given randomly (e.g., 4 threes are?, 6 sevens are?, etc.) Also, *division by tables* (6 by 3 is?, 12 by 4 is?), etc. (Grade 3)

By the end of second grade, the students should know, by heart, facts of addition and subtraction up to 20. (Grade 2)

ARTISTIC ACTIVITIES AND MISCELLANEOUS

'Free rendering': make a regular time every day for 10-15 minutes for free artistic, creative activity related to the main lesson content given the previous day(s). (Grades 1 - 8)

Have the children do more. Don't 'spoon feed' them. Have them help to clean the classroom, run your errands, etc. Spend time in the early grades teaching them *how* to properly wash the dirty wall, do the dishes, wipe the desks thoroughly, etc. (Grades 1 - 8)

Screening assessments of each student in second grade gives the teacher(s) a picture of *each* child's developmental status. (Grade 2)

When observing a child, don't take anything as 'conclusion', but only as an 'indication', contributing to a total picture. (Grades 1 - 8)

Always have something in your lesson that invites laughter or a smile. (Grades 1 - 8)

Sometimes having too much knowledge is very dampening to the humor; find a balance throughout the day. (Grades 1 - 12)

Children need plenty of movement especially in the lower grades, though it is not necessary to keep circle time so long; have them move in between other activities. Write with the feet. (Grades 1 - 4)

Create most activities from a picture image (a whole story is not necessary — just a picture image). (Grades 1 - 8)

Use Jean Hunt's beanbag exercises[2] intensively for six weeks, three to four times a year — not all year daily, nor once a week. (Grades 1 - 2)

Do two concentration exercises in the course of a six week block. When they can do them, choose two others.

Have a student (or a small group) walk a phrase, then a sentence forwards and backwards — speaking as the step is taken — to help strengthen memory forces. (Grades 2 - 8)

When a child has osteopathic help, this should be 'fastened into the etheric' with curative eurythmy and also Extra Lesson exercises.

A good curative eurythmist will usually know within three weeks or less when the curative eurythmy is going to work.

Science lessons give us the greatest opportunity to present material that may provide spiritual experiences. (Grades 5 - 8)

We need, in this country (US), at least 4-6 full-time (more if part-time) people consulting with faculties, giving in-service training, public lectures, parent education, etc.

Spend a few minutes of every faculty meeting sharing a quote that conveys an image from a poem or story written by a favorite author (metaphors and similes).

Handwork

In grades one, two, and three, the children need a great deal of help. Small groups with a more intimate atmosphere are important.

Foreign Language

In first and second grade, foreign language classes: using chalkboard drawings of stories and having the students make their own picture books is helpful. These pictures could help to build a basic vocabulary. (Grades 1- 2)

---

1   Mary Nash-Wortham, *Phonic Rhyme Time*.
2   Mary Nash-Wortham and Jean Hunt, *Take Time*.

Suggestions for Pedagogical Economy

Audrey E. McAllen

Before using spelling rules, a child needs to master the perception of words, letters, sounds, and the difference between vowels and consonants.

The following should prove helpful:

> 1. When introducing a poem, tell a story with words that are contained in the poem so that understanding is prepared (pedagogical economy). The child then takes this into sleep.
>
> 2. The next day, ask yourself what image is needed to introduce the poem. Tell the content of the poem in this image. This is again followed by an interval of sleep.
>
> 3. On the third day, the teacher recites the poem — ask what is the second word in the poem. Repeat the poem — ask what word came twice. An interval of sleep follows again.
>
> 4. Speak the poem, recite it as a group, then make sure that each child can say the poem by heart. This can be done as follows: stop the class while they are reciting and ask the choleric child to say the next verse alone, or, to begin with, the next line — continue the class recitation. Choose a suitable verse for a melancholic child and tell one (or a pair) of this temperament that you will ask him (them) to say that verse tomorrow at the appropriate time. Before the class begins to recite the poem, tell the phlegmatic child that he is to say the third verse. Tell the sanguine child that "next Tuesday you will say the second verse and the last verse of the poem."

Give time in the main lesson for free activity ('free rendering') out of the previous day's work (see previous article). The teacher selects the item and offers that each child may choose from drawing, modeling, writing, or handwork. This releases any congestion of the children's experiences and also prevents congestion of their perceptions. Teachers have often omitted time in the main lesson for children to work out what they have each individually matured in sleep. The child needs to bring this maturation process into conscious activity. The teacher needs to make space for the children to express this. Make a certain time — daily — a limited time (ten to fifteen minutes) — as a part of the recapitulation element in the lesson. When soul congestion is released, the child grows pink and healthy.

Here, we are using the curriculum pedagogically to awaken the children into their senses. Questions to the children in the first, second and third grades should not be on content,[1] but on words, letters, sound — auditory and visual perception. This helps the children realize that they are expected to listen. See that they really seize hold of their senses so that their ego is present.

Most teachers feel the importance of the curriculum, but there are some who feel all they have to do is to cover the curriculum and often far too much material is included. It is more helpful (healthful), i.e., that a fable or a Saint's story is given in homeopathic doses — beautifully done and fully worked through as indicated above. Then, one can use images and vocabulary from these stories to enliven the pedagogy, so there is repetition. If consciousness is involved, repetition then strengthens the will. (A useful aid to prepare this is *Phonic Rhyme Time* by Mary Nash-Wortham — a book of verse with repetitive words and alliterations which are both artistic and meaningful.)

UPDATE 1996

A research suggestion — here is a preparation for the time when 'virtual reality' will be as much a part of the home environment as video games and T.V. is now. Ever new means will be devised of engaging the children's interest in ways which will deflect the formative forces from their upbuilding work and their power of metamorphosis into capacities for later life.

Even as I write, technology is now providing a new 'teaching' play computer devised by an enterprising parent for his 18 month old son who had given his fathers' computer a playful whack, destroying the system. Research projects should be in our schools to see how the effects of such well intentioned technology can be mitigated.

The policy of the school where I started a class in 1950, was that pupils did not attend the cinema during term time. Many of the children in my class had never entered a cinema. But in 1953 when we were class three, television in the U.K. took over almost overnight. Everyone wanted to see the coronation of Elizabeth II. By the time we were class six, I noted many of the children no longer sat with the limb control which they once previously had. Teachers now recognize this lack of limb control as a symptom of the delicate disruption of the senses of balance and self-movement, nowadays exacerbated by the use of baby walkers in infancy.

It so happened that my class was the final one to have Saturday morning school (at that time the Upper School had classes on Saturday). You may imagine, I did not welcome the idea of teaching on Saturday. To my complete amazement, it was a wonderful day to teach. The children came quickly into class in the morning. They were inwardly content and responsive to the lesson and there was a real social feeling between them and a willingness to review the work of the week. In fact, one recognized the benign forces of Saturn working.

Contrast this with the usual Monday (moon) morning mood — all separate individuals 'stirring each other up', or wanting to gossip about the weekend activities, reluctant to receive the content of the lesson and to get down to work. Does this still sound familiar or have children changed dramatically for the better now that teachers have a more thorough training?

If the foregoing description is still a familiar scenario, then I suggest teachers start taking action. For example, begin Monday mornings with pedagogical exercises in painting and form drawing activities — the Blue/Red Spiral Exercises,[2] Secondary Color Exercises,[3] and Moral Color Exercises[4] could be used from the appropriate ages. Teachers could devise temperament exercises in painting or form drawing. Many variations will suggest themselves from the main lesson. Follow this with dictation from content of the previous week, or set a composition. Work at spelling, mental arithmetic and then when the class has settled, 'call on' *expectancy* by telling them what they will be learning in the coming week — concluding with class recitation. There should be teachers in the latter part of the class teaching period who would be interested in carrying out such a 'program' for a six week period and assess the result with the effects the subject teachers have experienced that day. Think of the Norse Gods and their names and qualities!

Teachers need to learn to work with the qualities of the other days of the week. Also, try to recognize which subjects are best taught in winter and which in summer. Indications were given by Rudolf Steiner in the supplementary course to teachers when upper school classes commenced in the first Waldorf school.[5] Working with these indications, I found, for example, that history in the summer term was more easily received by the children than in winter; quite a different mood was achieved in the summer time. The indications Steiner gives raises the question, "Do you take an incarnating subject when the seasonal tendency is to 'excarnate' — should one go with the opposite effect of the subject to the season?" What effect does this have on discipline? Some indications have already been researched by Paul Platt[6] at the Great Barrington School and these could be used as a basis for further research. Dr. Zimmerman, when speaking to teachers of the Pedagogical Section in his Michaelmas address in Dornach (1995), asked if we rely too much on our traditions. How do we bring ourselves up-to-date; how must the curriculum and school life be modified to suit climate or cultural differences?[7] Have we at our teacher's conferences considered how to implement the suggestions, stemming from the conversations with Rudolf Steiner which Karl Ege gives in his book?[8] Our school movement needs to prepare itself for the new demands which the next decades will make on our pedagogical insights in learning and in the social capacity of the classes, as well as upon individuals.

It is unlikely that the deleterious effects in the environment — pollution, chemicalized foods, etc. — will soon change. They will have already had their impact on the children before their coming to us. We cannot expect parents to alter their life-style overnight — if at all.

Waldorf/Steiner teachers have the responsibility to provide a daily oasis where the child is nourished in his soul and where his individuality can take hold of his body in a strong and helpful way.

1. Rudolf Steiner, *The Kingdom of Childhood*, Lecture 4.
2. Audrey E. McAllen, *The Extra Lesson*, pp. 161-164.
3. Ibid., pp. 164-166.
4. A. E. McAllen, *Sleep* (2004 edition), pp. 49-64.
5. Rudolf Steiner, *Waldorf Education for Adolescence*.
6. Paul Platt, *Qualities of Time: Contribution Towards a Modern Understanding on How the Cosmos Works in Man*.
7. Heinz Zimmerman, *What is Happening in the Anthroposophical Society*.
8. Karl Ege, *An Evident Need of the Times, Goals of Education at the Close of this Century*, p. 11.

Helping Through the Feet

Jannebeth Roëll, RN

An experience of giving first aid through handling the foot:

Feet are a neglected part of our body in our modern society. We show much more respect for the brain than for any other part. So, one day I asked myself, "Who is wiser — the brain or the feet?"

It is with our feet that we walk step-by-step to our destiny. When we walk on a hike (not when strolling or shopping), we take as many steps in a minute as our heart beats. We are in time with our own rhythm, which is in effect a cosmic rhythm. The brain does not have this cosmic wisdom.

We talk about being 'well grounded'; in many situations this feeling is lost. There are circumstances where we literally cannot be in touch with the ground.

For example, when a child falls out of a tree, gets scared, and cannot stop crying, or when someone has to stay in bed for a long time, then a 'handshake' with the feet can be of practical help. The right hand 'shakes hand' with the right foot, or the left hand with the left foot. Then, placing the other hand firmly over the instep (top of foot), gently rub the skin. The hand should not move over the skin, but rather, the skin of the foot should be moved by the hand. This type of foot-rub can also be used for sleeplessness.

Jannebeth Roëll, RN, was born in Holland. She worked with handicapped children in Switzerland, completed her nurse's training in 1967 in the Hague, Netherlands, at the Rudolf Steiner Clinic, followed by extensive training in Boll, Germany. She practiced Anthroposophical nursing for ten years in Holland and started a "therapeuticum" in The Hague. Currently, she resides in Florida. She presents "home care workshops" in Holland, Switzerland, Germany, and the United States for doctors, nurses, and laymen.

Teachers, Look to Your Handwriting!

Irene N. Ellis and A. E. McAllen

In a Michaelmas lecture, Rudolf Steiner says:

> Today men do not have the writing, but "the writing has them." What does this mean? It means that in our wrist, in our hand, we have a certain train of writing. We write mechanically, out of the hand. This is a thing that fetters man. He only becomes unfettered when he writes as he paints or draws — when every letter beside the next becomes a thing that is painted or drawn.... When there is no longer what is called a 'handwriting'. Man 'draws' the form of the letter. His relation to the letter is objective; he sees it before him. That is the essential thing.[1]

In a Waldorf/Steiner school, if all goes according to plan, many children will be copying and later reading their teacher's writing on the blackboard for as long as eight years. In view of the above quotation, it is surely essential that the class teacher overcomes his/her individual handwriting when writing on the board for the children. Otherwise, whenever the children copy from the board they will be absorbing (all unconsciously) the characteristics of the teacher which are hidden within the writing — his habits, weaknesses, etc. If the teacher can develop a beautiful and well-balanced form of writing for the classroom, so much the better for all the dear children committed to his care.[2] Often seen is the teacher's 'own' handwriting on the board, showing their individual squiggles, incomplete loops of y's and g's incomplete, sometimes sloping slightly backwards and far too small for the younger classes. In one fourth grade, the teacher missed out a word and put it in thus:

Loki saw ∧^{his} chance

Several of the children copied it, showing the teacher's omission! The teacher should cultivate a beautiful, easily legible, clean way of writing, sloping slightly forward (a factor which leads into the future), with firm, strong downstrokes and lighter upward ones. Let teachers be quite conscious that they must help the child down onto the earth.

When introducing the CAPITAL letters to the children in first grade, in story form, it might be a good idea to introduce the small letter at the same time. (This is economy in teaching which Steiner is always recommending, and it will keep their thinking mobile.) As the vowels are more connected with the soul forces and the life of feeling, ways other than the 'picture' could be used, i.e., more gesture and movement.

After the letters have been introduced the children could be led straight away into cursive writing, using printed capitals where appropriate. Cursive writing brings rhythmic movement into the art of writing and keeps the whole word intact as a picture, whereas with script (printing) the word is broken up. I am convinced that cursive writing will facilitate the whole process of 'learning to read' as the children should always read aloud what they have written, both *forwards and backwards*. In this way, during the early days in second grade several children will 'discover' that they can read without ever having had a 'reading lesson' as such.

From the very beginning, it is essential to insist and encourage each child to develop a large, round and legible form of writing; in how each child's individual writing may develop over the years, lies a deeply embedded character forming process. Bring writing in script (printed letters) into the work whenever a poem or quotation is written; also in direct speech, *but not until the cursive hand is well established.*

A lively element can be brought into the art of writing through 'temperament writing'. The idea is from Jan van Bemmelen, founder teacher of the Hague School in Holland.

Once the cursive writing is established, the teacher can introduce four characters who are preparing a name board for their respective homes, for example:

Miss Sadly practices thus: *A B C D*

Mr. Rumpus next door thus: A B C D

Mrs. Fluttery writes thus: 𝒜 ℬ 𝒞 𝒟

While Mr. Pompous does so: A B C D

These letters should be 'drawn'. See that the stroke sequences are made in the correct order.³ Letter size 3" - 4" high in groups, well set out on the page.

By this means, any doubt about a temperament can be resolved as the child will show it, by his choice, as each child always identifies with his own! But to begin with, *all four styles should be practiced by the whole class,* and then the child can choose their 'own temperament'. This should be done for a short time only; for example, ten minutes in the main lesson for a week and then back to normal cursive writing. If the children are getting careless and need a stimulus for calling attention to their writing, then it can be repeated for one morning in main lesson. Nowadays, perhaps it would be necessary to work at each temperament for a week to maximize the effect of such an exercise.

Not only is this a pedagogical exercise for the present stage of development, but it is also relevant to the time when calligraphy is a main lesson in the upper school when, in exact construction, the young people will learn about wide letters, narrow letters, round letters, and the elaborate half uncials. Nothing is more strengthening to the will of the growing young person than being able to look back to his earlier classes and recognize how this has been a preparation for what he is now doing. This, too, is part of the work of our Colleges of Teachers: *that upper and lower school teaching consciously integrate and support each other.*

Repetitions of such a pedagogical exercise can be done after cursive writing has been used over time, for a few days only, and why not introduce alternate shapes for individual capital letters from time to time. Practice them in alphabetical order such as found in dictionaries or telephone directories (not as was seen in one classroom — in the order they were taught as pictures).

These changes help to keep both teacher and children alert, awake, and fully conscious and interested in their activity so that the writing will not become mechanical, i.e., "the writing has them." It can also strengthen their etheric bodies. As mentioned, when doing the cursive writing, quotations and poems can stand out in script (printed letters) — another change to cope with, and a healthy slowing down process. Keep the children constantly on their toes, and so engender a genuine enthusiasm and interest in writing for its own sake.

It is not necessarily recommended to use the temperament writing as a Main Lesson in itself, but rather incorporate it into a suitable Main Lesson, e.g., Legends of the Saints, Farming, as you will. Have the children use it during the time they do their usual written work, with a very brief practice of a sentence beforehand. Have all the children write in one of each of the four temperaments for four consecutive mornings, and then have one final day when each child could make his own choice.

The size of the letters for each temperament can vary — the larger the better! — the main object being to exaggerate the special characteristics of each temperament.

Melancholic: extremely thin and narrow and much elongated. Sometimes one can see how the striving to go right down to the bottom of the page helps the melancholic gain courage.

Figure 1: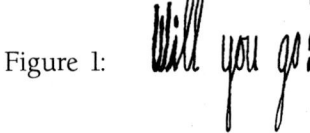

Choleric: accentuate the strength and the squareness — let the child feel his own strength in a good and healthy way. This can give great satisfaction to the choleric child.

Figure 2: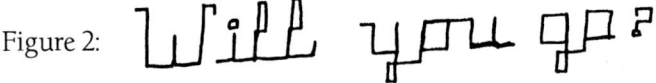

Sanguine: delight in all the twiddles and embellishments that a child can devise. This can help the sanguine's concentration around the different letters and *may* even bring in a certain thoughtfulness; it is also great fun!

Figure 3:

Phlegmatic: letters large and very rounded, even and level. This can be a beautiful writing but for some may be boring.

Figure 4: *Saint Francis was good.*

Even the dots and punctuation should take on the style of the different temperaments. It is hoped that teachers would evolve their own examples of temperament writing — these examples are only suggestions.

A handwriting practice book designed by Else Göttgens, is especially designed for handwriting practice in the 2nd and 3rd grades in Waldorf schools. Each page has seven soft green bars 1" wide. In the middle of each bar is a 1/4" soft pink bar. One writes in the pink bar and green on each side mark the correct length of the loops of the letters. The books are used in the Dutch Waldorf schools in combination with the extra thick Lyra colored pencils which are wonderful soft writing pencils. They are long lasting and write very smoothly, which make them ideal for flowing handwriting practice.[5]

---

1   Rudolf Steiner, *Festivals and Their Meaning*, Lecture January 13, 1924.
2   Joen Gladich and Paula Sassi, *The Write Approach Book I* and *Book II*.
3   Audrey E. McAllen, *Teaching Children Handwriting*.
4   Ibid.
5   For the above mentioned handwriting practice book designed by Else Göttgens write to Rudolf Steiner College Bookstore.

Hints for Waldorf Teachers in the Early Grades

Irene N. Ellis

How you yourself *stand* before children is very important.... Make yourself very straight and *upright* but essentially at ease.

Please, have the children *standing* to say "Good Morning" to you. This is the first stage of their learning to have a certain respect for you, which you will need very much in the higher grades.

For the most part, have the children *standing up* when they sing, recite poetry, play recorders ... they will be able to breathe much more freely in this position (as against sitting) and so develop a better posture. Also, alternating between sitting-down and standing-up can be a great help towards discipline — and it is something the class must learn to do all together.

Learn to work with the attentive children and give them due praise. Every child needs encouragement; try to ignore as much of the inevitable naughtiness as you can.

Avoid using the expression "O.K." (okay) in the classroom. Cultivate a beautiful, pictorial language — this will show very much in their later compositions.

Have much *repetition* and doing the same thing over again but *in a slightly different way*. Do the times tables and short speech exercises both forwards *and* backwards (in the tables do not repeat 36 = 12 x 3 but go straight back into 33 = 11 x 3). It is good when the children also *read* their early written work both *forwards and backwards*. This is a very great help in learning to read.

Be very particular about the truth of the terms you use in Math, e.g., when subtracting, we often use the term 'borrowing' when we have not the slightest intention of paying back! Surely 'taking' would be more truthful. In fractions, the term 'cancel' is equally incorrect — if it were, you would be left with a naught (zero) and not with a one. With decimals, it is not the point which moves, but the numbers. So, be aware!

During the first few weeks, it is wise to invite an experienced class-teacher and colleague into your first Main Lesson. I would recommend more visits between teachers into other classes as well.

Be particular about having the children sitting up straight and attentive for the storytelling. Also, see that they are *sitting properly* when they write, with feet together on the floor. The correct size of desk/table to chair is important.

See that the child *holds his pencil correctly* as it is necessary to cultivate these good habits from the very beginning.

You should try to cultivate a very special and beautiful writing for the blackboard; it should be other than your own, everyday writing. It is better if the children do not use the yellow pencil for writing in their books; yellow shows up well on the blackboard but not on white paper, and we write in order that another may be able to read it easily. For the same reason, it is better that the children do not do shading over their writing.

Be sure to do your *special meditation*, as well as briefly reviewing each child, *before* doing your preparation in the evening, and again first thing in the morning, when it is good also to recall your colleagues.

The initial interview with parents and child is very important. Be sure to have a colleague to share the interview with you. Find out all you can about the child's early development and try to prepare the parents, tactfully, about the later reading in our schools. Have an evening for your parents at least once a term and stress the importance of attending this meeting regularly. It can be helpful to have a few books on view already at the first interview, e.g., A. C. Harwood's *Way of a Child*, Francis Edmund's *Rudolf Steiner Education* and others, and where it seems propitious, you might even suggest that they buy one!

Start a study group with your parents and open it to others. The support and understanding of your parents is vital for the sake of children and teacher alike. A weekly study group can bring the greatest blessing into your classroom for the following morning — and onwards. Be sure to visit the parents in their home once a year; if they do not invite you (for sometimes they are shy), then invite yourself — the parents are generally delighted to have you for a meal! Make a point of being shown the child's bedroom; it is helpful to see the child's environment and playthings.

In these days, it is necessary to teach the children to say *please* and *thank you*, so use the words yourself as often as you possibly can.

See that the child starts off in the morning with clean hands — you may have to teach him how to wash them properly to begin with. Suitable clothing and tidy hair are also important.

When helping a child individually with his work, it is better not to squat down beside the child's desk but rather to bend over the child in a protective gesture. You thus surround the child with warmth, rather than having the child, all lonely, looking downwards onto you.

Ask parents to forego clapping when the children demonstrate from their schoolwork at a more intimate class festival. In this way, a very special mood can be engendered — a blessing alike for both children and parents.

It could be made more meaningful when the first day of the school year can begin on a Thursday, when possible. Each day in the week has its special character, and Thursday lends itself to being a festival day (a little Sunday) in a way that Monday does not. Also starting mid-week lets the children begin the term gently.

It can be a very special and beautiful moment when the end-of-year reports for the parents (handwritten of course) are handed out to the children in the classroom by the class teacher on the last morning of the school year, accompanied by a few appropriate words for each child.

Compiled by Irene N. Ellis — Class Teacher and later advisor to many pioneering Waldorf schools, from first-hand observations in more than one country. (ed)

GUIDELINES FOR THE TEACHING OF WRITING, SPELLING AND READING IN THE EARLY GRADES

Teachers' notes from lectures
by Audrey E. McAllen

In the curriculum lectures Rudolf Steiner says that when children are seven to eight years old, they should be able to write sentences (cursive writing) about what they have seen and done. This implies skill in the children's handwriting.[1] Printing the letters disrupts the thought flow; therefore, letting children become established in print script is not helpful either to writing or reading. Cursive writing of the alphabet in all variations and sequencing (e.g., nonsense words) helps the child to become fluent in 'seeing' letters together that they already learned as separate letters, and also familiarizes them with the correct joining of these letters. The teacher and children can have much fun with this: yabe, ydef, yghi, shabed, shdefg, shijk. Make it varied and interesting.

In class two, the teacher can place the children in groups of mixed abilities; in each group, would be one child who can tell stories, one who writes easily, one who has a good spelling faculty and two others. They write down part of a story they know and are encouraged to ask for help with spelling. If one group wants the spelling of a word, the teacher writes it on the blackboard, and if another group wants the *same* word (and this is the important thing), the teacher writes it *again* as the children want to live and learn from the teacher's *activity*. To point to a word already written is too much of an abstraction for them. Out of such situations, the teacher can then explain blends, the final 'e' and the change of the vowel sound with two vowels together. Make up a paragraph using a group or word family in an interesting activity. A.C. Harwood gives the following example: "Let a child come to the blackboard and rub out the two letters in words that sound the same, e.g., all the 'oa's, then have another child come, perhaps the next day, and write them in. Then they can collect them and write their own sentences... all in the context of a known story. Fantasy of their own does not come until age twelve."[2]

Spelling lists, sight words, oral reading and comprehension work unrelated to the content of the main lesson subject are all abstract and dulling to the imagination. Learning spelling lists is a meaningless activity to the child with conceptual perceptions, i.e., a child who sees a candle, electric light bulb, and a lantern and immediately thinks 'light'. A visual perceptual child will not 'think' this, he sees the separate identities. A visual perceptual child will recognize and group similar *forms* whose *function* is unrelated. If the teacher recognizes this, he can see how spelling lists will go with one and not with the other. The conceptual child will spell according to the sound in relation to what he is writing; hence, he will sometimes have three different spellings of the same word. This is not 'bizarre spelling', but a form of phonetic spelling, and the teacher only tortures him with spelling lists and spoils his spontaneity and interest.

To get over to these children the correct spelling of a particular word, a teacher needs only to make an arresting imagination, joke or comic scene that makes an impact, then they will never spell it wrong again. For instance, some words always wear their 'party-dress' — *gh* — right, height, high, sight, neighbor. Also, the abstract learning of spelling burdens the memory just at the time the rhythmic memory is developing (age nine to twelve). However, one can help with spelling words of similar sounds, but different spelling, e.g., enough, stuff, also words with ee and ea: see, sea, by having the children write them with different colored chalks. Choose opposite colors, for example, red-green. If giving them to learn, give them on different colored paper. Give a child a card with a word he can't spell and have him take it home. Tell him to look at it ten times during the day; then he is to have his parent ask him what word is on the card, and he is to practice the spelling. The card is brought back to the classroom and placed on the table. During the lesson, ask the child to remember it and write it on the blackboard. Make your own lists of words for the whole class so you can keep track which words have been given to which child. Abstract memory is not ready for use until at least age eight or nine years. Then the teacher may move around from one child to another, asking each child to spell different words that will be needed when the teacher prepares their compositions. Always teach spelling in relationship to what the children are going to do and will need to use. If the teacher puts the words up on the blackboard, and the children copy them incorrectly in their story, then the teacher can select these words and teach them as sight words, reminding them of the sentence. This is for fourth grade age (and onwards) where the teacher asks the children to write down an incident in a Norse tale, for instance.

If the teacher does the retelling of stories correctly — after the first three grades,[3] by having one child start and another follow, so that it is reproduced in its sequence, she helps to train the memory and the reading comprehension together. The teacher never retells the story by asking the children to fill in what happened next. This only uses the intellect memory.

The teacher uses rhythmic memory for poems, tables and retelling of stories. The rhythmic memory is strongest between ages nine and twelve. This is the time when a teacher lays up treasure for later years. Each child must know the poem by himself. The method used is as follows: learn the poem together, then each row says a different verse, then two or three children recite together, and then one child recites alone. Set the task so that one group or one child will have to say verses three and four by himself, and so on. Here the teacher can play on temperaments.

Just to sit down at the desk and to write in your best writing two or three words which a child needs to learn, with him *watching*, then have him write the words underneath *once* often does the trick. Give them something to imitate, attract their attention, and the memory will function. Spelling lists are a horror to sensitive children and a bore to most others. Watch children for a 'collecting craze' (usually around class two) and plunge into collecting obscure, exciting sounding words with blends and additions that you know as their teacher, that they need to know.

Concerning reading practice, the two writers, Peter Young and Colin Tyre,[4] who are very experienced and recognized people, vindicated our approach of 'thought-speech-writing-reading' sequence. They set up a project with parent participation which produced excellent results among groups labeled dyslexic and 'reading retarded' with age groups eight to thirteen years.

They tutored groups of parents on how to sit with their children, and for those under the age of twelve on going back to 'lap learning'. They taught the parents to read rhymes and jingles with the child sitting on their knee, or cuddled up close to them.

In 'shared reading' the child listens to the parent read and follows with his finger sliding along under the words as they are read. All the methods listed in *The Extra Lesson* are used. Always use material that the child finds easy, i.e., two years below his own reading age. This reduces the need for 'reading lessons' and reading groups. In any case, the slow readers should feel that they are 'careful' readers.

Fast readers, who are sometimes poor readers when reading aloud, should do an 'exercise' of reading aloud and taking a step at each word. This will make the 'careful' readers feel not so much out of the run of things.

One can have different groups read aloud together with good intonation, pauses and expression. This is far more important than each one individually reading out aloud and stumbling. Reading should happen magically — then the comprehension is there. If it's taught in a way that something is forced, it is never quite the same — that is, there seems to be a divorce between good intonation, breathing and intonation, breathing and comprehension. Speed tends to become dominant, rather than understanding the content as a whole.

Up to the 1950's, child culture educated faculty — now we are faced with uneducated physical bodies. The soul of the child is not able to assimilate what is being given. The child comes to us unable to take in the curriculum. We must change the emphasis in the curriculum so that we remove the impediments. *Children must not sit still so long listening to the teacher — reduction of talking and drawing is needed.* We can damage the able child by not challenging him, and the non-reader needs movement (see lists of skills children must accomplish in classes one, two, three and four[5]). Make sure *all* children can do these, then the able children will be challenged in their *will*.

The old methods have to be metamorphosed in an artistic/imaginative way, into a real sequence of methods that are applicable for the good reader as well as for the slow ones and for the ones in genuine trouble.

---

1 See Audrey E. McAllen, *Teaching Children Handwriting*, for deeper insight of the connection of writing with the development of spatial consciousness in the child.
2 A. C. Harwood, *The Recovery of Man in Childhood*.
3 Rudolf Steiner, *Kingdom of Childhood*, Lecture 4.
4 Peter Young and Colin Tyre, *Dyslexia or Illiteracy*.
5 See Ester Buekers, Section IV, 'Standards of Movement Skills'.

Language Teaching from the Whole to the Part

Else Göttgens

The cat sat on the mat... how can we do that in a Waldorf way?

Here are a few ideas that have been regarded as helpful by some teachers.

First and foremost, let us remember one of the fundamental principles of Waldorf education: to go from the whole to the parts. In this case, it could mean that the children learn their spelling words from poems, songs, stories, riddles, whatever occurs in Main Lesson, and not from word lists.

Language — spoken or written — is about meaning, so our spelling words should come from a meaningful whole. If St. Francis talks to the *birds* under a *fir* tree near the *kirk* we can expect more joy and better results than if these same words just appear in a word list, devoid of content.

Now I should like to go into a rarely mentioned aspect of spelling. 'Orthography' can be seen as a combination of three distinct skills:

1. Auditory discrimination (hearing the sounds)
2. Visual memory
3. Grammatical insight (i.e., past tense ends in 'ed').
   This plays a small part in English spelling, a larger one in many other languages.

Both 1. and 2. need to be practiced regularly during practically the whole school time.

LISTENING TO THE SOUNDS

I have seen this getting more practice in Waldorf schools than the visual memory aspect. It is a great help when the children are taught to use the 'sound-names' of the words when practicing (not the 'alphabet names'). "g(uh) - rrr - ah - sss - p(uh) - sss" — step on each sound — then back to front say, "sss - p(uh) - sss - ah," etc., will produce the word 'grasps' more readily than "gee - ahr - ae - es - pee - es."

Visual Memory

Well nigh 30% of English spelling! Just think of 'caught' and 'bought': no amount of listening will put you right. And unless you are going to learn by heart through the sing-song of alphabet: spelling "bee - oh - you - gee - aech - tee" — for most words in the English language, you will have to remember what it *looks* like!

One can do any number of visual memory games with the children — both unconnected and connected with spelling. It is very helpful to mount a curtain in front of one's blackboard so as to be able to pull back the curtain to reveal the writing done on it and to cover it up again as well, with questions such as: "What was the third letter from the end? Which letter occurs three times?" etc.

Essential is also to call the motor memory into play: "Now write it in the air with your right elbow. Now with your nose." One may also write words on paper or cardboard with a glue stick, sprinkle sand on the glue and let it dry with the sand stuck to it. Let children 'read' the words with their fingers while blindfolded.

A number of children have been helped by the use of a self-made 'rainbow-dictionary'. All children are given two or three pages of each color: pink, light red, dark red paper, etc., from 10 to 15 colors. By means of a clamp, a spiral or just threaded holes, they make those pages into a book.

Each page gets words written on it that *look* the same: plough, thorough, through, cough, bought, enough — all on the orange page; laugh, caught, etc., on violet paper (largest possible contrast in color). Weird, weight neighbor on let's say yellow, friend and fiend on blue. The words are written into the book as they occur in a text or dictation — and what hinders us to frequently manipulate these kind of words into a dictation? But reading-matter, poems, songs and dictations will be in connection with the main lesson block. The printed spelling lists which we the teachers keep at home will by and by get densely dotted: all the words that the class has practiced, and will also often remind us to bring in a word that we might not have thought of on our own.

That way the cat might jump off the mat to catch a rat: the rat of materialistic thinking that would forever have us try to assemble parts to a whole.

"There is only one temple in the world and that is the human body. Nothing is more sacred than that noble body."

— Novalis

VII

KINDERGARTEN

FORCES OF THE I AM

René M. Querido

It is now an acknowledged fact by educators in many parts of the world that children are in great need of remedial help. A return to the origins in order to understand the causes has led teachers, educators, psychologists to look more deeply into the events of early childhood.

Rudolf Steiner has shed much light on the magical development of the child in the first three years. The process of learning to walk culminates in uprightness, in achieving coordination between right and left, forward and back, up and down. The child experiences the forces of the *I am* so that a beginning can be made with finding the path.[1] It is exemplified archetypally in the words of Christ, "I am the Way." The moral overtone in learning to walk during the first year is expressed in becoming an 'upright' individual.

During the second year we learn to speak. This requires coordination of the rhythmic system centered in the activity of the heart and lung. We learn to 'give our word'; we strive so that our speech may be true. This is expressed in the words of Christ, "I am the Truth."

The achievement in coordination during the third year culminates in saying "I" to ourselves, in becoming conscious of self, and in the beginning of thinking. This is a more subtle, inward process. We become aware of the separation between self and world; for we can only say "I" to ourselves, if we feel separate from our surroundings. It is the beginning of a process that will lead a child ever increasingly to ask questions, to inquire, to search. But will our thinking be lively enough? This mobility, this movement in thinking will become a central concern in the learning process, especially later, when after the change of teeth, the academic work truly begins. Archetypally one might apply the words of Christ, "I am the life."

It is worth pondering that the mystery of each individual's first three years[2] is reflected in the words of Christ, "I am the Way, the Truth and the Life." And this contemplation can help us to understand more deeply the development of the young child; but all three — walking, speaking, thinking — issue forth out of movement. A path has to be trodden, a truth has to be found; and life itself only exists because of constant transformation.

Teachers and educators might also wish to consider how their remedial work is connected with some of the deepest experiences that every child goes through during its first three years on earth.[3]

---

1   René Querido, *The Wonder of Childhood: Stepping into Life.*
2   Audrey E. McAllen, *The Extra Lesson,* see Foreword by Claartje Wijnbergh.
3   Karl König, *The First Three Years of the Child.*

Birth to Seven Years

Audrey E. McAllen

Kindergarten teachers report that they are receiving questions from parents about the stages between birth to seven years and their incomplete development. They ask: "May the exercises in *The Extra Lesson* be used in kindergarten?"

An answer to this question could begin by stating that this arrested development which teachers are observing is due, in the main, to the modern trend which makes parents demand *too much, too soon* from the child. He is not allowed to mature at his own pace. For example, he is lifted into verticality too early for too long of periods of time. He is helped to stand, given a baby walker, tricycle, etc., and is asked too many questions involving him making decisions. All this calls the formative forces away from their bodily work and produces an intellectual age/ability in advance of his chronological age, e.g., a three and a half year old with a five-year-old IQ.

The delayed development between five and seven years, the growth into the legs, the uniting of the will forces, etc., may be seen as linked to the premature help onto the legs at the learning to walk stage with, of course, other factors playing in.

These developmental lags cannot be put right in the kindergarten by any form of 'exercise'. *The Extra Lesson* remediation is *only* for the class teaching and upper school period. Parents should not expect anything like this in Waldorf kindergartens.

The kindergarten heals by helping the child to regain his dream consciousness stage from which he has been pushed out too soon. The kindergarten allows the formative forces to go back to their proper functioning in completing, as well as they are allowed, their bodily work.

Developmental problems from birth to seven years can be seen through *The Extra Lesson* educational assessment after about seven years, nine months when full coordination is completed. Only then can the Extra Lesson teacher intervene. The class teacher in class one should be giving appropriate help for the completion of this stage of development.

Margret Meyerkort, in the article 'For Kindergarten Teachers', shows how the stages of spatial orientation, handedness and body geography should be cultivated in a kindergarten situation.

Kindergarten teachers should resist all parental pressures for specialized activities, and tactfully suggest a change in parental attitudes to allow the healing forces of our kindergarten to exert their maximum healing powers. Parents can become involved by being reminded that *imitative activities of the household and traditional childhood games help educate the developing young child on many levels.*[1]

---

1   John Thomson, *Natural Childhood*, guides parents from the birth of their child through age seven. Beautifully illustrated in full-color, this book offers: practical exercises in listening for good communication; games and activities for the whole family; and projects in creative and cooperative play, stimulating the imagination of the growing child.

Movement in the Earliest Years

Joan Caldarera

Children with certain weaknesses: limp limbs; sitting with legs to either side, like a 'W'; lack of imitation; inability to play; hitting and pinching; inability to pay attention or focus. The list is an increasingly familiar one that each Kindergarten teacher who was present at the Wednesday afternoon meeting with Audrey McAllen during the conference could add to from her own experience. Miss McAllen asked us to compile this list to launch into the main topic of her informal talk, that the proportion of children with such weaknesses is growing, and that there is one major cause.

The prime contributing factor in the burgeoning of these early childhood problems, according to Miss McAllen, is one that goes right to the heart of the conference theme: *lack of proper movement in the earliest months and years.* She reminded us of how often babies are forced into premature stages, receiving too much help when trying to sit on their own, to stand, and then *gradually* to walk, so that there is no real activity in the children's own limbs. These children, lacking the proper earliest movements, have not been able to use their muscles and senses sufficiently when standing, walking and speaking. We as teachers have to deal with this.

Miss McAllen emphasized that the head of the young child is in a dream state while the limb system is used and made skillful, but there is a danger in keeping children too long excarnated in this dream state. The child *wants* to be here in his limbs — in his will.

It was also pointed out that the self-education of the child through what can be called the culture of early childhood is no longer available for the child as it was earlier. Children no longer spontaneously play the traditional seasonal games. Now they need to be given games, finger-plays, etc. *This is an important task of the Kindergarten teacher.*

The Kindergarten teacher was further enjoined to give children worthy examples of balanced adults moving in the proper way, for young children are building their physical bodies through the imitation of what they are experiencing around them.[1] If our posture is cramped, the children imitate that *inner gesture* subconsciously. There was a question of teachers using child-sized tables and chairs, which is a practice Miss McAllen sees as unnatural and perhaps detrimental (except for the chiropractors!). The picture was advanced of the child looking up to the teacher, rather than on a level as to a peer.

Miss McAllen suggested that a gymnast in the Kindergarten, (trained in Spatial Dynamics[2]) moving with harmonious movements with the children, might be most helpful. This idea, giving Kindergarten children time for imitation of harmonious movements with a gymnast, as well as with a eurythmist, brought some comment from those in attendance.

There were many questions and some lively discussion, but two topics in particular might be mentioned here. The first had to do with the teacher's observation of the young child. Miss McAllen suggested that a teacher take two or three days to see how a few children walk, doing so very thoroughly, looking at the shoes to see how they are worn and so on. Make a formal list and check it off, so as to build up a picture to compare with one's imagined picture of the child. In this way, one could work on one's ability to observe, as delineated in 'Practical Training of Thought'.[3] Concepts of Anthroposophy, she counseled, awaken and enliven one's observation, producing in one a practical 'New Yoga' of the sense of sight. Our weakness is in connecting perceptions with pieces of knowledge. When these come together, there can be inspiration from the realm of the angels informing the Kindergarten teacher in their work with the young child.

The other subject was the use of *block crayons versus stick crayons* in the kindergarten, and the use of *black and brown crayons*. Miss McAllen spoke of the invention of the block crayons, which were intended for the use of students from fourth grade onwards for special drawing effects. With their more extensive use in the lower grades and the kindergarten has come a muddling up of what is painting and what is drawing. Blocks, she said, require a grabbing, cramping motion of the hand, over-emphasizing the gravity aspect (in contrast to the 'levity' aspect),[4] and can lead to later bad habits in how the hand grasps the pencil for writing. (Kindergarten teachers would benefit from studying the development of the hand grasp.) She also said that she is "not afraid of black" and finds its use valuable for the children (ravens, beetles, cats, obsidian and other natural objects are black). Brown is necessary as the archetypal tree color.

The above is a report on Audrey McAllen's speech to Kindergarten Teachers in February 1989, during a West Coast Teacher's Conference.

1   Rudolf Steiner, *The Human Heart*, Lecture May 26, 1922.
2   Jaimen McMillan is co-director of the School for Bothmer Gymnastics in Stuttgart (Germany) and director of Spatial Dynamics Institute, Inc., which offers conferences and workshops on the movement and spatial development of the child; its five-year in-service training program certifies movement education teachers and movement therapists for Waldorf schools and related institutions. For information, contact SDI, 129 Hayes Road, Schuylerville, NY 12871, tel (518) 695-6377, fax (518) 695-6955, sdioffice@earthlink.net, www.spacialdynamics.com.
3   R. Steiner, *Anthroposophy in Everyday Life*, 'Practical Training of Thought'.
4   See Audrey E. McAllen, Section I, 'Twofold Man as Archetype'.

Suggestions for Interviewing Parents

Marion Kerney & Sally Templer

Before sharing with us her experience of teaching children with learning difficulties and of the facts required at an interview, Audrey McAllen reminded us of the situation of the child's incarnation as a spiritual being:

The child leaves the womb head first. In this direction is mirrored the connection of the soul/spirit with the earth planet. The head and the planet go through metamorphoses, one stage to the next. The head is the result of one's past life; the earth is the result of the Old Moon incarnation. Everything else in the body is newly created. It is the picture of the heavens, of stars and planets, the working of the world of the Hierarchies in which we have been living prior to birth. This is archetypal, common to all human beings. The formative forces of the child also contain this cosmic pattern worked out and individualized, and he has the task of uniting it with the pattern of the physical body in its objective form presented to him by the stream of heredity. This is accomplished while the child's formative forces — streaming from the head — are in the protection of the mother's etheric body from which the child's formative forces will emerge at the change of teeth. This twofold head-trunk picture of the human being — the physical body[1] — is the basis of the development of the consciousness soul. This is the soul member which develops between the 35th and 42nd year; this soul member gives the Ego the ability to recognize itself as a spiritual being and to recognize that the same Spirit who created this body is working in the world around us.[2] That the birth of this soul member takes place in a healthy manner is the responsibility of the Kindergarten Movement.

In the child, the unifying process between the head and the cosmos starts as soon as the contractions of the birth process begin. Through the sense of touch, which extends over the whole body of the child, the nerves from the periphery of his body stimulate the brainstem during the passage through the birth canal. This brain stem is the center from which the brain becomes organized, and so can send its formative forces back into the body, forming it according to its destiny.

If the mother has had an epidural injection, or if she has taken drugs during labor, this process is weakened. It is one of the factors which can hinder healthy development of motor skills.[3] We need to know if the labor has been very long or very quick, or if at the end of labor there was a sudden expulsion. The long labor may result in oxygen deprivation; the sudden expulsion may result in compression of the skull onto the neck bones, inhibiting the coordination of the building up of the movement response patterning of the brain. These babies are the ones who often cry for no apparent reason. If this is in the birth history, it is advisable to ask the mother to have the child checked by a cranial osteopath, as we are finding children with motor and learning problems which have been caused by this kind of birth. Another cause we see is 'accidents' — rolling off the changing table, falling out of the high-chair, banging the head against the table leg, unexpectedly stepping backward from a chair or table, etc. — in other words, falls which take the child by surprise. Broken noses, broken jaws — even a broken arm — can result in displaced neck bones impeding the brainstem in its coordinating function with the brain. Thumb-sucking, where the thumb is pushed right into the mouth as far as it will go, is often a sign that there is trouble in this realm. The child is trying to relieve pressure by sucking the thumb. These subtle injuries are not readily recognized, so it has been the work of cranial osteopaths who have greatly helped in this area.[4]

Babies nowadays have no period of 'recuperation' after the strenuous journey down the birth canal. Once upon a time, it was considered necessary to keep babies quiet and protected for the first six weeks after birth. This allowed any subtle injuries from a long labor, brain cells possibly affected by lack of oxygen, etc., to heal, for unaffected brain cells can take over for any damaged ones — so the latest neurological research has discovered. Hence, the wisdom in our grandmothers' time of the forty day interval of seclusion before baby was presented to the world at his christening at six weeks of age!

The next things we need to know are: was there severe baby jaundice? Did the child shuffle on his bottom instead of crawling? Many children with learning difficulties have this in their life history. If crawling, i.e., moving while stretched out on his tummy, or creeping on hands and knees, has been missed, immature movement responses may still be present. These are normal reflexes in the baby when he is a 'whole' before head-trunk differentiation takes place. We have all seen how, when the baby turns his head, the arm he looks at extends and the other arm contracts. This disappears as he starts the crawling and creeping activity. If this movement response remains, then his free movement is impeded by the body forcing this reaction which subtly blocks his intended movement. Motor coordination, writing and copying problems result, not to mention the difficulty of doing eurythmy. It has also been found that antibiotics can cause a yeast allergy which can produce a return of already integrated movement responses.

Information coming to light in research through the study of children's drawings is that the last stage of the first seven years of development is so often incomplete, i.e., the five to seven stage of growth into the limbs — into the will. Too many drawings remain at the four to five year old stage (body, arms and legs) and do not progress to the threefold figure, where the neck and waist are delineated and the limbs extend from the lower trunk. It would seem that this arrested development at the four-year stage may be due to the interference that modern parents make in 'getting the child on': helping him to sit up, so that he does not have to practice pulling himself up and flopping back and trying again; playpens where he hangs over the edge gazing, instead of creeping and staggering around; and the use of walkers, baby bouncers and reins, the use of which inhibit the child's normal movement development. All these 'good' intentions mean that the movement and balance systems are not being fully developed, and that the five to seven year old child does not grow properly into the legs as this has not been prepared at the earlier stage. In many instances, incomplete coordination causes reactions that are patterned so that eventually the child becomes 'nervous', won't run along a wall, is afraid of steps, etc.

These are some of the reasons why we need to ask such questions about the first years so that we can compensate and allow the child to re-experience in play activity those things which have been denied to him by the current fashion in child upbringing.

These remarks by Audrey McAllen were made at a regional Kindergarten conference in England and are reprinted from the magazine of the Kindergarten movement in England courtesy of their Editor, Stella Jurmen.

---

1   See Audrey E. McAllen, Section I, 'Physical Body as Archetype of Man's Spiritual Being'.
2   Rudolf Steiner, *An Outline of Esoteric Science*.
3   Jane Field, *Vicious Circle*.
4   See Elizabeth Hayden, Section II, 'Osteopathy for Children'.
5   See Dee J. Coulter, Section II, 'An Immature Movement Pattern which Interferes with Reading'.

For Kindergarten Teachers

Margret Meyerkort

The Remedial Research Group for learning problems at Rudolf Steiner College received requests from kindergarten teachers asking for guidance as to ways in which they could help the pre-school child — aware now as they are that the causes of learning difficulties are connected with the development stages of the first seven years.

The Research Group contacted Audrey McAllen and she arranged a meeting, in England, with her, myself and Amelie Firman who is active in kindergarten teacher training. Margaret Duberley, another experienced kindergarten teacher was also present. The following is a report of this meeting.

Audrey McAllen gave us a summary of the development of the first seven years from a 'learning disorder' point of view, that is, spatial development, immature movement responses, the ambidextrous stage, good body image and coordination.[1]

As a basis for further work we are looking together at the Old Saturn evolution and the beginning of the Earth period from Rudolf Steiner's book *An Outline of Esoteric Science*[2] Meanwhile, I suggest that kindergarten teachers should look at the following aspects in relation to *spatial development*.

The first step in this direction is the coordination of eye, hand and ear which develops when the baby, lying on its back, follows the mother's movements in the room; when the baby turns the head in the directions of sounds; when the hand reaches out for objects. Sight, hand and ear are stimulated in every variety of combinations by what is happening around the tiny child.

For this reason, it is important that the baby should have the experience of rolling over to the tummy and onto the right and left sides, from lying on the back, so that the full range of the muscular system is activated and used. This prepares for the momentous moment when standing upright takes place and full movement exploration in space begins.

We have to be awake to gadgets which prevent children from having the experience and awareness that they need during the toddler stage. By gadgets, I mean guiding reins, push trikes, walking aids. Mother holding on to the reins 'rescues' the child from falling; in doing so, she disturbs the balance sense which comes into play as he topples over, or staggers quite normally from left and right to keep his upright position. Every step a human being takes establishes the balance between left and right, overcoming the extremes. We deprive the child of these experiences when he sits and pushes himself around the room on a trike or in a push car. Children need to walk. It is in walking that laterality establishes itself. Today, they do too little walking. How good it is to see kindergarten buildings set well back away from the road entrance of the school, so that the children can get out of the car and walk along a path to meet their teacher. Here, too, this can work both ways, as it gives the teacher an opportunity to see how the child walks and steps on the earth, how he places his body into gravity.

Walking in every variety of terrain geometricises the bodily organs which are still growing and being formed. Children like to jump — here above-below — up-down is brought into play. Let them jump *into* puddles, across them, jump down from walls, walk along branches and swing on branches. A homemade seesaw, a branch over a log, make the senses active, as eye, hand, leg, all have to adjust to the irregular movements.

Another activity for movement forward and back is walking in mud, barefooted or in rubber boots according to place and season. Children need to feel resistance to their movement. Walking in water, of course, does the same. See that children have many pieces of irregularly shaped branches — not blocks. Each piece of wood could have an end cut or sawn so that it can stand firmly. The children have to move about, crouch, lie on the tummy when building with these. They have to peer in the building, they have to make judgments in relation to space and gravity: Will it fit? Will it fall if I put another log on top? Eye and hand have to coordinate with these judgments.

The foundation for development of spatial orientation is natural bodily movements, and we teachers have to keep our eyes open to see what nature offers us. Nature is full of opportunities if we are alert enough to recognize them. For example, when it is autumn and the gardens are full of leaves, let the children rake them together with their hands, let them have sacks and, holding the sack in the left hand, put the handfuls of leaves into it with the right hand, a left-right movement *across the vertical midline*; this also leads the older child through the ambidextrous stage. Using a wheelbarrow, for example, to collect leaves is too static, too easy, too mechanical. So, gather your apples in baskets. If loads are heavy, have a bag with a string top and let the child put it on himself like a haversack, so that he experiences behind and before as he walks along. It is better, too, for girls to carry their dolls in an arm sling, rather than always in a pram. With the sling support, the child has the doll's head resting on the left arm, and the right arm is free to move and arrange the doll's clothes. Here, a consciousness of left and right is unobtrusively begun.

Let children jump into the piles of leaves they have gathered, experience them from down below as they crawl into the piles, the scrunching and crackling awakening the hearing. In summer, in drought, big cracks appear — let the child see how far their arms go into them. Let them be a 'Rumpelstiltskin', plunging a foot into the crack. Roll snow balls, larger and larger, in the winter. As they get bigger and bigger, the body has to orientate to them differently.

Kindergarten teachers need to develop a 'seeing' of what is there, to take hold of the opportunity and bring to the child the experiences his growing body needs.

---

1   Audrey E. McAllen, *The Extra Lesson*.
2   See A. E. McAllen, Section I, 'Physical Body As Archetype Of Man's Spiritual Being'.

ON FIRST GRADE READINESS

Margret Meyerkort

In class assessments, it has been found that a number of children are too young for their classes. For example, the etheric body is only just consolidating its birth while the rest of the class is comfortably in the nine-year change. This is seen in certain motifs in the children's assessment drawings. It was noted that these children have entered class one when their sixth birthdays were from May to September or October. Indications that children are 'school ripe' in the kindergarten from my observations that have been made in the course of my forty plus years of work with kindergarten children, can be grouped according to:

1. Physiological readiness, that takes the period of seven years and nine months.
2. Readiness in the etheric realm — the gradual birthing of the three stages of the child's etheric body from that of the mother's etheric body.
3. The first delicate appearances of soul phenomena, which we begin to sense as the above stages progress.

PHYSIOLOGICAL READINESS

a. After three plus years of age, the formative forces are at work on the middle system. As this stage completes itself (five plus years), we can observe how the waist and neck become definite. This is an indication showing the border of the rhythmical system situated below the head and above the waist. Here, we have confirmation that there is a *physiological readiness of the middle system* for the artistic education which we shall give between seven and fourteen years.

b. The *stretching of the legs* (the arms lengthen earlier in conjunction with the rhythmic system) occurs between five and seven years nine months and provides the basis for the will forces for the young person after puberty, when education will be directed to the thinking. With the growth into the legs comes the individualizing of the face and the loosening of the teeth.[1]

c. Being able to touch the ear with the opposite hand while the arm is resting on the head and reaching to *take hold of the ear lobe* is the third physiological growth sign of maturity.

Birth of the Etheric Body

The birth of the etheric body, that is:

a. The emancipation of the child's etheric body from that of the mother. This also has three stages: first the head is freed at approximately three years, then the middle system at five plus and lastly the legs at seven plus years.

b. During the last stage, five to seven years, we see two new things happening. The child begins to *eat more in quantity*. The etheric body, as it is being born, becomes individualized into the legs and brings this change in eating. The child develops an awareness of the metabolism which is expressed in the tummy-aches which are now noticed by the child at this stage.

c. The *element of time* which belongs to the etheric body expresses itself in the way a child can individualize himself in the group by slowing down or speeding up his singing or speaking of the verse. The group may be singing a song, "Mulberry Bush" or, "All on a frosty morning" and one child will gabble it, "Allonafrostymorning," and stand and smile triumphantly looking around, while the rest are completing it together in its rhythm. The opposite also happens, the group finishes and one child plods on with the end of the line, solo.

d. In drawing, the individualizing element of the birth of the etheric body shows itself by the *use of the diagonal line*, the ladder leaning against the tree, the stairs going up inside the house, the appearance of the arching rainbow, and the hill with a well or house on it. It takes at least until seven years and nine months for these processes to consolidate, so we should not jump to the conclusion that the process is finished when these symbols first appear!

The Beginning of Soul Life

a. As the physical growth enters the limbs, so the head begins to awaken and we have the first intimation of the thinking element. A kind of logic appears. In speaking, this shows itself in the use of new words, "You do this *because*." "Therefore" and "if" enter the vocabulary. The word "so" is often used instead of "because."

b. In creative play, string is used now for tying things together. 'Logic', *one thing after the next* (not yet true cause and effect thinking which arrives at about age 12) appears.

c. *Friendships* now begin. As children play together, an authoritative element comes, "You be the horse; I'll hold the reins." There is a *giving and receiving of authority* between the players. One child likes to mediate between two younger rivals: "You give it to him," the mediating child may command. Consciousness is entering into the will, reflecting the limb growth. A child may set himself an *aim in his play*. The sand castle is no longer built for itself as a castle, but so that a car can go through it. What was instinct-desire, now becomes directed will. The children begin to *play with words*; they find inconsequential rhymes — muddle, duddle, etc. They start using numbers as words — note how traditional rhymes and songs reflect this stage, as in "One, two, buckle your shoe."

d. We must let this new stage settle down before we ask the child to do daily tasks. He is not ready for this new capacity until *after he is six years old*. Then he may run errands, collect things together, for now with the soul-element glimmering, he can enjoy being helpful.

e. The soul expresses its advent in whispering — it still is something which keeps itself hidden. The child talks about *dreams*. He likes to *make and give surprises* — he likes to hide so that you can't find him. It is the time when he starts to want to *give presents* — and to make the presents with you. Riddles, guessing, getting the giggles, all presage the maturity of his bodily development. He feels the future dawning, the new stage coming, he says, "I hope...."

---

1   Rudolf Steiner, *The Kingdom of Childhood*, pp. 23-27.

"Linked by a common goal well beyond us, only then are we breathing. And this shared experience teaches us that to love is not to look at one another, but to look together in the same direction."

— *Antoine de Saint Exupéry*

VIII

On Left-Handedness

An Interview with Else Göttgens

Audrey E. McAllen

Audrey McAllen: The findings of neuropsychology more and more confirm Rudolf Steiner's pedagogical insights. Drs. Goebel and Glöckler's book for parents on bringing up children[1] contains a chapter on left-handedness, giving the essential reasons for the need to write with the right hand, reiterating with modern research the indications by Rudolf Steiner on this matter. Will you share with us your experiences of putting this into practice, namely *how left-handed children should learn to write with the right hand?*

Else Göttgens: One of the most vital things is that, on the first day in Class One, the children are told that people all have a writing hand and a drawing hand. With some people, the same hand is both the writing and drawing hand, and with other people, they use different hands. Then, using one's authority as a teacher, one says, "The hand on this side," indicating one's writing hand (right side of the body) "is our writing hand, and you shall *all* learn to write with this hand, and we are going to start right now...." The teacher introduces the straight line and the curved line, telling the children, "Later on, we shall find these lines in writing." When they first start to draw the straight line and the curve, it is good that they *all* hold something beautiful in the left hand — a flower or a crystal.

The importance of using the right hand for handwriting should be made clear to parents at the initial interview and suitable literature references given them.[2] The parents should support the process described here.

If the parents are convinced their child is left-handed and not ambidextrous, tell them that this will be checked with educational and medical assessment. In the meantime, ask them to observe, over a period of three weeks, exactly how many times the child uses his *left* hand, and for what tasks, and note this down. They should also note when he uses his *right* hand, and when and for what he uses his *left* foot. The same observations can be made for his *right* foot as well. Observing how he listens is also important. The observations are to be exact. They can be given a book in which to record their observations. The class teacher must make similar observations and records in the classroom and at play time. All these observations will be required at the medical/pedagogical conference with the parents.[3]

After this period of observation and the appropriate tests, the consultation with the parents, doctor and class teacher takes place. *If it is seen that the child consistently uses left hand, foot, eye and ear he is only required to learn to write with his right hand; for all other activities, he may use his left hand, leg and eye.* The parents are given every opportunity to ask their questions, share their concerns and give their input. If they still do not agree with the process, the teacher may ask them to give it some more thought before they make their final decision. *The teacher should only follow through with having the child write with the right hand if the parents are supportive.*

Audrey McAllen: Parents who have the true left-hander may say that what you suggest will leave him cross-lateral and produce the likelihood of learning problems.

Else Göttgens: This is a mistaken concept. Writing is a learned skill, and one is no more making a child cross-lateral by writing than by expecting him to play scales with the right hand when he is learning the piano. The right-hander acquires many skills with his left hand without causing problems, so a skill where the left-handed child uses the right hand is the same requirement.

If assessment shows the child has unconfirmed dominance (cross or mixed laterality), he is given the appropriate therapy and remedial exercises to make him thoroughly at home in the right side of his body.

Secondly, during this time (and after), the teacher must be aware of the child all the time. He must put the left-handed children temporarily in the front row where he can see them, and in a friendly way insist that they do all their writing with the right hand. *When there is resistance on some days because a child is tired, give him some drawing task to do instead — with which he can use his left hand. To anticipate and guard against fatigue is most important.* Ambidextrous children will change from using the right to using the left hand when tired, and parents often consider this a sign of left-handedness. It is better for Mother to have 'fun' feeding him than to allow him to use his left hand when eating.

The above interview came about during a teachers conference in Eindhoven, The Netherlands. (ed)

---

1   Michaela Glöckler and Wolfgang Goebel, *A Guide to Child Health.*
2   M. Glöckler, 'Aspects of Left-Handedness', from *Developmental Insights*, David Mitchell, ed., p. 273.
3   In conferences with teachers, Rudolf Steiner gave indications for having left-handed children use the right hand especially for writing. See *Faculty Meetings with Rudolf Steiner,* sessions of May 10, 1922 and May 25, 1923.

Rudolf Steiner's Indication for Confirming Dominance

Audrey E. McAllen

To serve the needs of the children of the present time, the following is an extension of indications given by Rudolf Steiner in the conferences for teachers and eurythmists. *For children seven to ten years old:* The child should stand with his feet slightly apart for good balance and with his arms at his sides. The teacher then places a *blue* cloth on her own index finger and when she moves it, the child follows the movement with his eyes. The blue-covered index finger is brought to the *left* shoulder and *slowly* travels down the child's arm to his left hand and fingertips, and then back up his hand and arm to his shoulder. The child relaxes his eyes a moment, then this movement is repeated twice more, always moving slowly and steadily down the child's arm and back to the starting place. With a *red* cloth on the teacher's finger, follow the above directions moving from the child's *right* shoulder and slowly traveling down his arm to his right hand and fingertips and back up his hand and arm to his shoulder — three times altogether on the right side, as well.

The following version is a strengthened form of the previous exercise. It can also be used if the pupil has a *tendency to be ambidextrous or lacks fully established dominance.* With a child from ten years, the teacher should still do the movement with the colored cloth.

Start with the child extending his *left* arm straight in front of him. The teacher places her index finger with a *blue* cloth gently on the child's left shoulder, and *slowly* travels down his arm to his hand and fingertips and back again; same as above. The child returns his arm to his side to relax it. Repeat this twice more, relaxing between each movement and the following one. Next, the same *left* arm is extended out to the side at shoulder height and the same movement is done three times, relaxing between movements. Last, the *left* arm is placed alongside the body and the same movement is done three times, relaxing between movements. After the sequence is completed on the left side, it is repeated on the *right* side, with a *red* cloth on the teacher's index finger following in the same order and the same number of times, relaxing between movements. The child's *eyes always focus* on the index fingers during all of the movements.

After age eleven, the older child should use his own index fingers and place them on his own shoulders *without any colors*. Start with the child extending his *left* arm straight in front of him. He places his *right index finger* on his left shoulder, and *slowly* travels down his arm to his hand and fingertips and back again. The child returns his arms to his sides to relax them. Repeat this twice more, relaxing between each movement and the following one. Next, the same *left* arm is extended out to the side at shoulder height and the same movement is done three times, relaxing between movements. Last, the *left* arm is placed alongside the body and the same movement is done three times, relaxing between movements. After the sequence is completed on the left side, it is repeated on the *right* side, with the child's *left index finger* following in the same order and the same number of times, relaxing between movements. The child's *eyes always focus* on the index fingers during all of the movements.

Confirming Dominance with a Child

Melinda Turner

The following report concerns confirming the dominance of a fourteen-year-old female student — Annmarie, a quiet, thoughtful, gentle child. Annmarie does not go to school but is home-schooled. At the time of this report, exercises from Audrey McAllen's book *The Extra Lesson* had been given weekly for ten months.[1]

Background Information

Details of birth: Two weeks after the due date, labor (which was very long) was induced. The after-birth (placenta) was broken up. The mother was advised not to have more children, so she didn't.

Annmarie is an only child and attended two different state schools and one private one before 'giving up'. Her parents undertook to educate her at home when she was thirteen years old. (This is a legal right in Britain.) They knew something about Steiner education and considered it for awhile, but it would have meant too much upheaval, including moving to get her into a Steiner/Waldorf school.

Assessment

The Extra Lesson Handedness Pattern Assessment[2] showed a fairly strong indication that Annmarie was right-footed, right-handed, right-eyed (it was noted that she could not close her right eye muscularly), and left-eared. She wrote with her left hand and did most tasks left-handed, except cutting with scissors.

Lesson Progress Report

After seven months of fairly solid Extra Lesson work, I discovered that she was still writing with her left hand for her math and English lessons while doing lessons with me she used her right hand. She quietly challenged me a few times about why it would be better if she wrote with her right hand. It forced me to think about the whole subject more deeply. One suggestion I gave her was that in order to get the information from her mind to her hands, there was some rather complicated 'wiring'. And that, partly due to the difficulties of her birth, this wiring had become 'twisted'. By doing the exercises and changing over to her right hand, she would be 'unraveling' the twists and allowing everything to flow more smoothly and efficiently.

Annmarie must have digested this picture I gave her, for one day, following the Copper Ball exercise, she offered a picture herself (while drawing the Moving Straight Line and Lemniscate exercise[3]), "It is like when you've got several blankets on your bed," she said, "and during the night some get pushed down toward your feet, and the only way to sort it all out is to fold back all the blankets to your feet and peel them back towards you one at a time." I think she understood what I had been trying to explain.

Soon after, I told her it was now up to her to make that extra effort. Her parents and I had done all we could; the rest was up to her. She immediately took up the challenge, and the following week proudly told me that she had used her right hand every time for writing. A week or two later she commented that she now noticed that she was not so lazy. Whereas before she may have wanted to do something, then couldn't be bothered, now she just gets on with it and does it. I was very moved when she said that and suggested that this was a blessing for all her hard work. She really seemed at peace with herself.

She has continued to write with her right hand since mid-January, although I think there are several tasks she does unconsciously with her left hand (e.g., lighting a candle). I have slowly suggested that she become more aware of other tasks, for example, unlocking the front door with a key.[4]

Annmarie's parents are pleased. They noticed an improvement in her ability to remember things and to concentrate. Her confidence improved too. She is not so shy and withdrawn in company. Annmarie herself noted several improvements in her scholastic ability.

Annmarie also received monthly treatment from a cranial osteopath for about eight months. The osteopath recently sent me a report. Briefly, he found overall compression at the base of the skull, poor circulation of the cerebro-spinal fluid, and inflexibility in the vault of her head and in her facial bones, particularly around the eyes and nose. (She is a mouth breather, although this is much less marked now.) Although Annmarie is still not fully established in the use of her right hand, I will be seeing her once a month for the next few months.

About herself, the author writes: I work full-time as an optometrist and in my spare time have taken on the Extra Lesson work with two children in the last two years. I have always been interested in remedial work, having come across the American optometrists' approach during my studies in Australia.

---

1   See Lalage Craig, Section III, 'David's Story — A High School Student'.
2   Audrey E. McAllen, *The Extra Lesson*, pp. 42-51.
3   Ibid., pp. 147-150.
4   Julio B. de Quiros and Orlando L. Schrager, *Neuropsychological Fundamentals in Learning Disabilities*, Chapter Three, Sections 17-20; see A. E. McAllen, Section II, 'Comments and Extracts'.

Confirming Dominance with an Adult

Mary Ellen Willby

The following letter was addressed to the Remedial Research Group:

> To Whom It May Concern:
>
> I am 34 years old and until recently I have used my left hand to do almost everything. About three months ago I had a strong urge to write with my right hand. I have continued to do so and since then I have also begun eating with the right hand. What has developed is a conscious effort to try to do as much as possible with the right hand.
>
> Is it possible at my age to be able to 'change to the right side'? I am still in an awkward stage with all of this. What is the definite reason for right-handedness?[1]
>
> Any help that any of you could give or any advice that you have would be greatly appreciated. The strange thing about all of this is: I need to know, but what it is I need to know has not been revealed yet....

In response to this letter, the Remedial Research Group sent Gerda Hueck's *The Problem of Left-Handedness*, and Audrey McAllen's *The Extra Lesson*, with suggestions by the writer for a program of exercises from *The Extra Lesson*, to accompany the efforts already under way. Some weeks later, the letter below was received.

> I am so very grateful for what you have shared with me. There has already been a big change in my life and it's only beginning! The Copper Ball Exercise[2] seems to be so mild, yet I find that the movements have a powerful effect on the body as well as on the spiritual being. I am keeping a little journal to record certain things that occur so that it can be used as a reference in the future. I will keep in touch. Thank you so much....

Four months later, Elizabeth (not her real name) called on the telephone to share her progress. Here is a transcription of her conversation with the writer:

Elizabeth: I just had to call you to tell you how wonderful I feel and how I am progressing in confirming dominance to my right side.

Mary E. Willby: Yes, how is it going?

Elizabeth: Well, I do most everything with my right hand, except I still find I sometimes want to eat with my left.

Mary E. Willby: That sounds reasonable. Anything else you are noticing?

Elizabeth: My way of speaking has changed. I'm more open, not so one-sided, not so closed in.

Mary E. Willby: Could you elaborate on that a little more, please?

Elizabeth: Now let me see; my understanding has grown, my whole life has enlarged, changed. I'm happier, my thinking has changed. It isn't the same closed-minded pattern it used to be. I mean, I used to see things in a certain way and only in that way. I was closed off to a wider viewpoint. I'm more useful now to my family and others. My attitude has changed; I'm very positive now. I still occasionally feel some resistance, but I wouldn't give up the effort because I feel so much better.

Mary E Willby: When do you especially feel resistance?

Elizabeth: When brushing my teeth or when writing — something in me doesn't want to do it.

Mary E. Willby: Have you been doing the exercises from *The Extra Lesson*?

Elizabeth: Yes. The exercises have helped me tremendously. I feel so peaceful after doing them. It's a subtle feeling, but I feel so positive doing them. The Extra Lesson exercises have opened the door for me. My family is as happy as I am about these changes, and I wish to express my gratitude for all your support and help.

---

1   A. A. Tomatis, *Education and Dyslexia;* in Chapter Seven, Dr. Tomatis considers right-handedness an essential element in attaining full human stature; Michaela Glöckler and Wolfgang Goebel, *A Guide to Child Health.*

2   Audrey E. McAllen, *The Extra Lesson,* pp. 122-126.

Glossary

The Terms —Primordial Creative Beings; the Gods; the Hierarchies; all embrace the following:

Rudolf Steiner's Usage	Christian Terminology
Holy Trinity: the Father, Son & Holy Spirit	
Spirits of Strength	**1st Hierarchy**
Spirits of Love	Seraphim
Spirits of Harmony	Cherubim
Spirits of Will	Thrones
Spirits of Light	**2nd Hierarchy**
Spirits of Wisdom	Kyriotetes/Dominions
Spirits of Movement	Dynamis/Mights
Spirits of Form	Exusiai/Powers/7 Biblical Elohim
Spirits of Soul	**3rd Hierarchy**
Spirits of Personality	Archai/Principalities
Spirits of Fire	Archangeloi/Archangels
Spirits of Life	Angeloi/Angels

Twofold Man: "I have often said that man is a twofold being. He is a being composed of many more than two parts; but particularly is he a twofold being, and consists as such of head and the rest of the body."

— Rudolf Steiner
"Anthroposophical Life-Gifts" April 1, 1918

The Human Being - Ninefold Man

The "I" or ego is the core of the human being membered into this organization. According to context it is differentiated into higher and lower ego. The task of this "I" or ego is to transform the bodily members in order that it can live consciously in its highest organization.

Spirit Members	Spirit Man
	Life Spirit
	Spirit Self
Soul Members	Consciousness (Spiritual) Soul
	Intellectual (Mind) Soul
	Sentient Soul
Body Members	Astral Body
	Etheric (Ethereal) Body
	Physical Body

Faculties of Astral Body — Consciousness & Form (Patterns)
Faculties of Etheric Body — Growth & Multiplication
Faculties of Physical Body — Mirror for Ego Consciousness

The Body of Formative Forces is a specific enhancement of the etheric body. The term 'Body of Formative Forces' designates an etheric body, which is impregnated by the forces emanating from constellations of the zodiac, which produce in certain combinations, for example, a rose in the plant kingdom or a frog in the animal kingdom. Working as a totality, the zodiacal constellations create the structural and neurological functions of the human body. The planets provide the formative forces for the organs of the constitutional body. (See *An Outline of Esoteric Science* by Rudolf Steiner, Chapter III, pp. 63-64.)

The Terms *Old Saturn, Old Sun, and Old Moon* designate the earlier evolutionary stages of the earth planet.

On Old Saturn, the structural archetype of the human form was laid down.

On Old Sun, the life processes for the constitutional body were added.

On Old Moon, structure and processes were further organized for consciousness to develop.

On the present planet, the principle of the ego was added and self-development becomes possible.

Another aspect: The archetypal structural body of the human being has been formed out of the Imagination, Inspiration and Intuition of the Hierarchies (see 'Twofold Man as Archetype', page 5). This "spiritual physical body is a transparent body of force" and has been rescued from the effects of the fall of humanity into material substance by the death and resurrection of the Christ. Rudolf Steiner uses the term 'the phantom' for this perfected resurrected body (see *From Jesus to Christ*, lectures 6 and 7).

Essential Reading by Rudolf Steiner:

An Outline of Esoteric Science

Theosophy

The Spiritual Guidance of the Individual and of Humanity

A Psychology of Body, Soul and Spirit, especially lectures given on October 23, 25, 26 and 27, 1909.

From Jesus to Christ, lectures 6, 7, 8.

Editor's Afterword

From the many queries received about the *spiral* and *cube* in Audrey McAllen's work, the references below are added as a guide for further study.

Rudolf Steiner:

Apocalypse of St. John, The. AP/RSP 1993, lecture 12. Reference to the New Jerusalem as a Cube.

Balance in the World and Man, The. For reference to the cube, see pp. 30-31, lecture given on November 21, 1914 in Dornach, Switzerland. Left-right currents which appear in the original German were left out of the English translation.

'Calendar of the Soul', *Anthroposophical Quarterly*, Spring 1963, lecture given in Cologne, Germany, May 7, 1912. RSP. Available from Rudolf Steiner Library, New York, London.

Foundations of Esotericism, RSP, London, 1982, p. 81.

Planetary Spheres and Their Influences on Man's Life on Earth and in Spiritual Worlds, all of Lecture 2 and pp. 58-59 of Lecture 3.

Occult Signs and Symbols, lecture 4 given September 16, 1907, AP 1972 (GA 101).

Other authors:

Revelation 21:16. Reference to the New Jerusalem as a cube.

D. J. van Bemmelen, 'The First Goetheanum as a Modern Mystery Temple', published in *Anthroposophical Quarterly* (UK), Vol. 9 #1, RSP, Spring 1964. Available from Rudolf Steiner Library, 65 Fern Hill Rd., Ghent, NY 12075/ Tel (518) 672-7690, Fax (518) 672-5827

Margarete Bockholt-Kirchner, 'A Grail Castle in the Brain', published in *The Golden Blade* (U.K.), 1975.

Callum Coates, *Living Energies: An Exposition of Concepts Related to the Theories of Viktor Schauberger*, Bath, U.K.: Gateway Books, 1996.

Keith Critchlow, *Time Stands Still*. Page 109, regarding the 'Canon of Man' ($12 + 7 = 19$) in relation to the cycle of the year, embodying both Lunar and Solar calendar, pp. 93-94.

Adalbert Graf von Keyserlingk, *The Birth of a New Agriculture*, based on a conference held in 1924 in Koberwitz, Germany. London: Temple Lodge, 1999.

Lawrence Edwards, *The Vortex of Life*, p. 82, pp. 106-134.

Harold Falck-Ytter, *Aurora*, published by Floris Books/AP, 1985. Plate 15, p. 84.

John Fletcher, *Art Inspired by Rudolf Steiner*. Plate 28, 'The Seal of the Holy Grail', executed from a sketch by Rudolf Steiner which includes the cube and spiral.

Liane Collot d'Herbois, *Colour*. Spiral diagrams with text.

Robert Lawlor, *Sacred Geometry*.

R. A. Schwaller de Lubicz, *The Temple in Man*. 'The Canon of Man', 'The Golden Section' (sacred architecture and the perfect man); includes excellent illustrations.

Ernst Marti, *The Four Ethers*. Page 10, Note 21: 12 plus 7; forces of zodiac and planets gives number 19, which is the 'canon' of the human being as temple for the Eternal I.

Sergei O. Prokofieff, *The Spiritual Origins of Eastern Europe and the Future Mysteries of the Holy Grail*. The cube and the New Jerusalem, Part One, Sections 10-12.

Michael S. Schneider, *A Beginner's Guide to Constructing the Universe. The Mathematical Archetypes of Nature, Art and Science, A Voyage from 1 to 10*. The author shows what property makes the spiral a shape that occurs frequently in nature.

Theodore Schwenk, *Sensitive Chaos*. Remarkable photos and drawings of the spiral form in water, inspiring text.

Simon Singh, *Fermat's Last Theorem* (also published as *Fermat's Enigma*). This is the 'biography' of Pythagoras written for the layman with 'asides' for those with the knowledge of mathematics. It is a very readable book and can be recommended to class teachers. The Pythagorean theorem provides the equation which is true of all right-angled triangles and defines the right angle itself. It is the archetype of the structure of three dimensional space (*Last Theorem* p. 19, *Enigma* p. 18). This theorem is the basis of the Right-Angled Triangle Exercise given in *The Extra Lesson*.

Gordon Strachan, *Christ and the Cosmos*. The cube and the New Jerusalem in Chapters One and Two with End Notes and Appendix.

Remedial Teacher Trainings that Include Extra Lesson

For information regarding educational programs for teaching children with specific learning difficulties, contact the following:

AUSTRALIA
The Institute for Learning Difficulties
Graduate Diploma in Educational Studies
(Extra Lesson™)
Lalage Craig and Mariane Judd
P. O. Box 232
Pennant Hills, NSW 2120 AUSTRALIA

www.extralesson.com

lalage.craig@extralesson.com
mariane.judd@extralesson.com
Tel/Fax + 61-2-99807891

BRAZIL
contact: Maria Eugenia Obniski

www.recursoespeciais.com.br

ENGLAND
The Learning Difficulties Course
Gordon Woolard and Cathy Day
105 Plymouth Road
Buckfastleigh
Devon, TQ11 ODB
England, UK

Tel: + 44-1364-644241

GERMANY
Fortbildung für Förder Lehrer
Düsseldorf, GERMANY
contact: Uta Stolz

Tel: + 49-2242-900616
Fax: + 49-2244-900618
LerneninBewegung@t-online.de

HOLLAND
Hogeschool voor Opvoedkunst Helicon
Socrateslaan 22-A
3707 GL Zeist HOLLAND
contact: Joep Eikenboom
extralesson4europe@ilse.nl

www.hhelicon.nl
Tel + 31-30-6937900
Fax + 31-30-6911440
Tel + 31-78-6187815
Fax + 31-78-6315178

HUNGARY
Varázsvirág Egyesület
Hungaria út 23
Budapest 1192 HUNGARY

varazsvirag@yahoo.com
Tel/Fax + 36-26-343-405

SPAIN
Formación en Pedagogía de Apoyo Waldorf
(Dificultades de Aprendizaje)
Apartado 25
28230 Las Rozas (Madrid) SPAIN
Laura Pellico + 34 91-856-82-54
Antonio Adáñez + 34 91-313-22-65

nebreda@hotmail.com
acadanez@yahoo.es

USA
Rudolf Steiner College
Remedial Education Program
Ingun Schneider, director
9200 Fair Oaks Blvd.
Fair Oaks, CA 95628 USA

www.steinercollege.edu
ingun@steinercollege.edu
Tel + 916-961-8727
Fax + 916-961-8731

Sunbridge College
Remedial Education Program
Joan Ingle, co-director
Mary Jo Oresti, co-director
285 Hungry Hollow Road
Spring Valley, NY 10977

www.sunbridge.edu
joaningle@aol.com
mjoresti@aol.com
Tel + 845-425-0055

Assn. for a Healing Education
Mary Jo Oresti
24228 Edgemont Dr.
Southfield, MI 48034

www.healingeducationassociation.org
mjoresti@aol.com

Gradalis Seminars
Therapeutic Education Course
Bonnie River, director
San Jose, CA

www.gradalisway.org
gradalisway@aol.com
Tel + 408-286-7474
Fax + 408-286-7475

For a Current World List of Rudolf Steiner (Waldorf) Schools and Teacher Training Centers:

Bund der Freien Waldorfschulen e.V.
Heidehofstrasse 32
D-70184 Stuttgart
GERMANY

Tel + 711-210-42-0
Fax + 711-210-42-19
bund@waldorfschule.de
www.waldorfschule.de

Association of Waldorf Schools
   of North America (AWSNA)
337 Oak Grove Street
Minneapolis, MN 55409
USA

Tel + 916-961-0927
Fax + 916-961-0715
awsna@awsna.org
www.awsna.org

Steiner Schools Fellowship
Kidbrooke Park, Forest Row
East Sussex, RH18 5JA
UK

Tel + 44-1342-822115
Fax + 44-1342-826004
Mail@waldorf.compulink.co.uk
www.steinerwaldorf.org.uk

The International Extra Lesson Association
This association has chapters in Australia, Europe, and the United States.
www.extralesson.com

BIBLIOGRAPHY AND WORKS CITED

Publishers:
AP   Anthroposophic Press, New York
RSP   Rudolf Steiner Press, London
RSCP   Rudolf Steiner College Press, California
TLP   Temple Lodge Publishing, London

Steiner, Rudolf

Anthroposophical Leading Thoughts, RSP, 1973.

Anthroposophical Life-Gifts, 7 lectures given March 30-May 21, 1918 in Berlin. Transcript available from Rudolf Steiner Library.

Anthroposophy: A Fragment, AP, 1996.

Anthroposophy in Everyday Life, AP, 1995. 'The Four Temperaments', lecture given March 4, 1909; 'Practical Training in Thought', lecture given January 18, 1909.

Apocalypse of St. John, The, AP/RSP, 1993.

Balance in the World and Man, The, three lectures, November 20-22, 1914, Steiner Book Centre, Inc., N. Vancouver, BC, Canada, 1977. (Also published as *The World as the Working of the Product of Balance*, RSP.)

Balance in Teaching, Mercury Press, NY, 1982.

Challenge of the Times, The, AP, 1941.

Cosmic Forces in Man, November 4 to December 24, 1921, lectures given in Christiania, Norway.

Deeper Insights Into Education: The Waldorf Approach, AP, 1983.

East in the Light of the West, The, Garber Communications Inc., NY, 1986.

Education for Adolescents, AP, 1996

Education of the Child, The, RSP, (lecture given January 10, 1907).

Etherization of the Blood, The, RSP, 1971. Lecture given October 1, 1911 in Basel.

Faculty Meetings with Rudolf Steiner, AP 1998. Also published as *Conferences with the Teachers,* given in Stuttgart, Germany, 1919-1920, Steiner Schools Fellowship, Forest Row, East Sussex UK, 1986.

Festivals and their Meaning, The, RSP, 1996.

Foundations of Human Experience, The, AP, 1996. Also published under the title *Study of Man.*

Four Mystery Plays, The, RSP, 1982.

Four Seasons and the Archangels, The, RSP, 1984.

From Jesus to Christ, RSP, 1991.

Gospel of St. John, The, (Kassel), AP, 1982.

Human Heart, The, Mercury Press, 1985.

Initiation, Eternity and the Passing Moment, AP, 1980.

Inner Nature of Man and Our Life between Death and Rebirth, The, RSP, 1994.

Intuitive Thinking as a Spiritual Path (also published under the title *A Philosophy of Freedom*), AP, 1994.

Invisible Man Within Us, The, lecture given February 11, 1923, Dornach, Mercury Press, Spring Valley, NY.

Karmic Relationships, Volumes I - VIII, RSP.

Kingdom of Childhood, The, AP.

Man as a Being of Sense and Perception, AP, 1981 (Archive Edition).

Mission of the Folk Souls, The, RSP, 1970.

Modern Art of Education, A, RSP, 1972.

Meditatively Acquired Knowledge of Man, Steiner Schools Fellowship, UK, 1982. Also published as *Balance in Teaching.*

Metamorphoses of the Soul, RSP, 1983.

Moral Configuration of Man in Sleep, The, lectures November 12-13, 1921, Rudolf Steiner House Library, London, or The Rudolf Steiner Library, 65 Fern Hill Rd., Ghent, NY, 12075.

Mystery of the Universe: The Human Being, Image of Creation, RSP, 2001. Previously published as *Man: Hieroglyph of the Universe,* RSP, 1972.

Outline of Esoteric Science, An, RSP, 1997.

Pastoral Medicine, AP, 1987.

Planetary Spheres and Their Influence on Man's Life on Earth and in Spiritual Worlds, RSP, 1982.

Psychology of Body, Soul, and Spirit, A, AP, 1999. Previously published under the title *The Wisdom of Man, of the Soul, and of the Spirit: Anthroposophy, Psychosophy, Pneumatosophy.*

Renewal of Education through the Science of the Spirit, The, Kolisko Archive Publications for Steiner Schools Fellowship, UK, 1981.

Significance of the Senses after Death, The, August 13, 1916, Rudolf Steiner House Library, London, UK, or The Rudolf Steiner Library, NY.

Spiritual Ground of Education, The (Oxford Course), RSP, 1947.

Spiritual Guidance of the Individual and Humanity, AP, 1992.

Three Stages of Sleep, The, lecture March 24, 1922, Rudolf Steiner House Library, London, UK, or The Rudolf Steiner Library., Ghent, NY.

Twelve Senses and the Seven Life Processes in Man, lecture August 12, 1916, Dornach, Switzerland, published in *The Golden Blade,* RSP, 1975.

Waldorf Education for Adolescence, see *Education for Adolescents.*

World of the Senses and the World of the Spirit, The, AP, 1979 (Archive Edition).

Zone of the Senses, The, lecture given in Dornach, December 30, 1917, Rudolf Steiner House Library, London, UK, The Rudolf Steiner Library, NY.

Other Authors:

Anderson, Adrian, *Living a Spiritual Year,* AP, 1993.

Ayres, A. Jean, *Sensory Integration and the Child,* 1979; *Sensory Integration and Learning Disorders,* 1972, Western Psychological Services, 12031 Wilshire Blvd, CA, 90025, US.

Barfield, Owen, *Romanticism Comes of Age,* Wesleyan University Press, Connecticut, US, 1986.

Belgau, Frank A., *Learning Breakthrough Program,* Perception Development Research Associates, 1983, P.O. Box 837, Port Angeles, WA, 98362, USA.

Bemmelen, D. J. van, 'The First Goetheanum as Modern Mystery Temple', *Anthroposophical Quarterly,* Vol 9, Spring 1964. Available from the Rudolf Steiner House Library London, UK, or the Rudolf Steiner Library, 65 Fern Hill Rd., Ghent, NY, 12075, US.

Blythe, Peter and David J. McGlown, *An Organic Basis for Neurosis and Educational Difficulties,* Insight Publications, 1981, 4 Place, Chester, CHI 2IU, England.

Bockholt-Kirchner, Margarete, *Fundamental Principles of Curative Eurythmy,* RSP, 1977; 'A Grail Castle in the Brain', *The Golden Blade,* RSP 1975.

Child, Gilbert, Ph.D., *An Imp On Either Shoulder,* Fire Tree Press, Bisley, Stroud, Gloucestershire, GL6 7BL, UK, 1995.

Christie, Agatha, *An Autobiography (1890-1976),* Dodd, Mead & Co., NY, 1977.

Coats, Callum, *Living Energies: An Exposition of Concepts Related to the Theories of Viktor Schauberger,* Gateway Books, Bath, U.K., 1996.

Critchlow, Keith, *Time Stands Still,* St. Martin's Press for Lindisfarne Association, New York, 1982, and Gorden Fraser Gallery Ltd., UK.

Crimley MD, Ann and Ian A. McKinley, *The Clumsy Child,* Association of Pediatric, Chartered Physiotherapists, Ilkley, W. Yorkshire, UK., 1977.

Ege, Karl, *An Evident Need of the Times,* Adonis Press, NY, 1979.

Edmunds, Francis, *Rudolf Steiner Education: The Waldorf Schools*, revised, RSP, 1986.

Edwards, Lawrence, *The Vortex of Life*, Floris Books, Edinburgh, Scotland, UK, 1993.

Emmichoven, F.W. Zeylmans van, *The Foundation Stone of the Anthroposophical Society*, RSP, 1963.

Falck-Ytter, Harold, *Aurora*, Floris Books, Edinburgh, Scotland, 1985.

Field, Jane C., *Helping Specific Difficulties by Correcting Physical Causes*, 1989; *Talking to Teachers*, 1990; *Why Don't You Listen*, 1991.; *Your Vision Is Perfect: Why Don't You See?*, 1992; *Accommodating the Neuro-Developmentally Delayed Child Within the Classroom*, 1992; *A Vicious Circle*, 1993; *The Role of the Corpus Callosum in the Acquisition of the 3 R's*, 1994, privately printed: Janes C. Field, Gatepiece Cottage, Highfields, Wichenford, Worchestershire, WR6 6YG, England.

Fletcher, John, *Art Inspired by Rudolf Steiner*, Mercury Arts Pub., UK, 1987.

Gaddes, William H., *Learning Disabilities and Brain Function: A Neuropsychological Approach*, Spring Verlag, NY, 1985.

Gilmore, June and Rosemary Huber, *The Rape of Childhood: No Time to be a Kid*, J and J Publishing Co., Middleton, Ohio, US.

Gilmore, June, Rosemary Huber and James K. Uphoff, *Summer Children: Ready or Not for School*, J & J Publishing Co.

Gladich, Joen and Paula A. Sassi, *The Write Approach*, Books I and II, Rudolf Steiner College Press.

Glöckler, Michaela and Wolfgang Goebel, *A Guide to Child Health*, Floris Books, Edinburgh, Scotland, 2003.

Gold, Svea with Jessica Kline, 'No Miracles', *Academic Therapy*, vol. 21, no. 2, November 1985, 20 Commercial Blvd., Novato, CA, 94947-6191, US.

Goleta Union School District Personnel editors, *Sensorimotor Activities: A Workbook*, Academic Therapy Publications, Novato, CA, 1968.

Harwood, A.C., *Recovery of Man in Childhood*, Myrin Institute, NY, 1992; *Christmas Plays from Oberufer*, RSP, 1973.

Healy, Jane, *Endangered Minds*, Simon & Schuster, New York, 1990.

d'Herbois, Liane Collot, *Colour*, Stichting Magenta, Zeist, The Netherlands, 1985; *Light, Darkness and Colour in Painting-Therapy*, Floris Books, Edinburgh, 2000.

Holle, Britta, *Motor Development in Children: Normal and Retarded*, Blackwell Scientific Publications, UK, 1976.

Holtzapfel, Walter, *Children's Destinies*, Mercury Press, Spring Valley, NY, 1984.

Hunt, Jean and Mary Nash-Wortham, *Take Time,* The Robinswood Press, England, 1994.

Irlen, Helen, *Reading by the Colors,* Avery Pub. Group Inc., NY, 1991.

Jancy, Meryl, *Mappa Mundi, Map of the World in Hereford Cathedral,* Friends of Hereford Cathedral, Hereford, Herefordshire, UK, 1987.

Kellogg, Rhoda, *Analyzing Children's Art,* 1969; *Understanding Children's Art,* 1970: Mayfield Publishing Co., 1240 Villa St., Mountain View, CA 94041.

Kephart, Newell C., *Learning Disability: An Educational Adventure,* Indiana, US, 1968.

Keyserlingk, Adalbert, Graf von, *The Birth of a New Agriculture,* TLP, 1999.

Kirchner, Hermann, *Dynamic Drawing: Its Therapeutic Aspect,* Mercury Press, 241 Hungry Hollow Rd., Chestnut Ridge, NY, 10977, 1977.

Koepke, Herman, *Encountering the Self: Transformation and Destiny in the Ninth Year,* AP, 1989.

Kohen-Raz, Reuven, *Learning Disabilities and Postural Control,* Freund Publishing House Ltd., Israel, 1986.

König, Karl, *The First Three Years of the Child,* AP, 1969.

Kraus-Zimmer, Hella, *Erdenking und Weltenlicht.*

Kutzli, Rudolf, *Creative Form Drawing: Workbook 1, 2, and 3,* Hawthorn Press, Stroud, UK, 1985.

Lawlor, Robert, *Sacred Geometry,* Thames and Hudson, London, 1982 and NY, 1998.

Lievegoed, Bernard, *Phases of Childhood,* AP, 1997.

Lehrs, Ernst, *Man or Matter,* RSP, 1985.

Lovelock, James, *A New Look At Life On Earth: The Gaia Hypothesis,* Oxford University Press, Oxford, UK, 1979.

Marti, Ernst, *The Four Ethers,* Schaumberg Publications Inc., Roselle, Illinois 60172, USA, 1984; *Das Ätherische,* Edition Verlag Die Forte im Rudolf Steiner Verlag, Dornach, Switzerland, 1989.

McAllen, Audrey E., *Teaching Children Handwriting,* RSCP, 1999; *The Extra Lesson,* sixth edition, RSCP, 2004 (*Die Extrastunde,* Verlag Freies Geisteleben, Stuttgart, Germany, 1996); *Sleep,* second edition, RSCP, 2004; *The Listening Ear,* Hawthorn Press, Stroud, UK, 1989.

McGilmore, Timothy, Ph.D. editor, *About the Tomatis Method,* The Listening Centre Press, Toronto, Ontario, Canada, 1989.

Mesker, P., *De Menselyke Hand,* Dekker & v. d. Vegt, Nymegen, Netherlands, 1980.

Mesker, P. and J. Jofhuizen-Hagemeyer, *Kunnen En Niet Kunnen*, Dekker & v. d. Vegt, Nymegen, Netherlands, 1981.

Mitchell, David, *Developmental Insights*, AWSNA Publications, 1997.

Nash-Wortham, Mary, *Phonic Rhyme Time*, The Robinswood Press, Stourbridge, UK, 1995; 'On Goethe's Colour Theory', *Child and Man*, Vol. I, No. 13, 1978, Steiner Schools Fellowship, UK.

Nash-Wortham, Mary and Jean Hunt, *Take Time*, The Robinswood Press, UK, 1994.

Niederhauser, Hans R., and Margaret Frohlich, *Form Drawing*, Mercury Press, 241 Hungry Hollow Road, Chestnut Ridge, NY, 10977, US, 1974.

Phillips, Dr. D.A., *Secrets of the Inner Self: The Complete Book of Numerology*, Angus and Robertson, Unit 4, Eden Park, 31 Waterloo Road, North Ryde, NSW, Australia 2113; Angus and Roberston 16 Golden Square, London, W1R 4BN, UK, 1986.

Platt, Paul, *Qualities of Time: Contribution Towards a Modern Understanding of How the Cosmos Works in Man*, Star Cross Press, Box 1029, 110 Root Lane, Sheffield, MA, 10257, 1986.

Prokofieff, Sergei O., *The Spiritual Origins of Eastern Europe and the Future Mysteries of the Holy Grail*, TLP, 1993.

Purce, Jill, *The Mystic Spiral*, Thames and Hudson, Inc., NY, 1992.

Querido, René, *The Wonder of Childhood*, RSCP 1991; *The Esoteric Background of Waldorf Education*, RSCP, 1995.

de Quiros, Julio B., MD, Ph.D, and Schrager, Orlando L., MD, *Neuropsychological Fundamentals of Learning Disabilities*, Academic Therapy Publications, 20 Commercial Blvd., Novato, CA, 94947-6191, US, 1988.

Salter, Joan, *The Incarnating Child*, Hawthorn Press, Gloucester, 1987.

Sanders, Barry, *A is for Ox*, Pantheon Books, NY, 1994.

Schneider, Michael. S., *A Beginner's Guide to Constructing the Universe*, Harper Collins, NY, 1994.

Schwaller, R. A. deLubicz, *The Temple In Man*, Inner Traditions International, Rochester, Vermont, US, 1981.

Schwenk, Theodore, *Sensitive Chaos*, RSP, 1996.

Singh, Simon, *Fermat's Enigma*, Anchor Books, U.S., 1997; published as *Fermat's Last Theorem*, Fourth Estate Ltd., London, 1998

Smith, Sally L., *No Easy Answers: The Learning Disabled Child At Home And At School*, Bantam Books, NY, 1981.

Spock, Marjorie, *Eurythmy*, AP, 1980.

Strachan, Gordon, *Christ and the Cosmos*, Labarum Publications Ltd., The Abbey, Dunbar, East Lothian, EH42 1JP, UK, 1985.

Strauss, Michaela, *Understanding Children's Drawings*, RSP, 1988.

Sutherland, Adah Strand, *With Thinking Fingers*, The Cranial Academy, Indianapolis, IN, 1962.

Thomson, John, *Natural Childhood*, Simon & Schuster, New York, 1994.

Tomatis, A.A., *Education and Dyslexia*, AIAPP, Fribourg, Switzerland, 1978, dist. The Listening Centre, 99 Crowns Lane, Toronto, M5R 3P4, Canada.

Tyre, Colin and Peter Young, *Dyslexia or Illiteracy*, Open University Press, UK, and Milton Keynes, Pennsylvania, US, 1983.

Upledger, John, *Your Inner Physician and You*, Upledger Institute, 11211 Prosperity Farms Road, Palm Beach Gardens, Florida 33410-4449.

Wyatt, Isabel, *The Way Down*, The Michael Press, Hawkwood College, Stroud, UK; Stars Roundelay, Hawthorne Press, Stroud, UK, 1985.

Wisby, Aubrey, *Learn to Sing, Learn to Read*, BBC Publications, London, UK, 1982.